D0053395

KITCHENER

BOOKS BY PHILIP WARNER

KITCHENER

THE MAN BEHIND THE LEGEND

Philip Warner

ATHENEUM   NEW YORK   1986

Copyright © 1985 by Philip Warner
All rights reserved
ISBN 0-689-11805-8
LCCN 85-48285
Manufactured by Fairfield Graphics, Fairfield, Pennsylvania
First American Edition

Contents

Acknowledgments

This biography was made possible by the kindness and co-operation of members of the family of the late Field-Marshal Earl Kitchener, their relations and their friends. I wish to express my special gratitude and appreciation to Earl Kitchener, the Field-Marshal's great-nephew, to Lady Kenya Tatton-Brown, to the Hon. Mrs Charles Kitchener, to Major and Mrs G. O. C. Probert, to Mr and Mrs Richard Probert, to Mr and Mrs John Chevallier Guild, to Mrs Peronelle Guild, and to Mrs Margaret Miller.

For permission to consult the correspondence between Lord Kitchener and the 3rd Earl of Salisbury and the Countess of Salisbury, I am indebted to the 6th Marquess of Salisbury; for permission to quote from the writings of the late Field-Marshal Lord Birdwood, I am indebted to Lord Birdwood; and for permission to quote from the letters of her father, Brigadier-General Frank Maxwell, VC, CSI, DSO, I am indebted to Mrs W. H. Lambert.

I have also received much helpful advice from well-wishers, notably from Mr John Hunt, Mrs Michael Wright, and the Staff of the Library at the Royal Military Academy, Sandhurst, the Staff of the Public Record Office, the Staff College, Camberley, the India Office Library, and the Library of the Ministry of Defence.

Much assistance and encouragement was provided by Dr John Sweetman, Head of the Department of Political and Social Studies at the RMA Sandhurst, and by Lt-Col Alan Shepperd, MBE, former Librarian at Sandhurst. Mr John Wing, Librarian of Christ Church, Oxford, Mr Philip Ziegler, Mr James Leasor, Mr Richard Holmes and Mr Robin Harcourt-Williams very helpfully answered enquiries.

List of illustrations

Chapter 1

The Hour and the Man

In times of peace generals become slightly comic figures. Often the characteristics and qualities which have carried them to the top of their profession and to victory appear bizarre and eccentric. Julius Caesar was vain and erratic, Marlborough brave but devious, Wolfe a hypochondriac, MacArthur self-opinionated, Montgomery unscrupulous in his ambition. The civilian public is not naturally at ease with the idea of generals, being both awed and disgusted at the thought that one man can direct campaigns in which thousands of his own countrymen, as well as numerous others, are killed. The thought of Haig and Ludendorff hurling millions of conscripted soldiers at each other in a continuous bloodbath can only really be tolerated from a peace-time perspective if the generals are seen as intriguing, imperfect, obsessed individuals. It cannot be a natural human impulse, so the reasoning goes, to preside over scenes of mass slaughter, much as it may be done in the name of patriotism, liberty, manifest destiny, or any other battle-cry. Even the fact that later generals such as Eisenhower and Montgomery were intent on saving lives does not alter the fact that they directed events in which thousands of men were killed and wounded. When the catalogues of death belong to the distant past they have less impact, but when they are part of an all too recent history, which may be repeated in a not too distant future, the rôle of generals comes under a very severe scrutiny. One of the questions which springs to mind is: can the men who ordered the slaughter of thousands and then returned to die in bed have had normal human emotions? Serving soldiers express doubts freely; historians wonder.

Kitchener was a hero in his day because his name became a synonym for success. Subsequently there have been many attempts to minimize his achievements. The dramatic poster 'Your Country Needs You' has been parodied in advertisements. In 1985 it seems

1

unreal, totally unconvincing. Dying for one's country has a diminished appeal in the late twentieth century. Men, and women, are prepared to die for religious or political beliefs but to die for one's native land is not a popular thought. In fact the whole idea of patriotism has become suspect in many European countries. In Britain there seems to be a widespread credo that to be proud of one's homeland and heritage is wrong. The ideas and beliefs of immigrant peoples must be given equal place to the ones traditionally associated with this country. In consequence, Kitchener's statement that 'your country needs you' has been rendered almost meaningless.

This development is probably the result of a long period of peace. Forty years have now passed since the last major war came to an end. There have, of course, been other wars, in Korea, in Vietnam, and in the Falkland Islands, but these have been so remote that they aroused little apprehension except in those either more involved or likely to be involved. They were news items among many other competing news items. They were thus vastly different from the wars which had brought the possibility of invasion close to these shores, which had seen air raids, which had involved hardship, shortages, rationing, and widespread casualties. When that type of danger threatens, public attitudes change rapidly. In Britain in 1940 the public looked for a leader and found him in Churchill, although Churchill had been a far from popular figure in the past. (The moment the European war was over, and immediate peril at an end, the British public discarded him; the war in the Far East, which was still in full spate, did not appear to threaten this country.) In 1941 Stalin, who was hated and feared rather than admired, became the symbol of heroic Russia battling against her brutal adversary; nobody was aware that Stalin had repeatedly ignored warnings about an imminent German invasion. In 1942, when America was shocked by the attack on Pearl Harbor, and lost so many ships in the process that people living on the western coast of America thought very seriously of the possibility of a Japanese invasion, Roosevelt, a far from universally popular figure, became the symbol of wise statesmanship and the efficient direction of war. The hour, it is said, brings forth the man. It might be more accurate to say, 'The hour brings forth the symbolical man.'

The esteem in which Kitchener was held during his lifetime was not based on a feeling that this was a man who would protect us in our time of peril but on the belief that here was a man who, faced with the difficult task of safeguarding the country's interests, would do so with the minimum of fuss, dislocation and casualties. He was

2

seen as an architect of victory, rather than as a heroic figure leading men spectacularly into battle. (He was, of course, quite ready to take his place at the front of the battle and often did.) Kitchener was not a man to produce impressive but messy victories. His genius lay in strategy, rather than tactics. Gustavus Adolphus, Cromwell, Saxe, Marlborough and Napoleon were not averse to battles which would bring satisfactory conclusions at the price of heavy casualties to their own side; Kitchener, Auchinleck, Slim and Montgomery were. In the long run the verdict of military history on who was, and who was not, a great general, depends on the way victory was achieved rather than its appeal to the general public. Brilliant generalship is cost-effective generalship, not a series of charges of Light Brigades into complete destruction.

At the beginning of every war there is an optimistic belief that on this occasion everything will be different. The waste, muddle and stupidities of former wars will be avoided, the generals will be a different breed, and all will end well and quickly. It is understandable that such thinking occurs and that sometimes even those involved believe 'it will all be over by Christmas'. Thus at the beginning of the First World War there was a firm conviction that the dash of Sir John French combined with the cunning of Foch would bring rapid victory. Kitchener's more sobering view that the war would last for three or four years was decidedly unpopular. At the outbreak of the Second World War Generals Gort and Ironside were Britain's leading generals, the former a holder of the Victoria Cross; with such men in charge, success, it was thought, would be painless and complete. But it was not, alas, Gort and Ironside who were to be the architects of victory; it was Wavell, Patton, Slim, Ridgway, Auchinleck and Montgomery. In military planning it is essential to allow for 'the worst possible case' and for full attention to be given to the possibilities of unexpected disasters. Few generals seem to take 'the worst possible case' into proper consideration: these generals, and Kitchener, did. At the outbreak of the First World War Kitchener had had adequate experience on which to base his views. He had seen the early disasters of campaigns in the Sudan before he brought his own to a triumphant conclusion; he had observed Buller and Roberts in South Africa before putting his own plans into effect; he had planned for 'the worst possible case' on each occasion and he had been right.

Although he became a national hero, Kitchener never courted popularity. He was, as we shall see, a much less forbidding figure than he appears in the famous recruiting poster (in which he seems more an intimidating, humourless automaton than anything else), but it was also in his character to be judged by results rather than personal popularity. Had he lived to see it, he would have enjoyed the poem which Siegfried Sassoon wrote when he was serving in the trenches:

'Good morning, good morning,' the General said
When we met him last week on our way to the line.
Now the soldiers he smiled at are most of them dead
And we're cursing his staff for incompetent swine.
'He's a cheery old card,' grunted Harry to Jack
As they slogged up to Arras with rifle and pack
But he did for them both by his plan of attack.[1]

All through his life Kitchener regarded victory in war as the result of careful planning, persistence, the overcoming of obstacles, and attention to detail. But he also saw it as something more; he saw it as an ambition achieved. Military planning can be an art form, just as the achievement of victory in a sporting event can be art: the training of a racehorse or an athlete, of a cricketer, tennis player or footballer is designed to produce a skill which is artistically beautiful in its execution, as well as its result. In Kitchener's early days the most thorough military training was probably to be found in the cavalry (it took two years to train a lancer to a proper pitch of efficiency) and eventually perfection in cavalry manoeuvres became an end in itself. The cavalry believed that properly handled cavalry would always be able to defeat opponents by outflanking them; cavalry generals never completely rid themselves of this delusion. Cavalry expertise was beautiful to see but it was not war.

Kitchener's attitude to war was the viewpoint of the engineer, not of the infantryman, cavalryman, or gunner. Sappers—engineers— are trained to think of roads, bridges, demolitions, obstacles, supplies, transport: they have to see the campaign as a whole in relation to the terrain over which it is fought. Camouflage and deception fall naturally into the province of the sappers, not merely because they have materials for making replicas and deception targets, but also because engineers look at landscapes with a more understanding eye than most other soldiers do. During Kitchener's lifetime the art of deception and concealment took a vast stride forward. In the Sudan British troops realised painfully that what might appear to be harmless bush or tuft of grass could have a lethal, fanatical dervish concealed in it. In South Africa, Boer troops would suddenly appear from an apparently deserted landscape and, after making a swift

[1] Siegfried Sassoon, 'The General'.

4

attack, would disappear again. Camouflage was not a new tool of war; it had been seen throughout the history of warfare, though often using somewhat primitive methods like the one by which Shakespeare's 'Birnam wood came to Dunsinane'. But Kitchener was one of the first to appreciate its possibilities and limitations in modern war, although his reactions were those of the artist rather than the materialist. It is interesting to recall that when Kitchener was a boy his father invited to the house a cousin who was a master at Rugby. The cousin was asked to report to Kitchener's father on the standard of young Kitchener's educational attainment. He pronounced it appalling, but noted that the boy had a facility for figures and also showed distinct promise at art. It later turned out that this judgement may have been over-harsh. The cousin in question, Francis Elliot Kitchener, had been precociously brilliant, able to repeat the entire catechism at the age of six and said to have read all the classical authors by the time he was fifteen.

Unlike many other generals, Kitchener never painted pictures. Like all officers of his time, he was trained in field sketching; perhaps his lengthy experience of surveying would have made it difficult to produce an imaginative study of a scene. Where his artistic tastes were more clearly shown was in his skill as a collector. On his various travels and assignments he assembled a remarkable collection of furniture, vases, ornaments, carpets, pictures, and screens. Undoubtedly a considerable part of the collection left at his death consisted of gifts, but it is unlikely that he would have received so many artistic gifts had he not made his tastes known.

Thus the real Kitchener was quite unlike the popular conception of him as a simple, determined, methodical soldier with no time for the irrelevances of military life. He was far from simple. His temperament was the result of mixed ancestry and an early education which, though inadequate in purely academic terms, laid the foundation for wise and perceptive judgements. Nor was he typical of the attitude and prejudices of his age. The fact that his father was a retired colonel did not automatically propel the son in the direction of an army career. Of Colonel Kitchener's four sons only three went into the Army. This was not an unusual state of affairs; the Army, in fact, took a very small proportion of the youth of the country. Military life was far from being held in universal esteem. Earlier in the century, when the long grinding Napoleonic Wars had come to an end, the army had been drastically reduced with more thought for economy than experience. And it stayed neglected until 1854, when it was suddenly called upon to fight a difficult war some five thousand miles from the home base. But after the Crimean War the lessons of past disasters were quickly forgotten. In 1879 a popular writer named W. H. G. Kingston published a boy's adventure story entitled *From Powder Monkey to Admiral*. Although the story did not glamourise naval life, nor underrate its hardships, it produced a strong public reaction on the grounds that it was militaristic and conducive to martial attitudes. Militarism and martial attitudes were thought to be characteristics of foreigners and therefore to be avoided. The publishers angrily refuted the criticisms of the book. They may have had some inward satisfaction later in the same year when the British public learnt of the massacre of British troops at Isandhlwana, and the heroic defence of Rorke's Drift. Kitchener had already been in the Army for eleven years by 1879, but he can scarcely have been unaware of the fact that his chosen career did not automatically make him an object of universal admiration. Kipling commented on the public's view of the troops whom Kitchener commanded:

> We aren't no thin red 'eroes, nor we aren't no
>   blackguards too
> But single men in barracks, most remarkable like you
> An' if sometimes our conduck inn't all your fancy
>   paints
> Well single men in barracks don't grow into plaster
>   saints.
> While it's Tommy this, and Tommy that, and Tommy,
>   fall be'ind
> But it's please to walk in front, Sir, when there's trouble
>   in the wind.[1]

Officers were more accepted socially but in order to be welcome had to have the right background and financial status. Impoverished half-pay officers of undistinguished breeding were, for the most part, ignored by those who saw themselves as the trustees of social precedence. In short, the Army was no short cut to financial or social advance at any level. The young man who cheerfuly and hopefully joined the colours at the age of twenty might easily find himself in poor health and without money or prospects at the age of forty. But it was no good his elders trying to tell him that, although many of them did. Fortunately for the country there always seemed to be a supply of young men willing to take a chance on a life of adventure, hardship, and danger. And for some it turned out better than anyone expected.

[1] Rudyard Kipling, 'Tommy'.

Chapter 2

Early Days

Horatio Herbert Kitchener was born on 24 June 1850, the third of a family of five children. The eldest was Henry (born in 1846), who eventually succeeded to the earldom, then came a daughter, Frances,[1] then the future field-marshal, then Arthur, who was a scientist, and lastly Walter who became a major-general after varied service. Some years later, after the death of his first wife, Colonel Kitchener married again, and this union produced a last daughter whom they christened Kawara (a name taken from New Zealand which they were visiting).

It was a happy childhood. The children were close in age. Two years separated each of the first four; Walter, the baby of the family, was the youngest by four years. Frances, although a girl, was a match for the boys at all their childhood pursuits. The only one who did not make great efforts to assert himself was the future commander-in-chief. As their father did not believe in the virtues of boarding schools, he engaged a series of tutors and governesses. The education thus gained was essentially modern, in so far as it went. While his contemporaries were translating Latin and Greek texts and making very tolerable verses in those languages, Kitchener was allowed to concentrate on mathematics, history, geography, French and German. This was accompanied by some instruction in the theory and practice of farming. In his education Kitchener seems to have shared the disadvantages which Churchill experienced. The latter spent much of his school life in lower forms which did not specialise in the Classics, and therefore concentrated more on the English language than most boys of his time and class were allowed to. (Churchill was, of course, idle and careless and, as his housemaster described him, 'regular only in his irregularity'.) Kitchener was

---

[1] Nicknamed 'Millie'.

studious but had all too little opportunity to exercise intellectual talents.

Kitchener's father had strong views on many subjects other than education. He had been born in 1805, almost in the middle of the Napoleonic Wars which, by lasting twenty-two years, must have seemed a normal condition of life for his elders. Since Admiral Horatio Nelson's great victory at Trafalgar took place in the year of his birth, the boy was christened Henry Horatio. (When the field-marshal was at the height of his fame in the early part of this century a number of boys were christened 'Kitchener'. Children who have been burdened with the cumbersome surname of an eminent figure who has died or passed into obscurity by the time they are growing up must regard this custom as a source of exasperation rather than inspiration.)

The Colonel had been a regular soldier, mostly serving in India, and had divided his military life between the 13th Dragoons (now the 13th/18th Hussars), the 9th Foot (later the Royal Norfolk Regiment), and the 29th Foot (the Worcestershire Regiment). In 1845, as a major, he had married Frances Chevallier, daughter of a well-to-do Suffolk clergyman. The Chevalliers had originally come from Jersey but had lived in East Anglia for several generations. The boy Kitchener was very much of an East Anglian. His own family had had East Anglian connections since the late sixteenth century when an ancestor, Thomas Kitchener, had moved from Binstead, near Alton in Hampshire, to Lakenheath in Suffolk. The family fortunes had improved considerably when the field-marshal's grandfather had abandoned the wool trade for the tea trade in London. This had enabled him to purchase a commission in the Army for his son. At that time, and also when Kitchener himself joined, all Army commissions, with the exception of those in the Royal Artillery and Royal Engineers, were bought before joining and sold on leaving. The practice stemmed from the days when landowners provided soldiers for service of the Crown. Originally the costs of providing, arming, feeding, and paying soldiers were defrayed by a share of the plunder from successful campaigns. On certain foreign assignments this could be very profitable; equally it was possible to lose everything. The practice had continued when regiments became permanent establishments instead of bodies of men raised for special ventures. 'Purchase' was eventually abolished in 1871. In the latter stages the system was manifestly absurd and unjust. Rich parents could purchase the colonelcy of a regiment for an infant who would then be entitled to a major part of the takings. Promotion could be gained without purchase, but only in extreme circumstances, such as conspicuous prowess in battle. The fact that rich people bought themselves positions in the Army meant that the style of life tended to be expensive and therefore a great strain for those with military talent but without money. Many of the latter chose to serve in India, where prospects were better and living less expensive. These factors had many social consequences. Not least was the consequence that the less affluent officers did not marry until they had attained a rank or sufficient money to support a wife and children. When they did marry it was usually to someone very much younger than themselves, perhaps to a girl who was visiting relatives out in India. Parents, for their part, made strenuous efforts to marry off their daughters to suitable men (and, for preference, suitable young men). The parties of girls who travelled to India to visit relatives and friends were eventually nicknamed 'the fishing fleet'; those who went back without fiancés or husbands were known as 'the returned empties'.

Colonel Kitchener was thirty-nine when he married Frances, aged nineteen, and the gap in age, though large in our eyes, was by no means exceptional then. There are numerous instances of much older men marrying young brides; bridegrooms of fifty or more did not necessarily seem absurd to the parents of young girls, or even to the girls themselves if they realised that otherwise they might be doomed to a life of spinsterhood. Some girls, of course, were genuinely attracted to and dearly loved their somewhat mature partners.

The Kitcheners returned to India and their first child was born there just over a year later. But Frances's health fared badly in the East. A year later Colonel Kitchener decided that drastic action was called for, so he gave up his regimental employment in India, went on to half-pay (a form of reserve), and came to England in 1847. There were no suitable military jobs for colonels that year, so, after some months of fruitless enquiry, he decided to sell his commission and make a new life. Back in England Frances's health improved and they had a second child. In 1849, the Colonel sold his commission and, with several thousand pounds in his pocket in consequence, went to Ireland to visit his cousin, the manager of the Dunraven estates. While there he attended a sale of land which was being held in Dublin and, observing a large tract of land in Limerick being offered to an apathetic audience, he put in a bid himself and secured 2000 acres for £3000. This occurred soon after the horrors of Ireland's famine, when potato blight brought starvation, death, ruin and misery to millions. The government, which had been slow to take measures to avert the hardships, now tried to make amends by passing a bill entitled the Encumbered Estates Act. This enjoined landowners to make certain improvements to their lands and also to relieve poverty among their tenants. As many landowners were already bankrupt, having received no rent from their wretched tenants, their estates were put on the market by creditors. This had been the government's intention, for it wished to replace poverty-stricken landlords by capitalists with money to spend on their new estates. Colonel Kitchener became one of the latter and gave a very successful example to his neighbours. His estate was called Bally-goghlan; the house in which Kitchener was born in 1850 was named Gunsborough House, though in fact it was twelve miles west of the township of that name. Kitchener was therefore Irish by birth and thus one of a long line of Irish-born or bred generals who served in the British army. Alexander, Auchinleck, Montgomery, Roberts, Wellington and Wolseley were others. However, Colonel Kitchener never thought of himself or his family as Irish, being far removed in temperament, outlook and experience from his Irish neighbours, whom he considered idle and feckless.

They did not care much for him either but accorded him respect for his skill and knowledge at estate management. Observing his father must have had a beneficial effect on young Kitchener, for the Colonel bred horses successfully, ran the estate efficiently, increased his productive land by successful drainage operations and made his own and other people's bricks. Both here and at Crotta, a much superior house nearby which the Colonel also bought, young Kitchener learnt the basic arts of estate management. He was described, in a letter by the blacksmith at Crotta, as 'a smart, intelligent, growing-up lad'. The expression 'growing-up' signified rapidly growing. Of boys who grew tall quickly, and proved unequal to tasks which they would not have been given if they had been shorter, it was frequently said that 'they had outgrown their strength'.

The Colonel, although kind at heart, had a mixture of orthodox and strange ideas. As an ex-Army man he was a stickler for punctuality and routine. His temper was short and, when frustrated, he was apt to express himself with military forthrightness. He taught self-discipline and mutual discipline to his children. On one occasion Kitchener was pegged out on the ground by his brother and sister with croquet hoops.[1] It was a hot day and he could not free himself, for his arms were tied firmly to the hoops with cords. Fortunately for him, his mother found him before the ordeal had lasted too long. It was not an uncommon trick for bored children to play on one who

[1] See P. Magnus, *Kitchener! Portrait of an Imperialist*, quoting family information.

10

had offended them or was merely an easy victim, but the remarkable feature of it was that Kitchener felt that it was a just punishment for some minor offence, and that he had no cause for complaint.

One of the Colonel's weird notions, picked up from his experience in India, which led him to believe that blankets harboured pests and germs, was that it was far healthier to substitute newspapers as a covering. Whether the children had to submit to this particular piece of crankery is not known. However, it was the damp Irish climate rather than the Colonel's spartan ideas which caused his wife's health to deteriorate once again. The Colonel was devoted to his wife, and although it was a wrench to leave the estate he had built up so carefully, there could be no question of staying in Ireland if it was endangering her health. He was essentially a man of action. He sold the estate – at a large profit – and took the whole family to live in Switzerland, where the combination of experienced doctors and the Swiss air might once more restore her. These efforts were, alas, in vain. Neither skill nor climate could avail and she died in Montreux in 1864. She had been in the country barely a year.

The Colonel was greatly and genuinely upset. The fact that he married again some two years later while in New Zealand indicated less that he forgot easily than that he missed his first wife greatly and hoped that a second marriage would restore his life to what it had been before. In this he was disappointed. He married his daughter's music mistress, Miss Emma Green. But the Colonel and the ex-music mistress were not matched in temperament.

When, after his first wife's death, the Colonel had found nothing to keep him in Switzerland, he decided to try farming in New Zealand and bought an estate near Dunedin. But his heart was not in it, and he soon resold it and retired for good to Dinan in Britanny. His sons did not accompany him on these global roamings. Instead they were put in a boarding school in Rennes on Lake Geneva. Here they were under the general supervision of the Chaplain of the English church at Montreux for three years.

A Swiss boarding school was a traumatic experience, although possibly less so than an English one at this period would have been. The boys had led a sheltered life. Kitchener had been very greatly attached to his mother, who thought he was perhaps too sensitive for his own good, and now at the age of fourteen he found himself in a hostile environment where he and his brothers were despised for their almost total ignorance of subjects with which their contemporaries were familiar. Physically they could look after themselves, but there was no avoiding the mockery and contempt which boys of no great educational depth themselves will enthusiastically lavish on companions of lesser attainment.

But the situation had its advantages. It made Kitchener realise that there was no way out of this situation except by his own efforts, and that the only means by which he might achieve any success would be by relentlessly working to 'catch up'. Unfortunately, although he had learned to ride in Ireland, he had no great skill as a horseman at this stage. Among boys, life is by no means bad for an ignoramus if he can display some physical skill outside the classroom, or has a reckless, lawless attitude which commands the respect of his contemporaries. Kitchener had neither.

However, shy, sensitive, backward and unathletic as Kitchener was, he never abandoned his ambition to obtain a commission in the Army. Although his father could have bought him a commission, this was not what Kitchener wanted. His eye was upon the Royal Engineers, colloquially known as Sappers. Sappers derived their name from the days (by no means over in Kitchener's time) when they burrowed under or towards fortifications through trenches known as 'saps'. Sapping was a slow, cunning, careful approach which required skill, perseverance and liking for the task. (The word 'sap' was also used to mean studying industriously: both this and 'swot' derived from Sandhurst and Woolwich.)

As commissions from the Royal Military Academy, Woolwich were awarded by examination rather than by the production of a large sum of purchase money, there was considerable competition to enter that establishment. There was an entrance examination for Sandhurst too, where educational requirements, though less specialised, were by no means optional. Entrants for both colleges made use of army 'crammers' who, from a knowledge of former papers, could usually forecast fairly accurately what might occur in examinations of the future. Cramming took many forms: there were 'army classes' in public schools; there were establishments run by retired army officers of academic bent; and there were specialist tutors.

In qualifying to become an officer, it was unnecessary for Kitchener to have even been a soldier, let alone to have spoken to one. Kitchener's experience, or rather lack of it, was no exception. In the present century there have been various efforts to see that officers spend a little time in the ranks before being selected for commissioning, but the belief that this is a valuable, even essential, experience, is held by politicians rather than senior officers. When National Service ensured that everyone would at least begin in the lowest rank, and was therefore thought of as a great democratic experience, the possibility of the public school boy making friends with the boy from the state school was neatly circumvented by the former being put into potential officer companies, in which he would mix mainly with young men of similar background. The practice was not mere snobbery. Long experience has taught the Army that an officer who sees the point of view of the 'other rank' too clearly may hesitate to order him to undertake certain unpleasant, perhaps fatal tasks. In short, he will be 'soft' in discipline. Equally an untalented private soldier, though never likely to become an officer, might be less inclined to obey, or follow, a person whom he suspects (from experience) is not quite the god-like figure he is meant to be. The ultimate test of an army is how it functions in war; the Soviet Army, which began by abolishing 'officer status', quickly restored it and now has a less democratic army than any other in the world. Viscount Esher, who worked with Kitchener and knew him well, said of him in his later years 'he was never seen to address or even notice a private soldier'.

In the early days after commissioning, Kitchener was posted to the School of Military Engineering at Chatham and from there to a mounted troop of Royal Engineers at Aldershot. It is impossible to be stationed in Aldershot and not have some contact with soldiers. Kitchener was specialising in field telegraphy, precursor of the Royal Corps of Signals. He was also devoutly religious, and spared no efforts to increase the congregation of the garrison church. But he was shy and self-conscious with soldiers, whether British or from any other nation. He probably terrified most of them, for he was much taller than they were and stared down at them with icy-blue eyes.

However, although Kitchener missed seeing the harshness of Army life in the lower ranks, this does not mean that his early experience of the Army can have been pleasant. It seems unlikely that any of the gentleman cadets at Sandhurst and Woolwich enjoyed their time in those establishments. They were regarded as a necessary evil. In the late nineteenth century, Sandhurst was known to Wellington College, itself no bed of roses, as 'hell over the hill'. As many Wellingtonians went on to Sandhurst, which was only four miles away, Wellington was doubtless kept well-informed.

Kitchener arrived at the RMA Woolwich in January 1868. Nine years earlier the college had been the scene of a spectacular mutiny by cadets protesting at the spartan conditions. (Sandhurst, where conditions were slightly better, had one the following year.) Although conditions at both colleges improved after the mutinies, the régime still remained extremely harsh.

The first term lasted until the end of June. There then followed six weeks' holiday. Then came the second term and a further six weeks

13

over the Christmas period. The process was repeated during the second year with examinations occurring termly. The daily time-table was:

6.30 a.m. Reveille.
6.45–7.15 a.m. Extra drill for those undergoing punishment.
7.30 a.m. Prayers and breakfast. [Food was now adequate: tea, coffee or cocoa, bread and butter, fish or meat.]
8–11 a.m. First study.
11.15 a.m.–12.15 p.m. Drills.
12.30 p.m. Luncheon. [Soup or cold meat or sandwiches, bread and cheese. Beer was extra.]
1–3 p.m. Second study [Except on Saturday, which was a free afternoon.]
3.15 p.m. Dinner. [Hot meat, vegetables, puddings or tarts, bread. Beer could be purchased as an extra.]
6–8 p.m. Third study.
8 p.m. Prayers [And tea or coffee with bread and butter. Cold meat or eggs could be purchased as an extra.]
10 p.m. Roll call.
10.30 p.m. Lights out.

On Sundays Reveille was at 7.30 a.m. but most of the morning was taken up by church or other parades. There was a church parade at 5.45 p.m. to make sure cadets had not strayed outside the grounds.

Although there seems to have been little enough time for recreation, it is recorded that cricket was popular, and that there was a rifle club, a taxidermy club, a photography club which did all its own developing, and a billiards club. Up till the 1860s, billiards had been regarded as a wicked and pernicious game, likely to lead to drinking, gambling and evil habits, which, as it was usually played in seedy public houses, does not seem surprising. But most of these recreations would have been impossible before 1867, for the fixed timetable as described above did not exist, and a cadet had no agreed allotment of free time.

Smoking was also well known as the road to physical, moral and mental ruin, but in the 1860s was permitted on the basis that if it was forbidden, it would occur illegally, but if condoned could be controlled. Smokers were not, however, allowed the wild freedom of a pipe in their rooms, but had to go to the billiard room or the lower storey of the school-at-arms to indulge in their new privileges. Once smoking was made legal it became much less popular.

Kitchener, like all his fellows, started with mathematics, practical geometry, topography, drawing, French, German, gymnastics, and infantry drill. (Mathematics was always known as 'swot'.) Later his course included riding, artillery, surveying and chemistry.

Needless to say, the Woolwich cadets (it was always known as 'The Shop') did not comport themselves blamelessly throughout their two years. They broke the numerous rules, they idled, they endeavoured to bluff their instructors, they damaged their uniforms and their barracks, and they were often rowdy. But, as Colonel Alan Shepperd aptly put it in his history of the companion college at Sandhurst: 'It could be said that the unending struggle between the College authorities and the Gentleman Cadets must have inculcated in the latter the invaluable qualities of constant alertness and a high sense of self-preservation.[1]

It is recorded that Kitchener worked extremely hard at Woolwich. One can but wonder how he did. If a cadet was not being harried by the authorities for not working, he would be enduring a far worse time from his fellows for doing so. Kitchener had not arrived from a public school from which there might have been a few friends to stand by him. It is said that his health broke down at one point from overwork. It seems just as likely that the breakdown came from the frustration of trying to work and catch up as he had been able to do in Switzerland. Up until quite recently, 'brain-fever' was thought to be an illness caused by overwork. Schoolboys thought they were prone to it; insensitive schoolmasters expressed unclinical scepticism. If Kitchener actually made himself ill by studying too hard, his case may well be unique at Woolwich and Sandhurst. Cadets do occasionally miss a term through illness, but the cause is usually diagnosed as something less exotic than brain-fever: glandular fever, tuberculosis, or pneumonia, perhaps.

By the time Kitchener left Woolwich he would probably have lost much of the sensitivity of his earlier years. He would have been shouted at, reprimanded, ragged, and bullied. In the middle of it all, he would have made a few friends. He had probably been instructed with military thoroughness. Some of the Woolwich instructors were eminent and good instructors. Some were eminent but bad instructors.

A more detailed account of daily life at Woolwich is given in the appendices. It was written by a fellow Royal Engineer who was at the college just before Kitchener. He was one of 138 who competed for thirty-four cadetships: 'Of these one was rejected as medically unfit and one was dismissed for writing rude remarks on the papers.'

So although Kitchener never served in the ranks, his time at

[1] *Sandhurst*, London 1980.

Woolwich may well have been almost as gruelling. That he probably gave as good as he got to those who tried to override him is suggested by his subsequent experience with the French Army. Having passed all necessary examinations by December 1870, in spite of the term lost through illness, he went to stay with his father in Dinan.

The conversation that Christmas was almost all of the war. In the previous July the French Emperor, Napoleon III, had foolishly allowed himself to be provoked by Bismarck into declaring war on Germany. Subsequent events were disastrous for him. He was defeated and captured at Sedan in September. Other defeats followed. Paris was besieged. However, there were still French armies in the field and one under General Chanzy in the west and another under General Faidherbe in the north looked as if they might yet have some success. Britain was, of course, neutral, though watching the situation keenly. To Kitchener and a friend named Harry Dawson it seemed a wonderful opportunity to see what modern war was like. Neither they nor Colonel Kitchener could see any objection to their joining a French field ambulance unit. Clearly this would be a humanitarian gesture and would provide first-class experience of battle. They proceeded to Laval to join Chanzy's courageous but ill-trained and equipped army. Here they saw enough of battle, casualties, wounds and destruction to rid them for ever of any illusions about the romance of war. Kitchener showed that, sensitive or not, he had courage and stoicism. The scenes around the field ambulance station were enough to turn strong stomachs, but Kitchener stayed at his self-chosen task and displayed indifference both to horror and danger. The lesson he seems to have learnt was that to go into battle ill-prepared has extremely unpleasant results; certainly all his own battles in the future would occur at the end of long, careful preparations. Kitchener was to belong to the school of generals who believe that battle should only be offered if it is thought to have been won already.

Chanzy was finally beaten in a bloody battle which began on 9 January 1871 and lasted for three days. Sporadic fighting continued after it. The French were already very much aware of the value of balloons for observation on the battlefield. The Sappers, on the other hand, would not have a balloon section till 1890, although once it was formed it would prove very useful in the South African War. When Kitchener saw the French using a balloon to observe German troop movements, he persuaded the two French officers in charge of it to let him make an ascent. This was a somewhat non-neutral action, and subsequently all information about the ascent was officially denied and Kitchener told not to speak of it. Later, when the war was over, he was able to confess that it was true.

But by this time the insanitary conditions on the battlefield were beginning to prove too much for him. He was badly equipped for the type of work he was doing and soon fell ill with pleurisy and pneumonia. When news of this reached his father he was rescued from the hovel in which he was lying. It was a close call but he recovered fairly quickly at Dinan and was soon on the way back to England.

There he received a considerable shock. The activities of the young English officer with the French Army, and his narrow escape from death, had not gone unreported. To make matters worse, he was now not a mere cadet under training, whose escapades would be overlooked or condoned, but a commissioned officer in the British Army. While he was in France his commission had been gazetted and it was dated 4 January. This was a serious matter. It was so serious that he was summoned to appear before the commander-in-chief, Field-Marshal HRH the Duke of Cambridge. The duke was renowned for putting so many oaths into his sentences when moved that his meaning was often altogether lost. However, on this occasion the significance of his words was all too clear to Kitchener. The wretched youth had imperilled his country's neutral status. He deserved to lose his commission. And even that might not be the end of the matter. Just when Kitchener thought his military career was at an end the old duke took his hand and said, 'Don't worry, my boy. I should have done just the same if I had been in your position.' Or so one version of the conversation goes.

That was not quite the end of the matter. In 1913 Field-Marshal Kitchener received a medal for being present at the 1871 campaign. This is probably a record length of time to elapse between earning a campaign medal and actually receiving it.

The young Kitchener then proceeded to Chatham, where the Sappers had their School of Military Engineering. Here he began to make a few more friends. Normally he was too shy to make friends easily and only did so when thrown into close contact by working with someone. Experience had made him a little more forthcoming, but he never ever shook off his shyness completely. He was always what is called 'a private person'. He knew his own strengths and limitations and hesitated to venture into fields, material or emotional, where the consequences could not be carefully gauged and calculated.

His first posting after Chatham was as ADC to Brigadier-General George Greaves when that officer was attending the annual manoeuvres of the Austrian Army. It was a very temporary appointment, but long enough for Kitchener to make a favourable impression on the Emperor Franz Josef. When General Greaves fell ill, Kitchener took over his duties, even to the extent of sitting in his place at formal banquets. Kitchener, however, was less interested in making a social mark than in learning the latest Austrian technique for river crossing: he therefore used his position to obtain permission to make a personal inspection of their equipment.

Then back to Aldershot, followed by a long visit to Germany where he improved both his German and his knowledge of German developments in field engineering. But he was beginning to feel that there was little more to learn in Aldershot and to experience the frustration of the keen young subaltern who, having learnt and practised all there is to know at one particular station, then has to study and practise it all over again because there is no other employment for him. But just when life seemed to have become stagnant and boring, an opportunity came which fulfilled all his dreams. He was given the chance to make a survey of the Holy Land. Not only would this be valuable professional experience and be interesting in itself, it would also offer an opportunity of seeing all those sites which, as a religious young man, he had longed to visit.

Chapter 3

Kitchener the Surveyor

The Palestine Exploration Fund had been opened in 1865 under the patronage of Queen Victoria. The purpose of the original trustees had been to identify the various biblical sites and, by a scientific survey of places which many people probably believed to exist only in myth or legend, to confound the sceptics. Of the latter there was an increasing number. Darwin's *Origin of Species*, which had been published six years before the Palestine Exploration Fund had been founded, had presented an apparently irrefutable argument against Christian belief, it was thought. Few people had actually read Darwin, but there was a large number who were prepared to believe that science had now made Christianity, in fact all religion, obsolete. In this they were like the later apostles of Marx who had never read *Das Kapital*, and the followers of Freud who had not only not read him but even misunderstood what he was supposed to have said.

The PEF was regarded benignly by the War Office, for at that time Palestine was part of the Turkish Empire, over whose moribund body the 'Great Powers' expected to be squabbling again before long. When that occurred, a knowledge of military geography of Palestine could well be of great value. The War Office was therefore happy to lend sappers and equipment to the Fund. Whoever envisaged Palestine as a future military theatre was certainly truly ahead of his time, which is not a characteristic for which War Office planners are generally noted.

One of Kitchener's few friends was Claude Conder, whom he had first met at his Army crammer. Conder eventually reached no higher rank than colonel, but had considerable distinction as a scholar. His subject was Altaic languages, those generally spoken in north-east Asia in areas such as Mongolia and Manchuria. At this point in Kitchener's career he had cause to be grateful to the chance which had made him Conder's friend, for Conder was already directing the

19

survey as a lieutenant. Conder had had a civilian assistant named Charles Tyrwhitt-Drake, until Tyrwhitt-Drake died of some form of fever in July 1874. He suggested to Kitchener that he should volunteer for the survey and at the same time asked for him. In consequence, Kitchener joined the expedition on the Plain of Philistia, once the home of the Philistines. The survey was already well advanced but climate, local difficulties, and the unceasing labour had combined to make the survey party jaded and dispirited. Kitchener's enthusiasm for the project, his technical competence, and his apparently limitless energy gave the small party fresh heart. In addition to himself and Conder there were three corporals and a local clerk.

This may well have been the happiest period of Kitchener's life. Not only was he doing the work of two men, but he was also finding time for studying Arabic, for taking numerous photographs, and for acquiring a knowledge of archaeological techniques. He was described by those who met him as cheerful and friendly. Almost inevitably he had a spell of what was descibed as dysentery but, as this cleared up fairly soon without long-term effects, may well have been some less deadly complaint. Prior to the ability of doctors to diagnose bowel complaints accurately, almost any stomach disorder could be given the impressive label of dysentery. Dysentery certainly existed, but as often as not it killed. Soon after the attack Kitchener was strong enough to save Conder from drowning when the latter got into difficulties while swimming in the Mediterranean. In Galilee the whole party had a narrow escape from being clubbed to death. Although their presence in the country was sanctioned and approved by the Turkish government, the presence of these infidels on their sacred lands did not go down well with the local Arabs. These, being Moslems, felt that the surveyors were defiling and despoiling their lands, perhaps even planning a means of stealing them. Although aware of a latent hostility, the survey party had encountered nothing serious until that July. On the 19th, a sheikh strode into the camp near Safed and started rummaging through the party's possessions. Conder heard the commotion and knocked the man over. The sheikh drew a knife but was overpowered and tied up. Unfortunately, this was not the end of the matter. He yelled for help and, to the party's surprise, several hundred men poured into the camp. This made the odds against the survey party, which only numbered fifteen including the servants rather high, and their situation looked very ugly indeed when the sheikh urged the crowd to 'Kill the Christian dogs'. The surveyors were better armed than their opponents, but hesitated to open fire. Scuffling continued while

20

Conder attempted to calm the situation but he himself was suddenly hit in the face and neck by a club wielded by an agile Arab. This encouraged the crowd and Conder would probably have been finished off had not Kitchener stood over him, enabled him to retreat, and held up the crowd by words rather than action. His newly acquired knowledge of Arabic was being put to a use he could hardly have anticipated. When the others had reached a position of safety on a nearby hill, he turned and made his escape. He was just in time, for someone discharged a musket at him as he left.

Fortunately for the party, rescue came in the form of a group of Turkish soldiers accompanying the British consular agent. They were preparing for a routine visit to the camp when an urgent message from Conder reached them. On their arrival all weapons disappeared, all threats and imprecations ceased, and there was nothing but a crowd of harmless sightseers. But the attackers were unduly optimistic if they thought that this was the end of the matter. They were, if they had known it, dealing with Kitchener.

He himself had been badly bruised by blows from stones and clubs. Conder had more serious injuries, some of which would trouble him for the rest of his life. These, followed by a bout of malaria, caused him to hand over command to Kitchener who, believing that the events at the camp might be followed by further and more serious incidents, felt that work should be halted until those guilty were punished. Furthermore there had been outbreaks of cholera in the north. He recommended that the survey should be stopped until the ringleaders of the attack had been dealt with and the cholera, which seemed to occur at certain seasons, had abated. Cholera, as is now known, is a water-borne infection and Kitchener, though ignorant of the cause of the spread of cholera, was right in his instincts about it. So he and the others packed up and went home, though not before giving evidence at the trials of the attackers, who were duly punished.

Kitchener spent another less eventful Christmas at Dinan and busied himself with his maps and the production of a book of photographs of biblical sites. There were twelve in all in the beautifully bound production, although it sadly sold very few copies.

The incident at Safed had been a very minor one, despite the possibility that it might have led to the termination of the life of the future field-marshal. Similar incidents occurred in their hundreds, perhaps thousands, in the course of the history of the British Empire. Solitary figures, or small parties of soldiers or police, faced turbulent mobs which were intent on looting and not averse to murder. British soldiers of whatever rank seem to have enjoyed facing crowds and treating threats, stones, or even bullets with nonchalant indifference. China, Africa, and India seemed particularly prone to such demonstrations. Kitchener's performance, though commendable, was in no way exceptional. Its interest for us rests in the fact that it underlines his coolness and resourcefulness in the face of danger. Had he not stood firm and looked immovable, the whole party could have been massacred. The incident demonstrates that he was not purely a textbook leader, although he missed the experience of all the campaigns which he might have known: the Zulu Campaign of 1879 where two young officers, one a Sapper, won Victoria Crosses at Rorke's Drift; the Afghan Wars of 1878; and the Ashanti War of 1873. None of these, of course, compared with soldiering in the Crimea, but they were dangerous and unpleasant enough to make it clear to all within the vicinity whether a junior officer was excited and improved by battle or whether he regarded it as an interruption to his plans to advance his career as a staff officer. Kitchener belonged to the former category.

Unfortunately, among all his photographs at this time, there was none of himself. Had there been any, they would have made an interesting contrast with those which appeared later in his career. A member of the party reported: 'We none of us thought much about our toilets, and he least of all. Why, after a few months in Palestine he looked more like a tramp than an officer in Her Majesty's Army. His clothes wouldn't have fetched a threepenny-bit at any "old clo shop" in Whitechapel!'

Somewhere, inside the formal, aloof Kitchener, there was a very different personality which occasionally showed itself. The author of the above description said that Kitchener was 'as good company as a man could wish to have, full of life and high spirits'. And later, in the South African War when his rank and eminence might have demanded some degree of smartness, he was described by an American war correspondent, Julian Ralph, as follows: 'His stars were gone. His buttons were dingy. His coat was stained, and the left-hand pocket was torn halfway down. His single eyeglass was as murky as a Whitechapel window in December. He had not shaved for weeks. He was sitting on splinters and leaning on Cape jam and he didn't care. He was like the rest of us—dirty, shabby, unkempt, unshorn—blending with the veldt, melting into the desert colour, going without a razor, a bath or a brush of any sort.'

After Christmas Kitchener and Conder worked together in London to produce an accurate map of Palestine. Much had been done, but there was still much to do. At the beginning of the following year Kitchener set off again, this time in command as

Conder's health did not permit him to travel. The departure was delayed at Port Said because the Russian steamer which was to take them to Beirut did not appear. The news Kitchener heard on arrival was disquieting: the Druse were causing much trouble, frequently murdering travellers on the road to Damascus, and further south there had been tribal clashes among the Arabs and many had been killed. Surprisingly, at Safed, of unpleasant memory, all was sweetness and light. The party was met by the local governor, and the sheikh, one Ali Agha Alan, who had started all the trouble, greeted him humbly and expressed deep sorrow for the events which had caused the cessation of the survey. Kitchener was unimpressed by the penitence, but eventually softened and became quite friendly with his former attacker. His comment on the repentance was, 'He might well be sorry. The fines have pretty well ruined him and his friends.'

However, the year 1877 was by no means without incident. Russia attacked Turkey on 24 April, which meant that all the local men were called up to repel the invasion while the women and the old men tried to harvest the crops. The withdrawal of all Turkish soldiers from the countryside to the front meant that there would be no rescue party available if the surveyors ran into another incident. London suggested that perhaps the party should be withdrawn, as its safety could not be guaranteed. Kitchener disagreed, saying he thought he could maintain a satisfactory relationship with what little authority remained. There were further incidents, they were fired on (by accident) in one place and stoned in another, but the survey was completed by the end of the following September. It was a major achievement. They had mapped some 3,000 square miles and recorded all the archaeological discoveries. They had photographed most of the sites. They had noted the names, religion, and state of the water supply of each village. They had corrected all the gross errors of previous map-makers.

It had been no sinecure. Conder's health had been permanently damaged; other members of the party had incurred various ailments. Kitchener had experienced sunstroke at one stage and snow-blindness at another. He had had several bad bouts of fever, one of which he seemed to have cured by his insisting on drinking beer to quench his intense thirst. And there was the sheer labour of it. The countryside was hilly and the surveying instruments were heavy and cumbersome. In heat and cold the party lugged their burdens around. Once over, hardship was soon forgotten; at the time it seemed almost insupportable.

Sir George Arthur, who published a lengthy *Life of Lord Kitchener* in 1920, described reports on the survey as 'lucid, graphic and precise'.

He added that Kitchener was 'keenly alive to the beauties of the country' and that the report read less like that of a survey officer than that of a very wide-awake diplomatic agent casting an administrative eye over the country, its people, its buildings, its history and its prospects. He underlined this view with a note saying: 'A well-known Jewish writer, Dr Daiches, has suggested that no other recorded period in the life of Kitchener gives a better insight into his disposition and his ways of work, or reveals to us his heart, mind and character, so well as the few years he spent in Palestine. "His indomitable energy, his unequalled thoroughness, his hunger for work, his mastery of detail, his preparedness, his economy in men and material, his making sure of success, his sense of duty, his ability to inspire others with a zeal for work—all these are characteristics of the Kitchener of a later time."'

Some estimate of this thoroughness may be made from the fact that his map included 2,770 place names, correctly spelt and located, whereas its predecessor had had only 450 and many of those of dubious authenticity. But too much should not be made of this painstaking, determined thoroughness. Doubtless many other young officers possessed similar characteristics but would never become field-marshals. What takes us further in the analysis of his character is that he could master so many different subjects and facts at once. He was single-minded in reaching his objective, but had an eye for everything else in the area too. This was a characteristic which would pay great dividends in the Sudan, in South Africa, and in the First World War where unobserved, unexpected, unimagined factors could easily destroy a strategic plan.

And undoubtedly, although Daiches stops short of saying so, this was Kitchener at his happiest. He enjoyed the hardships and the danger, he had a great sense of purpose in that his work was related to his religious convictions, and he enjoyed the companionship of a small team. Never again would he be able to be responsible to his own conscience alone, to be quite natural. Later tasks would bring increasing responsibilities, and he would find himself moulded into Kitchener the senior officer, a different and perhaps less happy man than the lieutenant surveyor.

After the completion of the survey Kitchener sailed for Constantinople (Istanbul) with various letters of introduction. There he obtained further letters which enabled him to visit the front in the Russo-Turkish war.

The cause of the war had been a combination of Turkish maladministration and Russian intrigue. Turkey administered her sprawling empire so badly that revolts occurred periodically (and were put down with excessive brutality), while Russia looked favourably on this turmoil, seeing in it a chance to intervene, preferably legally and with the approval of other European powers, and to benefit by acquiring a piece of Turkish territory. A recent anti-Turk rising in Bulgaria had been put down with such ferocity that Britain, stirred greatly by Gladstone's speeches, was at the point of intervening when Russia forestalled her by herself attacking Turkey with the excuse of freeing the Christians from oppression. Britain was therefore able to be neutral, even to show some admiration for the Turks for the courage they displayed in resisting the Russian attacks.

On his way to the front, Kitchener could not fail to notice numerous Bulgarian corpses hanging from lamp-posts. They represented a small fraction of those massacred by the Turks, but evoked no sympathy from Kitchener. He wrote in an article in *Blackwood's Magazine* that Bulgarians were 'physically and morally a most despicable race'. He felt that much sympathy had been wasted on them. He had probably absorbed some of these views from the Turks, though they themselves were no pillars of morality. The word 'buggery' is said to have originated in Bulgaria. However, what probably turned Kitchener conclusively against the Bulgars was the way in which a friendly fellow traveller, having borrowed a small sum of money to be repaid at the end of the journey, disappeared at one of the intermediate stations. How the Bulgars employed their spare time was their own affair, but when it came to swindling honest British travellers that was another matter altogether.

The railway on which Kitchener travelled appeared to wind about in an unnecessary and arbitrary manner. He discovered later that, in the Near East, railway contractors built lines at a fixed price per kilometre. With this in mind, as many kilometres as possible were constructed on level land, skilfully and at great length avoiding all geographical contours. Kitchener remembered this tendency later when he was ordering the construction of railways in Egypt.

Kitchener's articles in *Blackwood's* entitled him to a listing in the rolls of war correspondents. In view of his later, strongly expressed disapproval of war correspondents, this fact can scarcely have been to his liking. His reports included graphic detail. He recorded that though the Turkish sentries were relieved in the freezing conditions every fifteen minutes, no fewer than twenty-seven died at their posts in three nights. Frost-bite was, of course, widespread.

At the front Kitchener met Valentine Baker, of whom he would see more later in Egypt and the Sudan. Baker was at that time commanding a division of the Turkish Army with the rank of major-general. He had had a spectacular career already, and there was more to follow. He had fought in the Crimea, had commanded the 10th Hussars and had, at the age of forty-eight, been court-martialled and dismissed the service for the alleged rape of a young woman on the train between Aldershot and London. His accuser reported him when the train arrived at Waterloo, although as the trains on this line stopped every few minutes at stations, the offence seems rather surprising. After the trial, Baker went to Turkey and the military skill he displayed there later led to his being offered the post of Commander of the Egyptian Army in 1882. But Queen Victoria vetoed the appointment; it was said that she could not approve the appointment of a man whose record with young ladies in railway carriages would cause his brother officers to recoil from him in disgust. It did not seem to have that effect on Kitchener. (Valentine Baker's elder brother was Sir Samuel Baker, the redoubtable explorer, who gave Kitchener considerable help in the latter's next assignment.)

The war between Russian and Turkey ended in 1878, just at the point when Russia was advancing so closely to Constantinople that Britain was considering supporting 'the sick man of Europe'. (This was a favourite expression of the Russian Czar to describe Turkey.) Britain had no wish to be involved in another war with Russia so soon after the Crimea, but skilful presentation of the issues by Disraeli soon produced a wave of patriotic, belligerent fervour. A favourite music-hall song at the time went:

> We don't want to fight
> But, by Jingo, if we do
> We've got the ships, we've got the guns
> We've got the money too,

a heart-stirring ditty which has left us with the word 'jingoism' to describe bellicose patriotism.

The resultant treaty was the product of the Congress of Berlin, presided over by Bismarck, 'the honest broker'. Rumania, Serbia, and Montenegro were declared independent of Turkey; Bosnia and Herzegovina, though still belonging to Turkey, were put under Austrian administration (thus setting the scene for the outbreak of the First World War). Russia received a fort and a port, neither of much importance, and Britain was given control of Cyprus, which was thus detached from Turkey. Bulgaria was to be self-governing.

The British possession of Cyprus clearly called for a survey of this new acquisition, which was to be ruled by a form of trusteeship. Kitchener was the obvious man for the task, and although this by no means meant that he would be appointed to it, a little prodding by a cousin named Thomas Cobbold, MP for Ipswich and a successful barber and brewer, secured it for him. Kitchener was employed by the Foreign Office, which meant that he enjoyed independence and would eventually produce the report under his own name. This happy circumstance stemmed from the fact that the Intelligence Service and the Ordnance Survey Board of the War Office both laid claim to him, but could not agree who had prior rights. The simple solution was to give him to neither, but to attach him to the Foreign Office.

Kitchener approved strongly of this new territorial acquisition, which had even greater strategic merits than Palestine. By this time he was firmly imbued with the idea of Britain exerting a strong influence in the Near East.

The High Commissioner for Cyprus was Sir Garnet Wolseley, later to be Field-Marshal Lord Wolseley. Wolseley, twenty-seven years older than the young lieutenant, was an extremely capable, outstandingly brave man who had fought in Burma, the Crimea, in the Indian Mutiny, in China, in Canada, and in West Africa. He had worked closely with Cardwell over the 1871 reforms, and had helped to make a vast improvement in the efficiency of the British Army. After his term as governor of Cyprus, he would take posts in further brilliantly organised campaigns. Wolseley's drive, flexibility and bravery were an inspiration to many; the expression 'All Sir Garnet' was used by soldiers and civilians alike to denote efficiency, but eventually, like many a successful general before and after him, he met his match in the politicians, whose motives he mistrusted and whose intrigues disgusted him. In one particular he may have served as a bad example to Kitchener, for Wolseley was reluctant to delegate, and preferred to take all important decisions himself. Such a procedure may be highly satisfactory for minor campaigns with small armies, but becomes impossible when the forces involved run into millions rather than thousands. Some generals are, of course, first-class politicians and enjoy a campaign in the office nearly as much as they enjoy one on the battlefield. But they are not numerous. Most young men join the army to live in the open air and to avoid life in the office; if they rise high enough they experience little fresh air and all too much office. In 1944 Field-Marshal Alanbrooke was in the running to command the D-Day landings and subsequent campaigns. Unfortunately for him, he was indispensable in the War Office as Churchill's right-hand man. Neither Kitchener nor Wolseley was born to be anyone's right-hand man.

But apart from his pleasure in obtaining such an attractive appointment in Cyprus, this was not a very happy time for Kitchener. He had recently been going through an oriental phase, wearing a beard and scenting his room with incense. This was the sort of affectation an undergraduate at Oxford or Cambridge might have been expected to produce in his early twenties. Kitchener indulged in such frivolities late and not for long, but the fact that he did shows that he was not the unbending martinet he has often been portrayed to be. (The use of incense, incidentally, has no homosexual undertones.) But now life suddenly became sad and serious. His father's second marriage, which had never looked satisfactory, had reached a point at which the couple had decided to separate. The Dinan home which had been a happy retreat for Kitchener was no more. In the future his father, who never came to terms with his now rootless existence, would often stay with his son. But life was not the same.

There is a widespread assumption nowadays that in the nineteenth century the British people were earnestly and wholeheartedly behind the imperialist idea. This was not entirely true. There had always been criticism of imperialist policy ('We used to tax the colonies, now they tax us'). The cynics used to say that British policy was 'Philosophy and five per cent', but even the most patriotic citizen would question the wisdom of spending large sums of money in policing territories which few people could find quickly on a map. Some territories had been acquired for strategic reasons, others for their economic value, others to forestall European rivals, and yet others by missionary zeal; the last category produced almost intractable problems. Some territories begged to be put under the protection of the British government. Usually they were populated by uncivilised and gullible people who were an easy prey for unscrupulous traders. Annexation by Britain meant protection by the 'Great White Queen'. One recalls the pleasure of King Moshesh of Basutoland in his message to Queen Victoria: 'My country is your blanket and my people the lice upon it.'

Gladstone and many of his Liberal supporters had no faith in the Imperial Mission, but could not fail to see that the British version of imperialism had certain virtues. Liberal policy, when the party was in power, vacillated between a desire to shed all imperial commitments and a guilty feeling that Britain should not renege on its ethical obligations to subject peoples. Even to the most ardent anti-imperialist it was obvious that the British Empire was different from its predecessors and its contemporaries. Anti-imperialists were a minority; most British people, even though they would have been hard put to name half the countries in the Empire, were nevertheless convinced that 'wider still and wider should its bounds be set' and that they had a mission to convert and civilise 'lesser breeds without the law'.

When Kitchener made up his mind that the expansion of the British Empire would be to the benefit of the world in general, he had arrived at this process by his own observation and deductions. Most young men of his type and position would not have given the ethics of the matter a second thought. From childhood they had lived in a world which believed it was the duty of the British to protect the weak against the unscrupulous foreigner, that 'the colonies' offered great opportunities for making a fortune by enterprise and hard work, and that the British Navy was the greatest instrument of peace the world had ever known. They were, of course, not alone in believing that peace (except for minor wars) had been safeguarded by British seapower since 1814. In the public schools, which Kitchener had never attended although he would have met their products at Woolwich, the idea of 'imperial service' was taken for granted; it was almost an extension of the prefectorial system of the older and allegedly more mature, disciplining and training their inferiors. But the empire did not necessarily offer a quick and easy fortune. Investing money overseas in the nineteenth century offered equivalent risks to speculating in such territories as New Guinea, the Matto Grosso, or Antarctica to-day. It is often forgotten that more money was lost in colonial investment than was ever earned by it. Younger sons who went out to make their fortunes often made an early grave instead. Most of the judgements about the wickedness of British imperialism were uttered when countries such as Uganda, Burma, Zimbabwe, Sudan and Sri Lanka were living peacefully and prosperously.

Kitchener's awareness of the difference between a good and a bad empire had been sharpened by his experience of the Turkish Empire in decline. This he observed to be cruel, corrupt and inefficient. He would be happy to see it changed, but not for the worse. In 1878 he could see that if Britain did not take certain measures other countries would try to exploit the Turkish situation. Russia had already shown her hand by attacking Turkey four times that century, France would not sit idly by if there was territory to be acquired by military or diplomatic enterprise, and Germany, well, Germany's naked ambition was obvious to the dullest. Once his mind was made up, Kitchener never wavered in his conviction that the strengthening and extension of British influence, within or without the Empire, was essential for world harmony.

His relationship with Wolseley did not, however, begin on a cordial note. Wolseley thought that young Kitchener was a little too confident in himself and that the idea of a serving officer being employed by the Foreign Office instead of the Army was nonsense. He listened impatiently to Kitchener's ideas for producing a map of Cyprus like the Palestine survey, and brusquely told him that all that was necessary was a simple map which would be adequate for military and financial purposes. Kitchener tried to press his views, but was abruptly overruled. A general was in command, not a fledgling lieutenant. Kitchener did not give in lightly and wrote to the Foreign Office for confirmation, an act which annoyed Wolseley; although not actually challenging his commander-in-chief's authority, it came very near it. And it did Kitchener no good. Wolseley managed to arrange that Kitchener's expenses should be paid from the Cyprus revenues, rather than the Foreign Office, and then instructed Kitchener how much would be paid and for what purpose. Kitchener took the decision with bad grace. He was tempted to apply for a transfer to another post but decided that such an act might have unpleasant repercussions. Wolseley had seen the survey as taking at the most a year, possibly only a few months, but two years later Kitchener was still at it and his relationship with his commander-in-chief was, to say the least, cool. Then in April 1879 Wolseley was appointed commander-in-chief in South Africa. Kitchener promptly wrote to his friend Colonel Charles Wilson who had begun the original survey in Palestine, and asked to be posted; he suggested Anatolia.

This area, which lies along the southern shores of the Black Sea, seemed the place most likely to be the target of the next Russian attack on Turkish territory. At the Congress of Berlin, Britain had guaranteed to safeguard the territorial integrity of Turkey (although detaching Cyprus from it seems hardly in the spirit, let alone the letter, of the agreement) and in consequence had been able to persuade the Sultan of Turkey to allow British officers to help with his defence arrangements.

This enabled Britain to send a small military mission, which was officially part of the consular service. In Anatolia Kitchener made friends among the Turks, although generally horrified by their cruel and incompetent behaviour to their subject people. But the job lasted eight months only. Wolseley's successor in Cyprus was Major-General Sir Robert Biddulph, and his views of what was needed in Cyprus coincided with Kitchener's. Kitchener, to his surprise and pleasure, was invited back with better conditions all round and appointed Director of Survey for Cyprus. It was as well for him that he went when he did, for in 1880 Disraeli fell, Gladstone took his place, and the military missions were withdrawn from Asia Minor.

30

Kitchener's fortunes flourished during his second tour of duty in Cyprus. Not only did he complete the survey to his liking, but he also reorganised the Cyprus land registry into a form which he firmly believed should be applied in Britain. The project took three years. During this period he became a very good horseman, kept his own horses, was whip to the local hunt, and won numerous races both on the flat and over the fences. He shared a house in Nicosia with another ardent horseman, Lord John Kennedy of the Royal Scots. Kitchener had brought a bear cub with him from Anatolia and the two kept it as a pet. Kitchener, who had alternated between looking like a tramp and a dandy according to his employment, now began cultivating the enormous moustache which later seemed his most striking feature. Although in the 1980s 'heavy' moustaches such as Kitchener's strike one as being slightly absurd, they were very popular a hundred years ago, and moustache cups were much in evidence which possessed an upper rim which enabled the owner to drink without soaking his carefully trained creation in soup or some other liquid. Doubtless Kitchener had seen some very impressive moustaches worn by fierce-looking Turks and decided he could do as well, if not better.

There is no record of Kitchener's having any feminine attachments in Cyprus, a fact usually interpreted as a sign he must have been homosexual. There is absolutely no reason to suppose that he was, although homosexuals have often tried to claim him as one of their own. His celibacy seems to have been based on the fact that he was religious, moral, shy, and unwilling to make a fool of himself. He had been devoted to his mother, who had died when he was a mere boy, but had been equally ready to show affection to his stepmother when his father married again. He took the break-up of the second marriage badly, and yet it did not ultimately prejudice him against the idea of marriage. As a young man he had insufficient money to marry, even if he had wished to, and he also clearly had very little opportunity of meeting a suitable partner. There were none at Woolwich, and soon after commissioning he was posted to the exclusively male society in Palestine. Both here and in Turkey and Cyprus he was doubtless offered the local prostitutes. It is unlikely that these would have been both attractive and disease-free, and he probably thought they were revolting. Even a less sensitive person than Kitchener, such as the average British soldier, often prefers celibacy to the invitations to intimacy which he encounters wherever he goes. Kitchener would not have believed that he had to have sexual liaisons in order to remain normal and healthy. Many young men, of strong Christian training, believed they would be healthier and happier living a celibate life. Sex, it was believed, could be sublimated. Cold baths and hard exercise were considered adequate to dispel any uncomfortable desires. For men or women who had what is now called 'a low sex drive', it was quite easy to remain celibate. Jane Austen mocked at the ideas of her day when she wrote: 'It is a truth universally acknowledged that a single man in possession of good fortune must be in want of a wife.'

There seems little doubt that, by the time the Cyprus survey was nearing completion, Kitchener had developed a high opinion of himself. He was aware of his abilities as an archaeological surveyor and suggested to the Foreign Office that, on the strength of his experience in Cyprus, he should be appointed British Consul in Mosul. There, without neglecting his duties as consul, he would be able to make valuable surveys of the sites of ancient civilisations. He had been offered a chance to undertake work for the British Museum in that area, though only on a temporary basis, but had been refused leave to go. The post of British Consul seemed, to Kitchener, the ideal solution. It did not, however, seem as ideal to his commander-in-chief who, although generally sympathetic to his ideas, had formed the opinion that Kitchener was beginning to chase too many hares for a young officer in the British Army.

Kitchener looked around for a suitable area to which he might apply for posting. Somewhat optimistically he applied to Wolseley for a post in South Africa; Wolseley, as might be expected, had no vacancy. That left Egypt only. Egypt offered wonderful opportunities, and soon Kitchener became obsessed with the idea of it.

In so far as Kitchener was talented at creating order out of chaos, Egypt was certainly a suitable place for him to display his abilities. The country was in turmoil. A new phase in Egypt's millennial history had begun when it was conquered by the Arabs in 639 AD. By the Middle Ages it had become a powerful and influential country, but in the sixteenth century it had reverted to being a province of the Ottoman Empire, ruled by the Khedive (viceroy to the Sultan of Turkey) assisted by a corrupt and incompetent entourage. In the 1870s the Khedive, Ismail, had governed so extravagantly and incompetently that a country which should have been rich was instead on the verge of bankruptcy. This enabled Disraeli, in 1875, to purchase Ismail's holding of Suez Canal shares, which was nearly half the total amount issued, for four million pounds. As Britain was a principal user of the canal, this was a businesslike acquisition. It also gave Britain influence in an area which was vital to her imperial interests.

However, even selling the canal shares did not solve the Khedive's financial problems, and in 1879 he abdicated in favour of his son Tewfik. France and Britain therefore decided to safeguard their interests and investment by establishing the 'dual control' over the new Khedive and appointing ministers to take charge of Egyptian finances. Tewfik had no objection to these moves, which seemed the only alternative to national bankruptcy, but some of his ministers, and in particular a soldier named Arabi Pasha, resented the foreign interference bitterly. Arabi raised a revolt in 1881 and gained control of the government. A wave of anti-foreign sentiment swept across the country, directed not merely at the British and French but also against the Turks. In 1882 fifty Europeans were murdered in Alexandria. Britain invited France to assist in joint punitive measures, but the French, more apprehensive of Bismarck than of events in Egypt, did not wish to be embroiled in the Middle East. A British fleet was sent to bombard the batteries which Arabi's followers were constructing at Alexandria, but this only led to more massacres of Europeans. Britain, having gone this far, felt she had to go still further. Wolseley was instructed to raise a force and restore the safety of British residents in Egypt. This he proceeded to do at the battle of Tel-el-Kebir in September 1882. Tewfik was restored and some British forces were left in the country.

While the suppression of Arabi's revolt was in preparation, Kitchener made strenuous efforts to take an active part. He sent several telegrams to those he thought might arrange a posting, stressing his knowledge of Arabic. They had no effect. So far he had observed the French fight the Germans, and the Turks fight the Russians, but had never had an opportunity to show what he himself could do when Britain went into action. Now, it seemed, that moment had arrived. If he was to make headway in the Army he must do it in a campaign. Surveys and secondments would earn him good reports, but they could not lead to rapid promotion in the way military action could do. There had been few opportunities for campaigning in his lifetime; the Crimean War had ended when he was six. Here was the opportunity, but to be in a position to take it seemed almost impossible.

With a dishonesty which is difficult to reconcile with his normal high moral principles, he requested a week's sick leave. He was aware that nobody would enquire where he had spent it and, as soon as it was granted, hastened to take a ship from Cyprus to Alexandria. There he hoped that his knowledge of Arabic would prove indispensable, that he would be retained, and that the Cyprus situation could be sorted out later. At Alexandria he made his way to the military liaison officer to the commander of the Mediterranean fleet and

33

explained that his knowledge of Arabic would enable him to spy out the rebel government's defences. The liaison officer was intrigued with the suggestion and together, in disguise, they made a useful reconnaissance of Arabi's dispositions. They returned safely.

The success of this little mission seems to have gone to Kitchener's head. He applied for further employment; it was promised if the High Commissioner in Cyprus raised no objection. Needless to say, the High Commissioner, who had been very kind to Kitchener in the past, flatly refused to be steam-rollered in this way. Kitchener, suspecting that the answer from Cyprus might not be to his liking, kept well out of the way until the next boat to Cyprus had left. Then he came out of hiding and asked what answer had been given. As he expected, it was not the one he wished to hear. However he could not return to Cyprus immediately for there was no boat for another week. Like most people of high moral principles who abandon them for some temporary advantage, Kitchener did not know how best to extricate himself from this delicate situation. Everyone he met told him that war was inevitable and that if he could stay in Egypt longer he would be caught up in it. At the end of what could only be a victorious campaign he could then try to make his peace with the authorities, notably the High Commissioner for Cyprus. In the general euphoria all minor misdemeanours would no doubt be forgotten.

His view of the speed of developments was, however, incorrect. The bombardment duly took place, and he was able to witness it from the flagship. But his presence was entirely unofficial – he was not even in uniform, and after the bombardment his return to Cyprus could not be delayed any more. He returned. Sir Robert Biddulph appears to have acted with astonishing forbearance when he overlooked the deceit over the application for leave and the fact that Kitchener had overstayed his allotted week by another three. However, the former friendly relationship was clearly at an end. Kitchener wrote a pompous letter to the High Commissioner in which he said how pained he was over Biddulph's view of his absence in Alexandria and that he felt that Egypt was where his duty had called him. He would happily complete the survey or, if the High Commissioner would now let him depart for Egypt, he would gladly pay for some substitute to do his work. Alternatively, he would come back and complete the survey after a period of duty in Egypt. This episode reveals that Kitchener was so determined and ambitious that he could see his 'duty' as justifying what others might have thought to be sharp practice by an ambitious man. Doubtless Biddulph was not deceived but, being disappointed in Kitchener

34

and not wishing to have a sulky assistant on his hands, decided that if the young sapper was posted, a more than adequate replacement could quickly be found.

Within weeks of Kitchener's return to Cyprus, General Wolseley had finished off Arabi. It had been a small but brilliant campaign in which Wolseley took a number of risks. It was, however, conclusive only in so far as it removed Arabi. All the other problems remained, and in a worse condition than before. Politically Egypt was still regarded as Turkish territory, but in the absence of any effort by the Sultan to assist Tewfik to stabilize the situation or maintain law and order, it fell to the victor of Tel-el-Kebir to put the Egyptian house in order. That completed, the British force would gracefully withdraw.

The Egyptian Army, which had backed Arabi's rebellion, clearly had to be disbanded, but Egypt, which was also, if only nominally, ruler of the Sudan, could not be left without an army. Accordingly Major-General Sir Evelyn Wood, VC was appointed commander-in-chief of the armed forces in Egypt, with the brief to raise and train a force of some six thousand men.

General Wood's title was Sirdar, a Hindustani word which origi-nally meant 'leader and possessor'. It was frequently used when Kitchener himself later held that office. Wood was yet another example of those generals whose careers read like a boys' adventure story. He had first seen action in the Crimea, when he was actually in the Royal Navy but had been sent ashore for special duties. From then onwards, wherever there was trouble, Wood seemed to be in it, taking impossible risks and having hair's-breadth escapes. He too became a field-marshal.

Before returning to Cyprus, Kitchener had made useful contacts. One of these was Sir Evelyn Wood's ADC. It was no surprise therefore when the following December a message went from the Commander-in-Chief, Egyptian Army, via the High Commissioner of Cyprus that he would be glad to offer Lieutenant Kitchener a two-year engagement if he could be released from his Cyprus employment. Kitchener, who seems to have planned all this with a somewhat disagreeable degree of cunning, refused the offer, calcu-lating that Biddulph would be pleased at this demonstration of loyalty by his subordinate. Biddulph was indeed pleased. He would have been markedly less pleased if he had known that Kitchener had arranged with the ADC to cable a second time, on this occasion saying that Kitchener was urgently wanted for second-in-command of a cavalry regiment.

The appointment of a sapper to be second-in-command of a cavalry regiment seems to have been a whim of the new commander-in-chief who, as we have seen, began his military life as a sailor, exchanged that for the cavalry, and continued his career in the infantry. He said to Sir Reginald Wingate, 'You're a gunner, so I'll put you in the Intelligence,' and to Kitchener, 'You're an engineer, so I'll put you in the cavalry.' However it seems that both had previously expressed a keen interest in those arms.

An unorthodox and resolute approach was certainly needed. Wood refuted all criticism of the Egyptians by saying: 'Can't fight? They can. They have never had fair play. Treat them justly, train them well and they will go anywhere and do anything.' Kitchener echoed these remarks, and of the Egyptian soldier said, 'Give him a chance. The same blood courses in his veins as runs in those wild Arabs of the desert. Discipline, discipline, discipline – that is the one thing needful.'

In the late nineteenth century British cavalry was at the height of its prestige. It was heir to some three thousand years of cavalry development. In the battles of pre-Christian times, skilful cavalry commanders had shown how that arm could be decisive in battle, often bringing sudden and overwhelming victory. A late cavalry charge had won the decisive battle of Hastings in 1066, Cromwell had ended the first phase of the Civil War at Naseby by the skilful use of cavalry, Marlborough had won most of his victories with it, and at Waterloo, where cavalry had played a vital role, Kitchener's father's regiment had earned special distinction. And these were the merest fraction of the numerous battles and campaigns in which cavalry had won victory and prestige. Kitchener's father had served most of his military life in the 13th Dragoons and was unlikely to have left his sons unaware of the importance of the cavalry on the battlefield.

Kitchener was well aware of the social and military standing of the cavalry in all the armies of his day. As a sapper, with a foot-on-the-ground attitude to warfare, he must have been fully alert to the fact that the invention of barbed wire, and the development of the machine-gun (used successfully in the American Civil War some twenty years earlier) meant that, whatever its prestige and past glories, the cavalry had a doubtful future in European warfare. However, any warfare in which the Egyptian Army took part was likely to be against forces using extremely unsophisticated weapons. Thus in choosing the cavalry for his speciality, Kitchener knew that this was an area where spectacular, talked-of victories could be won. He may perhaps have envisaged leading cavalry charges himself: he was by now a good horseman and his courage was second to none. A few years later his knowledge of cavalry would stand him in good stead; in the Sudan his opponents would include not only some of the bravest cavalry the world has ever seen, but also foot soldiers whose ability to stop a cavalry charge seemed nothing short of miraculous.

The cavalry of the Egyptian Army was commanded by Lt-Colonel Taylor of the 19th Hussars. He may have been surprised initially at the appointment of a sapper for his assistant, but he was soon full of admiration for him. Our knowledge of this period is largely based on an article in a monthly magazine named *The Nineteenth Century*. The writer, John Macdonald, was also war correspondent for the *Daily News*. Macdonald wrote of Kitchener:

Taylor had invited me the night before to accompany him and his friend, and to witness the operations which they were both to supervise. A tall, slim, thin-faced, slightly stooping figure in long boots, 'cut-away' dark morning-coat, and the Egyptian fez somewhat tilted over his eyes—such as I remember him was the young soldier who was destined to fulfil Gordon's task of 'smashing the Mahdi'.

'He's quiet,' Taylor whispered to me as we were getting ready. 'That's his way.' And again, with a characteristic jerk of the head, 'He's clever.' And so, in the raw, greyish, early morning of 8th January 1883, the three of us drove in our dingy rattle-trap over the white dusty road Nilewards to meet the fellah cavaliers. Taylor did most of the talking. Kitchener expressed himself in an occasional nod or monosyllable.

At the barracks we found some forty men waiting. I remember Kitchener's gaze at the awkward, slipshod group, as he took his position in the centre of a circular space round which the riders were to show their paces. 'We begin with the officers,' said Taylor, turning to me, 'we shall train them first, then put them to drill the troops. We have no troopers just yet, though we have 440 horses ready for them.'

And now began the selection of the fellah officers. They were to be tested in horsemanship. The first batch of them were ordered to mount. Round they went, Indian file, Kitchener, like a circus master, standing in the centre. Had he flourished a long whip he might have passed for a show-master at rehearsal. Neither audible nor visible sign did he give of any feeling aroused in him by a performance mostly disappointing and sometimes ridiculous. His hands buried in his trouser pockets, he quietly watched the emergence of the least unfit.

In half an hour or so the first native officers of the new fellah cavalry were chosen. It was then that Kitchener made his longest speech. 'We'll have to drive it into these fellows,' he muttered, thinking aloud.

At that time Kitchener had been a captain for just four days, having been promoted on 4 January. But as it was the custom to promote British officers in the Egyptian Army to one rank (sometimes two ranks) higher than their rank in the British Army, Kitchener now became a major almost at once. Nobody was surprised at his rapid advance. Sir Evelyn Baring, the future Lord Cromer, noted that Kitchener seemed 'to have a finger in every pie'.

So Kitchener's name regularly figured in reports. He was respected for his efficiency, but not popular. Those who knew him well felt that he had spent too much time in lonely and dangerous places to be attracted to club gossip. And as the alternative to social life was work, Kitchener soon developed the reputation of being obsessively industrious.

Chapter 4

The Desert Scene

Taking service with the Egyptian Army was a calculated risk. The recent defeat of Arabi's army at Tel-el-Kebir had confirmed general military opinion that the Egyptians were little more than a bad joke on the battlefield. This view, though understandable, was unfair to Wolseley and his army who had executed a daring and dangerous manoeuvre to take Arabi by surprise. His night approach march had culminated in a pre-dawn attack, and such tactical moves, though highly effective when nothing goes astray, can easily end in disaster.

However, Kitchener, in spite of his reference to desert Arab blood in the Egyptians, must have been well aware that the material with which he had decided to work had no martial tradition at all. If an army like the Turks' was badly administered and led, it might still fight well in battle because the Turk was a doughty warrior. But the Egyptian fellaheen could not be relied upon to display similar characteristics. The only hope for the Egyptian Army was training and still more training. There was no middle class with a tradition of leadership and responsibility. Kitchener was recruiting his officers from the fellahs, the peasants. No one in the long years of cavalry history had taken such a course willingly or successfully. Even Cromwell had stressed the need for spirited young men: 'Do you think that the spirits of base and mean fellows will ever be able to encounter gentlemen that have honour and courage and resolution in them? You must get men of spirit that is likely to go as far as gentlemen go, or else I am sure you will be beaten still.' Even with these desirable qualities, Cromwell stressed the need for endless training. Kitchener was virtually trying to make bricks without straw. But then bricks had been made without straw in Egypt before, as Kitchener, as a keen student of the Bible, would know.

However, he was losing friends. Claude Conder, who had been with him from pre-Woolwich days and had given him the chance to

39

join the Palestine survey, was now greatly incensed by his feeling that Kitchener had passed off much of Conder's work as his own. Kitchener had, of course, taken command of the survey after Conder's injury (which but for Kitchener's intervention might have been fatal) and had produced the final report. It is impossible at this distance in time to know whether in fact Kitchener had given Conder sufficient credit for his work. It seems possible that he had not, if only for the reason that by the time he was writing the report he had probably forgotten just how much Conder had contributed to the survey.

Conder's sense of grievance went so deep that when in November 1883 he was asked to make constructive suggestions to help Kitchener in a survey of the Arabah valley (near Aquaba), he flatly refused to help. Kitchener was spending a two-month leave working with Professor Edward Hull, an eminent geologist, on the survey, which was being conducted under the auspices of the Palestine Exploration Fund. One cannot help feeling that there were faults on both sides, but that more perhaps lay on Kitchener's than Conder's.

In the end the Arabah survey was only a partial success. It has been said that Kitchener thought the professor unduly cautious; the professor, for his part, felt it was all very well for Kitchener, who was a professional soldier, to risk his neck in areas of dubious value, but that he should not expect a civilian to take the same chances. The survey ended unexpectedly soon, for the expedition was recalled by Sir Evelyn Wood. There had been bad news from the Sudan. The Arab world was extremely excited by the news that a new prophet had arisen and that Arab forces had wiped out a strong British expeditionary force. Kitchener decided to make his way back across the desert, two hundred miles of country which, as far as was known, had few wells and no roads in it. The professor advised against this route and himself went home more slowly and safely via Gaza.

In the event the professor was right. Kitchener arrived safely but the going proved much harder than he had anticipated. He was accompanied by four men and four camels on the journey. He wrote of it: 'We passed a good many Arabs of the Jerabin and Ma'azi tribes, and I was received among them as Abdullah Bey, an Egyptian official, thus reviving a name well-known and much revered amongst them: they supposed me to be a relation of the great Sheikh Abdulah. I was everywhere well received.

'But the last two days' travelling were the most trying I have ever experienced; a very strong west wind blew the sand right up into our faces, so that the camels could hardly face it. I travelled every day from 8 a.m. to 6 p.m. and with very little variation. One night we had

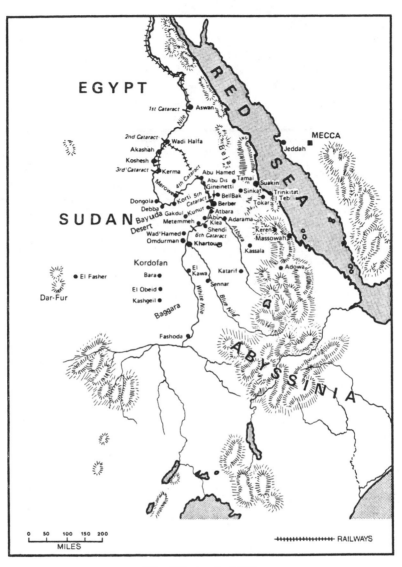

The Nile in the 1880s

to travel a good deal after dark to make a brackish pool of water, and I very nearly lost the party as we had to separate to hunt for the water.'[1]

The glare and fragments of scrub blown by the wind damaged his eyes, permanently though not badly. They also damaged the nerve endings in his face, giving him occasional pain later, and perhaps contributing to that somewhat bleak look of his later photographs.

Egypt and the Sudan were on the verge of stirring events, and heading for a crisis which would not be resolved for fourteen years. In 1844 there had been born on an island in the Nile a boy who was christened Mohammed Ahmed Ibn Al-Sayid Abdulah, but who would be known in future years by the shorter and more significant title of 'the Mahdi' – 'the Guided One'. His father, who was a boat builder, claimed descent from the Prophet. From an early age the boy demonstrated deep religious qualities, outstanding intelligence, and a belief, which others would soon share, in his special powers. In the early 1880s (the exact date is not known) he revealed to the Arab world the news that he was truly 'the Mahdi'. No one was greatly surprised; he looked the part and had an impressive personality. Even more convincing was the fact that he bore the distinguishing marks of 'the Expected One', a V-shaped aperture between his teeth and a birthmark on his right cheek. One mark would not suffice; the Mahdi would have both.

The followers of the Mahdi became known to the outside world as Dervishes, although they themselves preferred the term 'ansar' which means 'helper'. The original Ansar were the people of Medina who had helped the prophet Mohammed when he was in exile.

The title 'Dervish' was more usually applied to Moslem friars who had taken vows of poverty and austerity: the word literally means 'poor'. Some orders of the Dervishes developed highly individual practices—thus there were dancing dervishes, howling dervishes and singing dervishes—and these orders existed in a number of different countries. One characteristic of the Dervishes who followed first the Mahdi and then his successor, the Khalifa, was that they were astonishingly brave and enduring.

As the arrival of the Mahdi was taken as the sign that his followers would now be led to freedom in which they could practise their religion unimpeded, it is not surprising that there was soon consider-able unrest in the Sudan. At first the Egyptian government was inclined to assume that this was merely an expression of temporary

[1] Report to the Palestine Exploration fund, 1884.

local delusion. There had, in the past, been nearly forty Arabs who had claimed to be Mahdi. However, accepted military opinion, based on long experience, was that risings led by fanatical local leaders could do much damage before they were checked. Murder, rape, arson and looting were to be expected after initial victories. Later, when weight and steady pressure was brought to bear on marauders, who were probably already loaded down with plunder, the end would not long be delayed. Then the movement would crumble, the damage would be paid for and repaired, and all would soon be forgotten.

But this was different. The followers of the Mahdi adhered closely to the vows of austerity and poverty. They went to battle with primitive weapons and in ragged clothes. They did not fall apart after victory. They remained a coherent fighting force. Militarily, they displayed new and unexpected skills.

How dangerous the Dervishes were would be made all to clear to their opponents in the following years. When Kitchener heard the news of their early successes he realised that the cavalry he had been training might find themselves put to the test in the very near future. Kitchener was aware how well men will fight if they feel they have a cause and a true religion and he did not underrate the problems of the future. Nevertheless, he found time to complain that his work in the Arabah valley seemed to have been insufficiently appreciated. He was slightly mollified when Sir Charles Wilson wrote him a laudatory letter and the Palestine Exploration Fund voted him an honorarium of fifty guineas.

The Sudan, which was not to occupy Kitchener's attention, was vast, little known and exceptionally difficult for an invader. It is nearly a million square miles in area. This makes it almost equivalent in size to Western Europe. The northern two-thirds is desert country; the remainder is swamp, scrub and jungle. G. W. Steevens, who was there as a war correspondent, described the north in dramatic terms:

The Sudan has no colour and no age—just a monotone of squalid barbarism. Nothing goes green. Only yellow halfa grass to make you stumble and sapless mimosa to tear your eyes; dom palms that mock with wooden fruit and sodom apples that lure you with flatulent poison. For beasts it has tarantulas and scorpions and serpents, devouring white ants, and every kind of bug that creeps and crawls. Its people are naked and dirty; ignorant and besotted. It is a quarter of a continent of sheer squalor. Overhead the pitiless furnace of the sun, underfoot the never-ending treadmill of the

43

sand, dust in the throat, tuneless singing in the ears, searing flame in the eye—the Sudan is a God-accursed wilderness, an empty limbo of torment for ever and ever.

And yet—and yet there never was an Englishman who had been there but was ready and anxious to go again![1]

There is, of course, considerable variety in the Sudan, even if it all possesses a common harshness. The north of the country is Arab; the south African. The Nile is the only attribute they share, and the river, although vital to the country, is by no means easy or safe. In parts it is made dangerous by crocodiles, cataracts, and some of the people who live on its banks. By the time it reaches the Sudan it has already flowed down for two thousand miles. It is joined by other rivers in the southern Sudan, then later at Khartoum by the Blue Nile (never fully explored till 1969), which rises in Lake Tara, Ethiopia, then by the river Atbara at the town of Atbara. It flows into Egypt at Wadi Halfa and five of its six cataracts occur between Wadi Halfa and Khartoum. The principle exports in the time of Arab supremacy were ivory and slaves, and of these the latter was by far the most plentiful and profitable. Even in the early 1880s there were no less than 1500 slave traders operating in the Sudan, and the number of Sudanese slaves was said to be 50,000. Some slaves were sold in the Sudan itself but most in Egypt. The average Arab regarded a slave as an essential, much in the same way that Western men look upon a motor car. Attempts, notably by Gordon, had been made to stamp out the slave trade, but these had had little impact. Slaves were usually sold to traders by local sheikhs and the only development likely to stop this infamous practice was the exhaustion of the source of supply. A Slavery Abolition Act had been passed in the British Parliament in 1825 and in subsequent years the British Navy had conducted a continuous and effective campaign to stamp out the slave trade on sea routes. However, the overland slave trade proved more intractable, and even today a trickle of slave trading continues in certain remote areas of the world.

Although the twentieth century has been rich in condemnation of people like Kitchener, and the word 'imperialist' is a term of abuse, it is worth recalling that the motivation of many imperialists was to civilise other countries and stamp out abuses. They did not consider whether they had a God-given right to rule territories occupied by alien people; they merely considered it was best for all if they should do so. In 1883 Kitchener saw a need to train an efficient Egyptian Army so that political and financial reforms could be supported by a

[1] Steevens died of an unspecified fever at Ladysmith in 1900.

44

force strong enough to keep law and order at home and to protect its possessions abroad.

The news which came out of the Sudan in early 1883 suggested that the sooner Egypt had a proper army the safer life would become for many Sudanese and Egyptians. The Dervishes had already shown their feelings towards the Egyptians in the Sudan and had besieged two sizeable towns, El Obeid and Bara. The inhabitants of those towns could see little benefit from being 'liberated' by the Dervishes.

In consequence, a retired colonel of the Indian Army who was serving as chief of staff to the Egyptian Army by the name of Hicks Pasha,[1] was instructed to take an army into the Sudan and suppress the Dervishes before the situation got completely out of hand. He collected an expeditionary force from the remains of Arabi's army, half of whom had disappeared from the battlefield of Tel-el-Kebir without firing a shot. It included 1800 who had already been rejected for the new Egyptian Army. The low morale in Hicks' 9000-strong army was not improved by the hardships of the journey. A member of the expedition who left it before it was annihilated (having been sent back because of heatstroke) wrote of one part of it: 'Our camels sank into the fine quicksand at every step and we were glad to get on to firmer ground, however dreary. And a gloomier waste man never saw than that in which we encamped. There was no water, not a vestige of vegetation, nor of organic life of any kind. The loose black boulders with which the plain was strewn gave a terrible aspect to it. They looked as if they had been blackened by fire and the whole region seemed to be the debris of a vast conflagration—the cinders of a burnt-up world.'

When the ill-fated expedition reached Berber, Hicks learnt that El Obeid and Bara had surrendered with 7000 men, 10,000 guns, and a vast quantity of ammunition. Darfur and Kordofan had also been captured by the Dervishes.

Eventually Hicks reached Khartoum; here he began to drill and train his troops into the semblance of a fighting force. He then pressed on into Dervish-threatened territory. By now Hicks' army was beginning to look more soldier-like. Local chieftains became confident it should be able to protect them if they did not join the Mahdi. At the end of June the column was attacked by Baggara cavalry, which were the élite of the Dervish force. Nevertheless, these

[1] 'Pasha' is a Turkish word denoting an officer of high rank. There are four grades of pasha and they are distinguished by the number of horses' tails displayed on a banner. Hicks' grade was approximately equal to lieutenant-general in the British Army.

45

attacks were beaten off. After one battle 500 dead Dervishes were counted on the field. There was no difficulty over assessing enemy losses; Dervishes fought until they were dead or victorious.

Hicks, thinking that by now the Mahdi rebellion had spent its force, decided to begin the long march back to Khartoum. His ramshackle army had acquitted itself well and was a tribute to the leadership shown by Hicks and his officers, but now it was exhausted, as well as short of ammunition, supplies and water. By this stage the Mahdi had amassed an army of 20,000, on the basis that all who joined him would have 'Paradise and all its joys' and all who declined would have a hand and a foot cut off. It closed on Hicks' column and attacked in force in early November. Once again Hicks beat off the initial attacks, inflicting heavy losses on the Dervishes, but finally, surrounded and short of all supplies, his courageous force was overwhelmed. Hicks set a fine example himself, firing his revolver from the saddle until his horse was killed beneath him, and then continuing the struggle on foot with his sword. Eventually he was killed by several spear thrusts. Dervishes who had taken part in the final massacre (known as the battle of Sheikan) gave an account of the event later and had considerable admiration for Hicks' achievements.

In view of the fact that the Hicks' expedition has usually been dismissed as a ridiculous and expensive blunder which came to a deserved end, it should be noted that the venture came near to success, that the despised Egyptians put up a sterling fight, that Hicks himself displayed considerable courage and initiative, and that their experiences gave warning of the potential strength of the Dervishes. These experiences, and the successes and failures of the expedition, were carefully noted by Kitchener when he set about planning his own Sudan expedition many years later.

On hearing of the disastrous end to Hicks' venture, Gladstone's government found itself in a dilemma. It was clear that Egypt had now lost control of its Sudanese territory, and could not recover it without effort and expenditure which it could be no part of Liberal policy to provide. On the other hand, Egypt had now become a British dependency; its government contained many British nationals and was under effective British control. This meant that Britain had some responsibility for the safety of the Egyptian garrison and traders still in the Sudan; unless these were evacuated their fate was not likely to be pleasant. It was therefore decided that Egypt should proclaim a formal abandonment of the Sudan, but that help should be given in the withdrawal of the Egyptian garrison and their families. British soldiers could not be used to facilitate this, but an experienced general should be despached as soon as possible to arrange the evacuation.

The best available man for the task was clearly General Charles Gordon. Gordon, like Kitchener, was a Sapper, but was seventeen years older than the future field-marshal. He had fought with spectacular courage in the Crimean War and then followed this by distinguished service in China. There he had raised a 3500-strong peasant army and defended Shanghai with it for eighteen months, finally crushing the attacking rebels. Gordon was a brilliant organiser and leader; he was apt to lead troops into the hottest part of a battle carrying nothing more lethal than a walking stick. He was a Liberal and a devout Christian, and he had been in the Sudan before. On his previous tour of duty he had made strenuous and often successful efforts to impede slave traders. But in sending him to Khartoum to evacuate the remaining garrison in the Sudan at this stage, Gladstone was asking for a miracle which even the mythical powers of Gordon could not manage.

On 18 January 1884 Gordon met the Liberal Cabinet in London and was given his orders. On 18 February he arrived in Khartoum and took stock of a very unenviable situation. The garrison consisted of 7000 men of dubious loyalty whose numbers did not allow them to man the crude fortifications of the town effectively. He was well aware that all the Arab slave dealers hated him for actions against them in the past, and he suspected that the Mahdi had already infiltrated a number of spies and supporters into the city, probably into the very army with which he was supposd to be defending it.

Within less than a month of his arrival in the town, Khartoum was in a state of siege. Gladstone's government, which had hoped that Gordon would handle the awkward business of the evacuation swiftly and inexpensively, was annoyed to receive a series of letters pointing out the impossibility of the task they had given him. For his own part, Gordon was to begin with sustained by his religious belief, but as the weather in Khartoum became hotter and Gladstone's government appeared to be doing nothing to get him out of the unenviable position into which they had put him, even Gordon's patience became frayed. In desperation he suggested that the Sultan of Turkey should be asked to send an expedition; he felt the Turks would know exactly how to counter the Mahdi's movement. But neither this nor any other plan found favour with Gladstone's cabinet until it was too late to succeed.

However, the plight of Gordon and the besieged city of Khartoum was not lost on the people of Britain. Public indignation was fanned by press activity. Alarmed at this demonstration of strong feeling against the government, the cabinet held urgent consultation and decided to send a relief expedition. The only possible route was up the the Nile; all the other approaches were now in the hands of the Dervishes. But the Nile, as we mentioned earlier, had its own particular difficulties.

For a relief expedition of such urgency, as well as of such public interest, the government had to send the best possible general available. This, almost inevitably, was Wolseley. On account of his successes in various remote parts of the world, Sir Garnet Wolseley had earned the nickname 'Our only General'. He had been in the thick of the fighting in Burma, the Crimea, China, India, West Africa, and Zululand, and had won the decisive battle of Tel-el-Kebir by unorthodox and daring tactics. But perhaps his best qualification for the Nile relief force was the fact that in 1870 he had led an expedition 600 miles into the wilds of Manitoba to suppress a rebel who had proclaimed a republic there. His army had traversed almost unknown country and navigated rivers by means of portable canoes. He had forbidden all alcohol and tobacco to those taking part, but his unpopular methods were effective, for he took the rebel leader entirely by surprise.

Wolseley reached Cairo in early September with an army of 7000 troops from first-class British fighting regiments. He planned to transport them in 800 flat-bottomed boats which would be propelled by a combination of oars and sails. His meticulous preparations were a little too slow and deliberate on this occasion. The force set out on 5 October and made steady progress. The difficulties they overcame were immense; much of the route was either uncharted or, even worse, badly charted. In addition to its own supplies the expedition was carrying food for the thousands it planned to evacuate from Khartoum. They were attacked by Dervish troops but beat them off with courage that matched that of their fanatical adversaries. At the end of it all they arrived at Khartoum—two days after the city had fallen and Gordon had been killed.

Gordon had preserved hope until mid-December. It seemed inconceivable to him that he could have been besieged since mid-March without some effective force being raised to evacuate him and his troops. He showed on several occasions that the Dervishes could be routed but he had insufficient troops to do more than harass his besiegers. He sent a despatch down the Nile on 14 December 1884 saying that if he himself were in command of a mere two hundred men he was sure he could defeat the Arabs at Halfeyeh and then come on to Khartoum. But he added: 'MARK THIS, if the Expeditionary Force, and I ask for no more than two hundred men, does not come in ten days, the *town may fall* and I have done my best for the honour of our country. Goodbye.'

He held out for six more weeks. A ray of hope appeared when a message came from a spy in the Dervish camp to say that the relief force had inflicted a sharp defeat on an Arab force which had tried to stop its progress upstream. Unfortunately it was this event which sealed his fate, for the Mahdi realised that if he did not enter Khartoum at once the relief force would arrive and be more than a match for him. The final attacks went in just before dawn on 26 January. The Mahdi had given instructions that Gordon was not to be killed, but a small band of fanatics, probably imagining they were carrying out the Mahdi's true wishes, speared him to death. The Mahdi was genuinely angry.

The expedition, having failed to achieve its object, turned and went back downstream. The second journey was as hazardous as the first, the main difference being that upstream the voyage offered the prospect of a slow death; downstream the probability was a swift one in the cataracts.

Sir Evelyn Baring, later Lord Cromer, the consul-general, subsequently made an apt comment on the episode: 'A long course of misgovernment had culminated in a rebellion in the Sudan, which the Egyptian government was powerless to suppress. The abandonment of the Sudan, however undesirable, was imposed on the Egyptian government as an unpleasant but imperious necessity for the simple reason that after the destruction of General Hicks' army they were unable to keep it.'

But he went on to criticise the ministers who had allowed the loss of Khartoum and death of Gordon on the gounds that they had used arguments which 'appear to me to be rather those of debaters trained in the art of dialectics than of statesmen whose reason and imagination enables them to grasp in an instant the true situation in a distant country widely differing from their own'.

As the British government pondered on the events of 1884, the situation was already changing, and not for the better for them. The Mahdi died in June 1885 and was succeeded by the Khalifa Abdulla. The Khalifa, who belonged to the Baggara tribe, proved an extremely effective leader. In spite of his title, he was not a spiritual successor to the Mahdi; however, his despotic regime gave the Sudan more stability and unity than it had ever known before. The few local potentates who tried to challenge his authority met a swift fate. In consequence he held together as motley a collection of subjects as any tyrant has ever presided over. Although it is customary to talk of the Dervish Empire, the Khalifa did not succeed in extending the boundaries of his command beyond the Sudan itself. His attempts to expand into Egypt and Ethiopia were frustrated. Nevertheless, the success and range of his power were remarkable. A measure of his achievement is the powerful organisation eventually assembled by Kitchener to encompass his downfall.

In order to clarify an extremely complicated situation the main events of 1884 and 1885 have been outlined. However, outside the main theatre—which was the siege of Khartoum and the attempts to relieve it—there were a number of other incidents, most of which involved Kitchener.

Chapter 5

Kitchener the Adventurer

On returning to Cairo at the end of 1883 after the Arabah survey, Kitchener hoped to be able to complete his report on the territory at leisure. But by now the Mahdi's successes were alarming the Egyptian government and there was clearly going to be no time for unhurried report writing. In the event it was several months before a truncated version could be completed. There could be no question, for the time being at least, of sending another force along the route followed by the unfortunate Hicks' expedition. But pending British government action which, when it took place, meant the unwise move of sending Gordon to Khartoum, a small force was made up to operate against the Dervishes from a port named Suakin on the Red Sea. Suakin lay north-east of Khartoum and it was therefore thought to be in a useful position from which to harass the Mahdi's forces if they ventured in strength towards Egypt. The force was purely British and included the 19th and 10th Hussars. These took Colonels Grenfell and Taylor from the Egyptian cavalry, leaving Kitchener and Captain La Terrière of the 18th Hussars in charge. Kitchener and La Terrière shared a house, and from La Terrière's account of Kitchener at this time it is clear that he was taking his responsibilities more seriously than ever before, if that were possible.

Training began at dawn and included a steeple chase in which the Egyptian horsemen took a number of hard falls without complaint. Whether this was because Kitchener's faith in his material was being justified or whether a heavy fall was preferable to an interview with Kitchener is not easy to resolve. La Terrière mentions that Kitchener would often go straight from training to office work without even bothering to go in for breakfast. The hours he kept were arbitrary and unpredictable, to the despair of his juniors. One of these complained that he never knew 'at what times one was to get up or go to bed, at what hour one was to get breakfast, luncheon or dinner, or whether one was going to get a meal at all'.

Nothing, then or later, seemed to affect Kitchener's health. Lack of food or sleep, which would have brought another man to his knees, were matters of indifference. Hot weather suited him admirably, cold less so. If those who had known the delicate lad of Crotta had seen him now, they would not have been able to believe their eyes. In a contemporary pen-portrait quoted by Arthur he was 'very lean, with legs which seemed too long for his body, a narrow chest, and sloping shoulders. He had not an ounce of spare flesh on him. He was very sunburnt, which made his big light moustache look almost white; and he had thick and rather fair hair on a head with a very flat top to it, on which he always wore a tarboosh, even in the hottest sun. His slim appearance gave the impression of his being taller than he really was. He was brusque and cheery, and the curious cast in his left eye gave the impression that he saw right through you.'[1]

But he was not an inhuman automaton. La Terrière wrote: 'He did not often join in our little dinners and jaunts into Cairo, nor in our polo matches or paper chases; but he was not in the least shy in company, nor did he run away from the ladies. He had a few friends of his own, his taste in womankind tending rather to the motherly and "unsmart". He was certainly less a man of the world at that age than any one I have met, in many ways just a boy, with a boy's hearty laugh and cheery manner.'

On 8 February 1884 Kitchener was given orders to go to Qeneh (then spelt Keneh) on the Nile with a view to finding out the condition of the road to Quseir (then spelt Kosseir) on the Red Sea. Qeneh was 300 miles up the Nile. His report was so thorough that it was passed from the War Office to the Foreign Office. In it he exceeded his brief and included a scheme he had devised for recruiting a force of bedouins from the area to use against the Mahdi. This aroused interest. But the authorities were now considering landing a force of local levies at Suakin on the Red Sea and then sending it across to Berber, the nearest town on the Nile. So for the moment Kitchener went back to cavalry training. In the event the plan to send the force to Berber was abandoned because by the time it had been approved the town had already fallen to the Dervishes.

However, that event did not occur till late May and in April plans for the relief of Khartoum were still based on Egyptian possession of the town. Kitchener had been back with his cavalry regiment for a few days only when he was once again sent on his travels. This time it

[1] Op. cit.

was to take a party to Berber and from there to open up a route to Suakin. Opinions differed on the reliability of the governor of Berber, whose name was Hussein Pasha Khalifa. Gordon thought he was a traitor but Kitchener, who probably knew him better, decided he was as loyal as he could be in the circumstances. Kitchener was given a number of other assignments at the same time, such as checking the safety of the towns of Korosko and Abu Hamed, and was authorised to incur expenses of up to £10,000. With this he managed to organise a force of a thousand bedouins (all mounted on dromedaries) with a further thousand in reserve. In June he moved up to Korosko, but there the venture ended. Berber had gone, Abu Hamed was besieged, and even Dongola was threatened. The plan for the Suakin-Berber road was now clearly out of the question. He took the opportunity to send in a number of reports and assessments. In these he said that the Sudan would have to be reorganised sooner or later, and that it would require 20,000 troops.[1] (When he eventually defeated the Dervishes he had 25,000.) He went even further. He said that if the Dervishes were not checked now, and checked properly, Egypt herself would come under threat of invasion.

But at this stage neither the British nor Egyptian governments appeared to have realised the seriousness of the position. Kitchener's foresight in recruiting the bedouins turned out more valuable than even he had visualised. They roamed over the land between the Nile and the coast and, had they not been recruited by Kitchener, but instead given their allegiance to the Mahdi, the progress of the river relief column would have been vastly more difficult. Instead, Kitchener was able to establish strongpoints at various key areas in the desert. Money undoubtedly helped, but even then his task of making allies was not easy; the successes of the Dervishes in the remainder of the Sudan had not gone unreported in the areas where they planned to strike next. And he had his failures as well as his successes. One of the latter was at Dongola, where the local governor had already been promised by the Mahdi that he would be made an emir, a minor prince, if he threw in his lot with the Dervishes. On receipt of the news that a large British force was moving up-river he decided to put his army under Kitchener's direction. Kitchener found them lazy, inefficient and badly behaved, but they proved just adequate to repel a Dervish raid on Korti.

In July Kitchener received a further batch of instructions. They included making a reconnaissance of the country south of Korti, and enlisting on the Egyptian side as many of the local tribes as could be

[1] See Appendix.

persuaded or bribed. The financial inducements were kept as low as a prudent treasury could set them, but Kitchener made this parsimonious policy work by a careful selection of the right recipients. He occasionally expressed exasperation at the fact that he was sent coins of a type he had previously reported were the least acceptable. Gold was the preferred currency, because silver was depreciating in value; nevertheless the Finance Department continued to send some of his money in silver. An exception to official meanness was to offer to give a huge bribe of £10,000 to one tribe, the Kababish, if they would agree to relieve Khartoum. However, although they lived near to the town and knew all the exits and entrances, Kitchener very much doubted whether they were up to the task. Their prowess in a later battle showed him to have been right in his pessimistic view.

His latest brief gave Kitchener the opportunity to exercise his own initiative and negotiate at his own risk. His enterprise and achievements were so obviously consistent and valuable that, on the strength of them, Sir Evelyn Wood, the commander-in-chief, wrote to Sir Garnet Wolseley, who had now gone back to England to take the post of adjutant-general in the War Office. (The adjutant-general's responsibilities covered recruitment and service; the quartermaster-general was the overseer of supplies.) Wood recommended that Captain Kitchener, acting major with a local Egyptian Army rank, should now be made a brevet-major in the British Army. A brevet rank is a nominal rank only; it does not carry the normal pay of that rank but is usually understood to signify that when a vacancy for an appointment at the rank concerned occurs, the brevet holder will be in a favourable position to be appointed. This might seem a small enough reward for Kitchener's enterprise and courage, but the Army does not believe in encouraging people unnecessarily, and Wolseley turned down the request. Kitchener was unaware that this was in process and in any case was probably too busy to care. His mind was full of thoughts of the incompetence of the governor of Dongola and how much better he (Kitchener) could do the job himself. He felt that an Englishman would make an ideal choice for the post of governor of the town.

In September Wolseley, who had organised the relief column, now came out from England to take personal charge. The only good news was that the shifty governor of Dongola had succeeded in beating off the Dervish attack on Korti. Bad news soon followed. At this stage Gordon, who still had access to the Nile and in fact had steamers on it, had used one to send a party of forty downstream. The steamer carried Gordon's diaries and cipher book, the French and Greek consuls, and a mixed party including some Greek merchants and

54

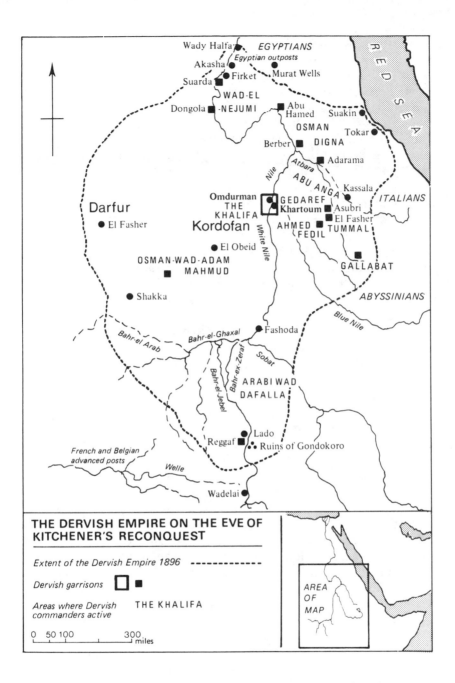

THE DERVISH EMPIRE ON THE EVE OF
KITCHENER'S RECONQUEST

Extent of the Dervish Empire 1896   ------------

Dervish garrisons   ☐ ■

Areas where Dervish   THE KHALIFA
commanders active

0   50 100   300 miles

AREA
OF
MAP

some Arab women. Gordon's steamers were quite unfitted for negotiating the Nile cataracts, even with the help of an experienced pilot, which they did not possess. The steamer ran aground on a shoal in the fourth cataract, close to Abu Hamed. Colonel Stewart, the senior officer who was carrying Gordon's papers, then received a friendly signal from the shore. He was rather doubtful about its value, but had little choice but to hope for the best. The party made its way to the shore and was massacred. Stewart was an old friend of Kitchener; they had both served in Anatolia and got on well together.

Kitchener did not hear about the attempt to run the gauntlet until it had begun but once he realised the party was on its way through potentially hostile country he sent stern warnings to all the tribes who lived along the banks of the part of the Nile through which the steamer would pass, that any attempt to molest the travellers would receive instant and severe punishment. The Mahdi, it will be recalled, was not yet at the height of his power. Khartoum was still holding out and Kitchener let it be known that a huge British force was on its way to drive the Dervishes before it like leaves before the wind. The perpetrator of the treacherous crime was Suleiman, Sheikh of Monasir, and Kitchener, suspecting his intentions, had sent him a personal message saying, 'If any harm befalls Stewart, for every hair of his head I will have a life.'

Unfortunately for Stewart, the message did not reach Suleiman until Stewart was dead. But it is said that, in time or not, Kitchener was as good as his word. (Somewhat confusingly there was another Stewart in the area at the time. This was Sir Herbert Stewart, who had been sent to Dongola to be in charge of administration.)

Meanwhile Kitchener moved from one tribe to another, making sure that loyalty—such as it was—never wavered. He was also busy collecting intelligence on Dervish moves. Most important, he maintained contact with Gordon through Arab messengers. He even managed to smuggle letters, sponges, soap and a toothbrush to him. Kitchener admired Gordon and subsequently considered that Gordon's last letter to him was his most valuable possession.

On his excursions Kitchener moved from one point to another as unobtrusively as possible, usually with a small escort of Arab scouts, perhaps six or ten.

In December the relief column had reached Korti where the Nile takes a huge U-turn before it comes back to a point just above the sixth cataract, a few miles from Khartoum. Here it was decided that the urgency of the situation necessitated a small column being detached and sent across the intervening Bayuda desert (a distance

Lord Kitchener's father, Lt-Col H. H. Kitchener, taken in 1870 when he was
sixty-five. A man of strong views and a keen sense of duty, but often
kind-hearted

Aspall Hall, Suffolk, the home of Kitchener's mother. The crinolines are of the 1860s style

Kitchener's birthplace, Gunsborough Lodge, Listowel

The main street of Ballylongford, through which Kitchener walked daily to a dame school. He had been sent there as a punishment by his father for neglecting the work his tutors set him

Kitchener on his mother's knee, with his elder brother (who succeeded him) and his sister Frances ('Millie')

Kitchener's early home, Crotta House, Kilflynn

Kitchener (*right*) with his younger brothers. Note the fashionable side curls

Kitchener at the age of seventeen

Kitchener as a cadet at Woolwich

Kitchener choosing cavalry officers
for the Egyptian Army in 1883
(drawing by G. J. Gillingham)

Kitchener as a major in the Egyptian
cavalry

Kitchener as Sirdar (Commander-in-Chief) of the Egyptian Army in 1896.
Note how far apart his eyes are set

The tomb of the Mahdi after the battle of Omdurman

An artist's impression (by Ernest Prater) of the meeting between Kitchener and Marchand at Fashoda, on the Upper Nile in 1898

of some 170 miles), in a desperate thrust to relieve the doomed town. Eleven hundred men were detailed for the task; the rest of the column was to proceed by water as planned. There were insufficient camels for the whole of the emergency force to cross the desert together and a staging point had to be chosen so that it could be transported one half at a time. This intermediate point was suggested by Kitchener. It was named Gakdul, and it had adequate supplies of fresh water.

The advance party, preceded by Kitchener and his Arab scouts, left Korti on 30 December. On 2 January 1885 they reached Gakdul, where Kitchener remained for the time being. Here, while the camels went back to Korti for more troops, he established a series of look-out posts. No hostile Dervish forces were seen, but several caravans of supplies for the Mahdi, mainly carrying dates, were observed and captured. On the 11th, the second part of the convoy reached Gakdul and brought with it the news that Kitchener must now return to Korti, which, in some disgust, he now did.

By this time he had become an expert camel manager, which was no mean feat. Some of his early attempts at riding camels had proved humiliating. He would have enjoyed staying with the Camel Corps for the dash across the desert, not merely because he wanted to be first into Khartoum and to rescue Gordon, but also because the bizarre appearance and unconventionality of the unit appealed to him. Although most of the surviving pictures of Kitchener show him as an immaculately dressed, upright, stern figure, he was undoubtedly happier when dressed in rags and passing himself off as a native. (Perhaps it was his certain dislike for photographers which accounts for the slightly hostile stare that characterises pictures of him.)

The Camel Corps was nothing if not informal. Its members wore red serge jumpers, yellow-ochre cord breeches, dark blue puttees, and white pith helmets, but by the time they had been in the desert for a few weeks the colours were almost indistinguishable. One member of the Corps, the future Lord Gleichen, who eventually grew fond of his unpredictable mount, wrote: 'A camel's hind legs will reach anywhere—over his head, round his chest, and on to his hump; even when lying down an evil-disposed animal will shoot out his legs and bring you to a sitting position. He will chew the root of his tail, nip you in the calf, or lay his head on his hump. He also bellows and roars at you whatever you are doing, saddling him, feeding him, mounting him, unsaddling him. To the uninitiated a camel going to you with his mouth open and gurgling horribly is a terrifying spectacle, but do not mind him, it is only his way. He hardly ever bites but when he does you feel it for some time.'

On the 17th the Corps was attacked by a force estimated at 10,000 Dervishes. It promptly adopted the traditional square formation and, with the advantage of better aim and discipline, held off the attack. This was at Abu Klea. In spite of heavy losses the column pressed on. High day temperatures alternated with bitterly cold nights. At one point they lost all sense of direction in a dense wood of thorny mimosa trees and wasted valuable time; then, just as it seemed they were almost at their objective, they were attacked by Dervish sharpshooters, who killed Sir Herbert Stewart and several others. At Metemmeh there was a well-defended little town, and here the Corps was fired on by Krupps guns, said to have been war surplus from the Franco-Prussian War. Here they waited for the second half of their party to arrive from Gakdul. As soon as it caught up, they prepared to march on at first light. But before they could start out, news was brought that Khartoum had already fallen.

Subsequently Kitchener was given the task of completing a report on the last days of Khartoum. His account of the sufferings of the citizens before the fall, and of the massacre which took place after it, makes disturbing reading.

Chapter 6

Taking Stock

After the loss of Khartoum, and the return, not without difficulty, of the relief column, the senior commanders made a fresh assessment of the overall military position. Wolseley considered that Dongola should be abandoned and instead outposts should be held at Wadi Halfa and Korosko. Kitchener and Buller (who was Wolseley's chief of staff and had commanded the river party in the first stages) felt that Dongola should not be abandoned and that the best policy would be to advance against Khartoum and bring the Mahdi to battle before he had consolidated his power. Kitchener, though the most junior, was the strongest advocate of this policy. His intelligence agents had assured him that the Mahdi's power now hung in the balance. If he advanced into the rich provinces of Darfur and Kordofan his strength and prestige would increase enormously; if, on the other hand, he was forced onto the defensive, his divine authority would be called into question and his army could well be split between factions. It was therefore essential to check him. This opinion seemed to be carrying the day when once more the Gladstone government gave its views. There could be no question of a military reconquest of the Sudan, or even of giving military support to those parts still under Egyptian control. Instead local sheikhs would be offered subsidies provided they remained loyal and kept the Mahdi at bay. This proposal seemed considerably more practicable in London than it did to the sheiks and provincial governors, who knew that some 50,000 Dervishes might at any moment be marching in their direction. Even the most avaricious flinched from accepting a subsidy which would involve their defying the Mahdi's troops.

Buller, who had won a Victoria Cross in 1879 in the Zulu War, was a newcomer to the Sudanese scene and therefore asked Kitchener to produce a report on the effects of the government plan, which had now been dubbed 'Operation Scuttle'. Kitchener was adamant that if the Dervishes were not checked at once, they would have to be defeated at much greater expense within a few years. The report contained a detailed analysis of the stresses and strains the Mahdi would be likely to encounter in his 'empire'.[1]

But it was of no avail. In July Kitchener, who had decided there were no future prospects with the Egyptian Army, resigned his commission in it and sailed for England. Here, with other survivors of the campaign, he was presented to Queen Victoria. The Queen was very impressed with this dignified, yet extremely brave and unorthodox young man; from that time on she looked upon him not only as one of her most valuable supporters but also as a personal friend.

He was now a brevet-lieutenent-colonel and entitled to two months' leave. He spent it in London, and occupied himself with a study of Turkish law. Experience in Egypt had shown him that most Egyptian peasants were virtually slaves to money-lenders. He studied how that tyranny could be broken legally; and many years later it was. While he was in London Gladstone's government was replaced by Salisbury's, but the policy towards the Sudan could not be changed immediately. This was perhaps as well, for Gladstone was back in power a year later.

Perhaps the most bizarre arrangement of Gladstone's tenure of office had been the acceptance of a proposal to control Egyptian finance with a joint board made up of representatives from Britain, France, Germany, Russia, Austria and Italy. Gladstone felt that this gave an air of international legality to the British presence in Egypt. It is doubtful whether anyone, even the Egyptians, cared whether British influence in that country was legal or not, but the creation of the board, which lent nine million pounds to Egypt, gave an eagerly welcomed opportunity for Britain's traditional rivals to criticise and frustrate any policies which the British government thought desirable. The French, at the last minute, had declined to take part in the defeat of Arabi in 1882, and had lost influence and face, and in consequence, naturally enough, hated the British for their subsequent success. The two countries were already rivals in the Middle East. The Russians were always ready to side with the French on the basis that anything which decreased British prestige in the Middle East could not but improve Russian prospects. These two made a formidable combination but could usually be outvoted by the Germans, Austrians and Italians. Since 1882 Germany, Austria and

[1] It appears in full in the appendices.

Italy had been linked in the Triple Alliance, which would remain in force till 1914. Germany was the dominant partner and Germany's undisguised ambition was to build an empire in Africa (and elsewhere). At this time Africa was being explored and annexed. European powers, for various professed reasons but mostly for economic and military ones, had no compunction about colonising and appropriating large portions of African territory. Portugal already possessed vast territories on both east and west coasts which had been taken over some two hundred years before. France was quietly extending her empire in the north and east. Germany was a latecomer to the party, but made up for the shorter time at her disposal by the size of her appetite. Britain had been quickly moving up from the Cape since 1814. However, the British entitlement to colonies was more paternalistic and less avaricious than that of some of her European contemporaries. The Cape had been acquired from the Dutch settlers by purchase; subsequently British expansion had been for the purpose of protecting their outlying Dutch subjects from the Bantu. On the west coast of Africa Britain had acquired colonies partly for trade, but mainly as a base for anti-slavery patrolling.

And this was Britain's second empire. The first had been acquired by settlement in America in the early seventeenth century and lost in the American War of Independence. That loss had left Britain with a few possessions in Canada, where there was a strong French element, and some trading posts in India which scarcely deserved the name of colonies. Then had come the Napoleonic Wars, as a result of which Britain had been exhausted but had once more, this time for strategic reasons, begun to build up an empire again. During this second phase, however, many British people, most of whom but not all voted Liberal, had grave doubts about the ethics and wisdom of an imperial policy. Kitchener, who had seen the way in which uncivilised people were tyrannised by despotic rulers, and and had on more than one occasion been asked to arrange for Britain to take over badly-administered Turkish possessions, had no doubt about the rightness of an imperial policy for Britain. He would no doubt have been interested to see Britain's almost frantic attempts to divest itself of its imperial heritage in the 1950s, 1960s and 1970s, and uttered a few words of warning about over-optimism. The progress of democratic government and economic prosperity in the former colonies has not been as sustained as had been hoped.

On the other hand Kitchener is thought of, by some, as being almost, if not quite, psychopathic in that he considered he had a mission to assist the spread of British influence. If one is to obtain a fair and balanced view of Kitchener it is therefore essential to see him as a man sharing the views of most of his countrymen, rather than inspiring them. At the same time it should not be overlooked that Kitchener had many vociferous critics in his own day.

An interesting example of what was known as the 'grab for Africa' took Kitchener to Zanzibar in November 1885. The island of Zanzibar, which has now become part of Tanzania, was an independent sultanate in 1885, and was extremely prosperous. Most of its wealth came from the trade in slaves and ivory, a trade which had been built up in the previous centuries when it was linked to Muscat and Oman. This thriving slave trade clearly needed to be checked, and therefore there was an excellent case, as it appeared to the European powers, for one of them to invade and impose a very different sort of government. Germany had already anticipated this and, in order to be in a favourable position, had been making treaties with minor sheikhs on the mainland. The Sultan of Zanzibar was by no means happy about what was happening in his domains which, in his view, extended over a considerable stretch of the land opposite the island. He therefore requested that a European commission should meet and give legal status to his claim. The Germans were in a comfortable position, for the treaties had been made between the German East African Company and the sheikhs and did not, therefore, commit Germany officially, although Germany still benefited from them.

The commission which was set up consisted of representatives of Britain, France, and Germany. The Germans were almost immediately up in arms, claiming that Kitchener, in league with the French representative, seemed to be determined to frustrate them at every turn. Kitchener was officially warned to be a little more impartial, in appearance at least. The Germans accepted the fact that Kitchener was much better qualified and more experienced than his colleagues in this type of work, but when he pronounced that a strip of the mainland some forty miles deep was part of the Sultanate of Zanzibar, they protested strongly. Eventually agreement was reached that the strip should be only ten miles deep. The commission therefore had completed its work impartially and satisfactorily. Five years later Britain arranged a protectorate over Zanzibar; ten years later she also acquired control of Mombasa, a port whose strategic and economic usefulness Kitchener had stressed. Meanwhile Germany had been allotted what is now Tanzania. Kitchener was awarded the decoration of CMG (Companion of the Order of St Michael and St George) for his work with the commission. (The Foreign Office irreverently describes this decoration as 'Call Me God' and its higher version—GCMG—as 'God Calls Me God'.) Kitchener was now well established, not only as a competent Sapper and courageous fighting soldier, but also as a man with diplomatic skill and experience. He was immediately appointed to be governor of the Eastern Sudan and the Red Sea littoral, at the port of Suakin.

'Eastern Sudan' meant little more than Suakin itself, where Britain retained a precarious toehold against the Dervishes. Even so, the appointment marked a significant advance in Kitchener's career. It gave him the opportunity to lead troops in action, which would be an experience he had not previously had, and which in the event he did not do particularly well. It placed him securely at the level of those who gave orders rather than those who have to execute them, and therefore meant that, unless there were serious setbacks, he would probably go much further in his career. However, there were setbacks at Suakin: he was wounded and nearly killed, and he made enemies among Liberal thinkers at home by his policies.

But at this period, he, for the first time in his life, did not much care whether he lived or died, whether his career prospered or not. He was recovering from the only really romantic attachment in his life. When he was in Egypt in 1883 he had, as we know from his colleague La Terrière, had a number of women friends of the more motherly type. But he had also been strongly attracted by the daughter of General Valentine Baker. The girl, Hermione, was a child when he first met her, but in 1883 she was sixteen and as mature as a girl of her somewhat cosmopolitan upbringing could be. Kitchener was thirty-three. Sixteen was too young for marriage and Kitchener was not yet ready for domestic ties either. But in three years' time Hermione would be the age at which Kitchener's mother had married his thirty-nine-year-old father. It was obviously a very sensible match. However, in January 1885 Hermione died of typhoid in Cairo, and her mother followed her soon afterwards. While this was happening Kitchener was in Korti, eagerly awaiting any news of Gordon, who was to die five days later. Kitchener cannot have known that his potential bride was even ill and must have heard the news when he returned to Cairo. It was at this point that he resigned his commission in the Egyptian Army and sailed for England. For his career it was a sensible move to make; the Sudan was being left to the rebels, and the Egyptian Army offered no prospects. But Cairo may well have become unbearable. Sir Philip Magnus-Allcroft, giving as his source private family information, says: 'It is certain that Kitchener wore at times for many years under his shirt a gold locket given to him by Valentine Baker which contained a miniature portrait of Hermione.'

Subsequently, Dr Bonte Elgood, who spent most of her life in

Egypt, confirmed the story in a letter to Sir Philip Magnus-Allcroft: 'At the time the Bakers were living at Shepheard's Hotel we were living next door. Hermione, whom I greatly admired (as little girls of ten do admire young ladies of eighteen), was frequently in their room there, and my mother living next door frequently went there with a specially-cooked diet. On one of these occasions I was with her, and I remember that as my mother had just opened her bedroom door to enter, a tall young officer came up and hurriedly spoke to my mother. My mother drew me back and we waited on a nearby couch while he went in alone. I remember clearly saying, "But why? Doesn't she want the beef-tea?" And my mother said, "Yes, but Major Kitchener is going to marry her and wants to see her quietly." She died, I think, not so long after and we were all very sad.'

That was probably the last time that Kitchener saw Hermione Baker. He had probably gone in to say goodbye when he was given his assignment with the relief column. She cannot have been very ill at the time if she was receiving visitors; typhoid, which at that time was usually referred to by the alternative title of enteric, does not usually last longer than two or three weeks.

Kitchener made a further move towards marriage fifteen years later. He was a national hero, a welcome guest in a number of patrician households, and a close friend of the Duke of York, the future George V. Doubtless it had been pointed out to him that a man in his position needed a wife to help him with entertaining and relieve him of the many responsibilities. He proposed to Lady Helen Vane-Tempest-Stewart, daughter of the Marquess of Londonderry, but she rejected his proposal. Two years later Lady Helen married the future Earl of Ilchester, whose military career had not taken him beyond the rank of second lieutenant in the Coldstream Guards but whose literary achievements would extend over many fields. He was twenty-four years younger than Kitchener. On this occasion Kitchener's pride was hurt, but his emotions seem to have been unruffled.

1885 marked the end of Kitchener's life as a John Buchan-type of adventurer. The nineteenth century produced an astonishing number of men who were prepared to set off on their own, without any special brief, into hostile territory. They relied on disguise, fluency in several languages, acute perception, and a good measure of luck to keep them out of trouble. Sometimes all of these failed them and they met an extremely unpleasant fate. The characters in books by Henty and similar writers for boys were not purely imaginary: often they were a compound of several people the writer had known. The authors, almost invariably, had travelled extensively themselves, and sometimes been war correspondents. Kitchener's life up until 1886 fitted him for a place in any schoolboy adventure story; and it showed that had he been a junior officer during the second World War he would almost undoubtedly have served most of it in a unit such as the SAS, or, given his ability at languages, the SOE.

On many occasions he had ventured deep into the Sudan, alone or with a few trusted companions. A somewhat incoherent account of one of these operations was given in a publication entitled *The Canadian Magazine* in March 1899. At Korti in late December 1884, Kitchener suspected that the Mudir (Egyptian governor) of Dongola was involved in treacherous exchanges with the Dervishes, that information about the relief column was being passed on, and that there was a plot to subvert the Egyptian garrison in Khartoum. (The fact that one of the gate commanders at Khartoum was subsequently given an important position in the Mahdi's army suggests that the belief in the plot was not unfounded.)

A Canadian journalist, Charles Lewis Shaw, and a friend of his called McBurney, were caught up in a fracas involving some Bashi-Bazouks, a tribe of uncertain allegiances. They were arrested and marched to the guard tent where they were confined overnight, pending an investigation of the trouble and whether they had contributed to it. Shaw wrote:

> A tall man, tied apparently hand and foot, was thrown amongst us. I thought he looked a different brand of Arab than I had been accustomed to. I didn't know much Arabic in those days but we could hear the Dongolese talk and talk in excited tones the whole night, the bound man occasionally saying a few words.
>
> When we paraded before the large open-faced orderly tent next morning we were almost paralysed to see Lord Wolseley himself sitting at the little table with Kitchener beside him, both in full staff uniform. A fine-looking Arab was being examined through the interpreter. He didn't seem impressed by the glittering uniforms or the presence of the commander-in-chief, or embarrassed by their questions. Once or twice an expression of surprise flitted over his face, but his eyes were always fixed on Kitchener, who would now and again stoop and whisper something in Wolseley's ear. Once he raised his voice. The prisoner heard the intonation and recognised him. With a fierce bound the long, lithe Arab made a spring and was over the table and had seized Kitchener by the throat. There was a short, swift struggle. Wolseley's eyes glistened, and he half-drew his sword. Kitchener, athletic though he was, was being overpowered and the Arab was throttling him

to death. There was a rush of the guard, and within ten minutes a cordon of sentries surrounded the Mudir of Dongola's tent. Within three days he was a prisoner in his palace at Dongola, guarded by half a battalion of British soldiers. The conspiracy was broken.

How widespread it was only half a dozen white men knew at the time, but that it embraced the courts of the Khedive, the Mudir and the Mahdi leaked out in after years. To it the treachery of the Egyptian garrison at Khartoum and the death of Gordon was due, and the preservation of the Desert Column can be placed to its discovery.

Bennet Burleigh, the *Daily Telegraph* War Correspondent, met Kitchener in Debbeh. Burleigh was alone, apart from one servant. He took many risks himself in his attempt to obtain news but whereas he could often relax in safety he felt that Kitchener risked his life all the time. Burleigh mentioned an occasion when Kitchener had to watch a captured spy being flogged to death, a fate which he himself risked daily. Burleigh was astonished that Kitchener could behave perfectly naturally and calmly in the most perilous situations. In the middle of Debbeh Kitchener managed to produce two bottles of claret, all he had, which the two drank at dinner.

Kitchener took up his appointment at Suakin with the firm conviction that the man on the spot knew more than the man in Westminster and that his best policy would be to act first and explain, if he had to, afterwards. He was well aware that the government regarded him as a potential liability, fearing that he would provoke a situation in Suakin like the one which had been so disastrous in Khartoum. The Liberals were determined to avoid further commitments in Africa. Gladstone was able to support his arguments for withdrawal from the Sudan by pointing to the potential danger of a Russian invasion of Afghanistan. This was no idle fancy, as the Russians had been making moves in the direction of Afghanistan, and thus to India, for several years. If they continued to exert pressure in that area Britain would certainly not wish to have her Army heavily engaged in the Sudan where British interests were minimal.

Although the Mahdi had died the previous July, the Dervishes had lost none of their drive and morale. And, after their recent successes, they had a large number of captured modern weapons at their disposal. The Khalifa not merely held the army together but significantly increased its strength. He despatched a force in the direction of Egypt in December 1885, more perhaps as a test of strength than a serious invasion. It was met by a mixture of Egyptian Army and British troops, and after a brisk fight was defeated with many casualties at Ginnis, on the Egyptian frontier. In a small sense Ginnis was a landmark in military history, for it was the last occasion when British troops went into action wearing red coats; in another it was a turning point, for it demonstrated to the Khalifa that runaway victories were not to be had for the asking and that further approaches towards the Mediterranean would need longer and fuller preparation. As a first step in that direction the Khalifa decided to capture Suakin, which could then be used to bring in supplies. While the British held the ports along the Red Sea, the Dervish Empire was landlocked.

From the early years of the decade the outstanding military personality in the eastern Sudan had been Osman Digna. He hated the British because they had put an end to his family's activities as slave traders; he had therefore offered his services to the Mahdi, who created him an emir. He belonged to the Hadendowa tribe, a people whose courage and ability were legendary. A Hadendowa would lie concealed in the grass over which cavalry was about to charge, then, at the moment a horseman passed over him, would slash at a leg, bring down the animal and spear the rider. This trick seemed to belong more properly to some barbaric circus, but the Hadendowa were able to repeat it effortlessly at will, and it made them redoubtable in battle. However, in spite of having a formidable army, Osman did not enjoy much success when he first went into action against the coastal forces.

Then he won the battle of El Teb, a minor encounter as battles go but one where victory gave him several hundred rifles and a large quantity of ammunition. With this he did even better when a force of Egyptians, sent to relieve Sinkat, was wiped out almost completely.

Consequently Valentine Baker had been sent to the port of Trinikat with a ramshackle army in February 1883. He expected to deal firmly with the Dervishes, who were still at an early stage in their rise to power. But the Egyptians he was commanding bore no resemblance to the Turks he had commanded when Kitchener had first met him, and in his first battle most of them tried to run away. Some two thousand of them were killed and even more arms and ammunition fell into the hands of the Dervishes. Baker escaped by charging through the encircling Dervishes and reached the shore.

A year later a stronger, largely British force, commanded by Sir Gerald Graham, VC, was sent to deal with the unsatisfactory situation in this area, where some towns were still holding out in

67

spite of Osman Digna's attempts to capture them. The new force met and defeated the Dervishes on the former battlefield of El Teb where the Dervishes had a strong position defended with Krupps guns, howitzers and a Gatling gun. British losses were very low; Dervish losses high. Encouraged by this success, the British force moved on to relieve the besieged town of Tamai. On the way it was attacked with great fury by 12,000 Dervishes. In the battle, to the astonishment and dismay of the British force, a square, the traditional defensive position, was broken into. The British, who often seem happier to recall their defeats rather than their victories (as Dieppe, Dunkirk and Gallipoli seem to suggest), gave an enthusiastic welcome to Kipling's poems about the incident. Fortunately for the rest of the force the Dervishes were driven out again, and after heavy losses withdrew.

Kitchener's task, when he reached the eastern Sudan, might well have seemed impossible. His brief was to keep Osman Digna and the Dervishes at bay by establishing a ring of friendly sheikhdoms; the friendly atmosphere would be created by subsidies. Suspecting that this was scarcely feasible, he began constructing fortifications. Meanwhile Osman Digna made various forays from his stronghold at Handoub, some fifteen miles away. Although Kitchener had been told to restrict his military activities to reconnaissance, he interpreted his brief somewhat freely by taking a mixed force of regular and irregular troops out of Suakin and attacking Handoub. The date was 17 January 1888. Unfortunately the irregulars lacked discipline and, after initial success, began looting. They were then attacked by Dervish reinforcements and driven back. As Kitchener tried to rally them he was hit by a bullet which penetrated his jaw and lower neck. It gave him great pain and made it almost impossible for him to talk. It is said that he managed to retain command and extricate his forces from the battle. This seems obvious nonsense, for a man does not conduct a difficult withdrawal by sign language. His second-in-command, Captain Hickman, appears to have taken the necessary steps.

The wound was too complicated to be dealt with locally, so Kitchener was sent back to Cairo. There he was visited by the commander-in-chief, Grenfell, who told him he ought to be court-martialled for exceeding his instructions, particularly as he had used some regular troops disguised as irregulars; but that everyone was proud of him for his enterprise. From this rash and ill-managed move Kitchener began to emerge as a hero. It transpired that he had news that many of the Dervishes were absent from Handoub at the time and that there had been an excellent opportunity to capture

Osman Digna himself. The Duke of Cambridge, Commander of the British Army for thirty years, who had rebuked him back in 1871 over the French incident, now sent him a congratulatory telegram. His old adversary Wolseley followed suit. Queen Victoria enquired tenderly about his health and made him an ADC. The army made him a brevet-colonel. It began to look as if Kitchener, though not necessarily a 'lucky' officer, was going to be rewarded for his defeats as much as, if not more than, for his victories. But the period also marked a significant step forward in his growing unpopularity in the Army. When somewhat unsociable officers begin to rise rapidly, they are immediately disliked as much as they are envied. Even popular officers are liable to attract sour looks and comments if they start to step ahead of their contemporaries. This was a time when a suitable wife could have made a great difference to Kitchener's standing in the Army. A 'suitable' army wife, who probably comes from an army family, knows all the necessary conventions. If she is beautiful and kind, her husband, however domineering, will be thought to share some of her virtues even if he does not himself display them. She can do much to help his promotion prospects by listening attentively to boring senior officers, who are flattered by the interest an attractive woman shows in them. One enterprising and clever wife of recent years, placed next to a general at dinner, enquired brightly, 'General, have you ever shot a tiger?' His detailed account of the occasion in the distant past lasted well past the dinner. Sometimes the contacts are less innocent and, although officially frowned upon, illicit liaisons flourish in the services.

Kitchener was well aware that the British aristocracy took a relaxed view of marriage vows, but he did not equate this with the casual immorality of Cairo society. He was enormously attractive to women—tall, handsome, outstandingly brave, mysterious, and unmarried, nursing a broken heart after the sad death of Hermione. Many women would have been only too glad to comfort him. He, for his part, despised them. Furthermore he believed that officers should rise in rank through merit and hard work, not from understanding wives. It could have been said of Egypt as was said of Malaya in the 1930s: 'It was a first-class country for second-class people.' Kitchener made a few attempts to be friendly but could not sustain them. He intended to gain his promotion through outstanding military service and sheer professionalism. The artificialities and antics of Cairo society may have amused the rest of the Army but they had no appeal for him. A wife might have bridged the gap.

Kitchener was by this time thirty-seven years old. He returned to his post at Suakin in March before his recovery was complete. In consequence he was soon forced to take a further spell of leave, and decided to spend it in England. For a time he stayed with the Prime Minister, Lord Salisbury, at Hatfield. While there he was told that he was to be appointed adjutant-general in Egypt. He returned to Cairo in September (1888). It looked as if a period of tranquil administration duty lay ahead but it was not to be. From Suakin it was reported that Osman Digna was even more active than ever and had now besieged the town. The irony of this particular situation was that while Baring had been encouraging trade with the tribes of the interior, on the basis that they were not wholly committed to Mahdism and would prefer a British allegiance, Osman Digna had taken advantage of the relaxation period to obtain some useful pieces of field artillery, which would otherwise have been used to defend Suakin itself. With these he was now bombarding the walls of the town. It seemed that Kitchener had been right in banning trade from Suakin to the interior: he was therefore sent back to defend the town.

The command structure in Egypt at this stage was demonstrably absurd. Baring, with his eyes always firmly fixed on the development of stability and prosperity in Egypt, regarded Kitchener as 'a gallant and efficient officer—though a headstrong subordinate'. Kitchener realised that Baring's good opinion could be of great value to his own career, but was not going to take overmuch direction from him all the same. Grenfell, as commander-in-chief, knew that Kitchener was an exceptionally gifted officer but of the type which obeys the orders he likes but fails to understand the others. He was a little worried by Kitchener's obvious unpopularity with the officers, but gratified by the devotion which 'native' troops had for him. 'Native' troops were not merely Egyptians whom Kitchener had raised from being a despised rabble into an efficient fighting force, but also the battalions of Sudanese which were now part of his army. The Sudanese were mainly Nubians and black (Sudan means the country of the black). They were superb fighters, which was as well, for they were going to be pitted against their redoubtable compatriots in the Dervish army. Undoubtedly Kitchener understood the psychology of his native troops, as we see later, but he was not interested in the psychology of his British officers, to whom he was curt, dismissive, and unsympathetic. He never seemed to relax but remained unapproachable. It was, of course, a period in which senior officers were expected to be aloof figures: Roberts was an exception. Not until the Second World War were officers regarded as a team; until then they were seniors or subordinates.

After his return from England Kitchener made some attempt to conform with what was expected of the adjutant-general. He attended dinners, receptions, dances, and other social functions, but without much appearance of enjoying himself. Everyone knew only too well how he had earned the nickname, 'He who must be obeyed.'

In December 1888 he settled his account with Osman Digna. On the 20th of that month Grenfell and Kitchener defeated the Dervishes at Gamaizeh, close to Suakin. Kitchener commanded the brigade with cool expertise. Five hundred Dervishes were killed, and the ease with which this was accomplished seems to have convinced Osman Digna that any further ventures in the immediate future would be unprofitable. But he was by no means finished.

The check to the Dervishes at Ginnis on 30 December, as described earlier, seems to have persuaded the Khalifa that any further advances must be made in much greater strength than hitherto. In June of the following year Dervishes appeared again, near Wadi Halfa, led by Wad-el-Nejumi, the emir who had been responsible for destroying the Hicks expedition. Nejumi had nearly 14,000 men at his disposal; it was rumoured that the Khalifa regarded Nejumi with suspicion as a possible rival for power, and was therefore happy to see him engaged in a trial of strength which might prove fatal to him. Grenfell allowed Nejumi to come forward until he was isolated in barren countyside, then confronted him at Toski (in August 1889). In a desperate battle Nejumi was killed with some 1500 of his followers; 4000 were taken prisoner. Kitchener was in his element commanding a cavalry detachment which was made up of one squadron of the British 20th Hussars, and his own Egyptian cavalry. His small force followed up some useful reconnaissance by heading off one of Nejumi's tactical moves. Kitchener was awarded a CB for his services in the battle. Some of the captured Dervishes elected to join their conqueror's forces; others contributed to a much needed labour force. Subsequently Kitchener spent a well-earned leave on a first visit to India.

He had good cause to be pleased with himself. He had proved that he could command a cavalry force successfully in action. Nobody had doubted that he could train cavalry—irritating though it might be for a Sapper to do so—but proving that he could handle cavalry in action was a different matter altogether. He felt he was justifying himself to his father, who had always wanted his son to follow him into the cavalry, but even that satisfaction was surpassed by the feeling that no cavalry officer would ever be able to tell him what to do in future. Cavalry officers tended to assume that commanding cavalry was an esoteric art which only the chosen few—i.e. cavalry officers—could manage. Criticism of the handling of cavalry could only come from cavalry officers, in their view at least; criticism from anyone else could be brushed aside as being mere impudence. But now Kitchener had proved he could handle cavalry as well as anyone. When he criticised cavalry later, everyone in that arm had the uncomfortable feeling that Kitchener knew what he was talking about.

The immediate satisfaction was short-lived. On his return from leave Kitchener was asked by Baring to combine his duties as adjutant-general with those of inspector-general of the Egyptian police. Kitchener had no objection to the extra work, and appreciated the challenge for the Egyptian police had previously defied all efforts to eliminate corruption and inefficiency, but he was concerned that it might be a divergence from the military career in which he was making such rapid strides. On being assured that he would lose nothing by accepting, he did so with relish. But he was too experienced in oriental ways to assume he could make drastic reforms overnight. He began gently: he persuaded the Mudir that they would gain in prestige by accepting British police 'advisers'. He did not attempt to abolish the tradition of bribery, but gradually made it less profitable. He stopped the torture of prisoners and witnesses and established clearly that the purpose of the Egyptian police was to help the poor, not to oppress them. Inside the force itself he made sure that promotion depended on merit and not on bribery, or other form of corruption. In one year his reorganised police cut major crime by 50%, doubled the number of convictions and, perhaps even more important, gained a new standing in the eyes of the public.

In April 1892 Grenfell resigned his post as commander-in-chief. Baring put in a strong recommendation for Kitchener to be appointed in his place. In less than ten years Kitchener had risen from being a lieutenant with no military experience to commander-in-chief, with the rank of major-general, who could look back on a record of proved military capability. He was no desk-borne general; he had won his promotion at the risk of his neck. And he was only forty-two. What might the future hold?

One thing which it was immediately clear the future did not hold was an increase in his personal popularity. The Army was furious. Its candidate had been Colonel Wodehouse, a man of wisdom, courage and military achievement. In this last he had a longer and better record than the new Sirdar, adequate though Kitchener's record was. It was assumed that Kitchener had been appointed because he had made friends with the right people in England, had Baring in the hollow of his hand. But there are very few high-level military appointments which do not arouse a certain amount of anguished, though muted, comment. Everybody, even the most indignant, knows that the initial disgust will soon settle into resentment and then grudging acceptance. A positive aspect of being an unpopular man in command is that it gives a certain stability. Instead of wondering if you will fall out of favour, you know you will never be in it.

Kitchener was well aware of his unpopularity and the resentment caused by his rapid promotion but realised that there was nothing to be done about it except make people respect him, even if they did not like him. He realised too that it can be a disadvantage to be popular. Subordinates are less likely to neglect their duties if they know that the man at the top is quite pitiless than if they believe the old buffer has a heart of gold. Kitchener had no time for condoning lapses of efficiency. He saw himself as a man with a mission. Gordon must be avenged, the Sudan must be cleared of fanatical tyrants, and Egypt must be left secure to rebuild itself economically and socially. He knew he was the man for the task and he was overwhelmingly glad that others had recognised it too.

Furthermore he felt he had the measure of the problems ahead. If anyone knew the Sudan, he did. He knew the language and many of its dialects. In order to spy he had learnt to think as a Sudanese. He was also well aware that he had an exceptionally gifted Intelligence officer in Reginald Wingate, and that between them they could make an excellent appreciation of the enemy's plans.

Habits which would later become a disadvantage were an asset at this stage. So far in his life everything had contributed to his keeping his plans to himself, and delegating as little as possible. He could still do so. Even though the forthcoming campaign would be exceptionally difficult, it would be on a small scale and could be controlled by one man—himself. He would not have to pay attention to the views of others, except in token fashion, and he would have no trouble with allies. It is said, no doubt with heartfelt emphasis, that any commander worth his salt finds the enemy causes him much less concern than his allies. At least he knows what the enemy is likely to do or think; allies, on the other hand, are totally unpredictable.

His expeditionary force was scarcely more than divisional strength: the Egyptian army numbered 18,000 but would be supplemented later by some regular battalions from England. (Nowadays divisions are much smaller.) There were thirteen infantry battalions of which five were Sudanese; there were eight squadrons of cavalry and three batteries of artillery. There was a camel corps. Surprisingly, in view of Kitchener's training, there were no engineers. The normal administrative tail scarcely existed.

The officers in his picked force were an élite. Many had been interviewed by him personally in England when he was on leave. There was no shortage of applicants. Not only were they promoted on appointment, but they also received nearly three times as much pay as they had been entitled to formerly. He chose them well and carefully. One of his stipulations was that he wanted no married men, or even men with marriage in view. Wives would have been unable to join their husbands until the conclusion of the campaign and he did not want wives or fiancées hanging around Cairo.

At the beginning of 1896 his army was ready for the task which he thought it should have. All that was needed was the authority to move. He felt that this could not be long delayed. The British government might be prepared to leave the death of Gordon unavenged, and to leave the Sudan to languish under a tyranny, but the deciding factor would surely be that if an Anglo-Saxon force did not soon reoccupy the Sudan another's army soon would. There were plenty of likely contenders, with France, Belgium, and Germany to the fore. The French were regarded as the most dangerous rivals. It was rumoured, and not without reason, that France was planning to occupy the whole of the area of the White (Upper) Nile. However, it was none of these countries which eventually spurred the British government into taking action; it was Italy, and not because Italy was getting too strong but because she was dangerously weak. In 1884 Britain, although preoccupied over Gordon's position in the Sudan, had not been sufficiently engrossed to miss the opportunity of establishing a protectorate over Somaliland, where Germany was suspected of having ambitions. France and Italy were quick to establish themselves in the same area with French Somaliland and Italian Somaliland, but in 1896 the Italians overreached themselves and were defeated by the Ethiopians at Adowa. It looked as if they would now be crushed by the Ethiopians on one side and the Khalifa on the other. It was reported that they asked the British government to make a military move to relieve this pressure. To the astonishment of all, the British government authorised an expedition to retake Dongola.

Whether this move was inspired more by a desire to help the Italians or by a wish to warn off the French from adventuring in the Sudan is not known. If the latter, it was only partially successful, but at least it put Kitchener in a position where two years later he could exercise his own particular skill in diplomacy.

Baring was not informed about the impending decision until it had been taken. He was surprised even more when he learnt that the British government had no intention of financing the conquest of

Dongola but expected it to be done from Egyptian revenue. By provident housekeeping Baring had put Egypt's finances in order and was earmarking certain sums to be used for building the Aswan Dam. That money went, and with it much more. However, the British government had to produce a loan of £800,000, which it eventually wrote off, because Egypt's finances were, as we saw, subject to the 'mixed tribunals'. Because the mixed tribunals (consisting of representatives from Britain, Germany, Italy, Austria, France and Russia) were officially acting in the interests of European bond-holders, their agreement had to be sought for any abnormal expenditure. France and Russia raised considerable opposition to Egyptian money being allotted to re-conquering a province in a move of which the chief beneficiary would be Britain. However, after much argument, the tribunal decided by a majority vote to sanction the expenditure. France and Russia promptly protested that the decision to allot the money must be unanimous and the sanction was therefore withdrawn. Britain therefore would have to pay for the war on its own. Although some attempt was made to be able to reclaim the money by calling it a loan, this was soon shown to be impracticable.

The re-conquest of Dongola appealed to the British government for two reasons. One was that the government was now Conservative and the fact that their Liberal predecessors had voted against re-conquering the Sudan seemed an excellent reason for voting it. Secondly, it now looked a practical proposition; five years earlier, in 1891, an Egyptian army under Colonel Holland-Smith, the governor of Suakin, had emerged from that town and, in a series of minor engagements and one major battle, had so completely defeated Osman Digna that he had withdrawn from the area. Osman Digna's forces were considered to be as good, if not better than, any other branch of the Dervish army, and if the newly-trianed Egyptians could defeat them there seemed every chance that they could clear Dongola of other Dervishes.

Baring approved of Kitchener's prudent attitude to army expenditure, but even he was surprised at the degree to which the new sirdar took it. In appearance the army resembled a procession of medieval paupers. Nothing was ever worn out until it had almost ceased to exist. Anyone who handed in worn-out clothing to the quartermaster to exchange for something better would probably get something worse—if worse was still able to hold together. Kitchener was no doubt aware that if new clothing had been issued, most of it would have been on sale in the bazaars (which it would have reached by pilferage or a straight deal with the wearer) by the following day

75

at the latest. There are some countries where thieving has been elevated to an art form comparable with the Great Masters, and Egypt is without any question one of them, perhaps the foremost.

The fact that the army was almost exclusively officered by the British had been resented by the young Khedive who had succeeded Tewfik in 1892. In consequence he had overreached himself and caused one of Kitchener's rare resignations. It had all been settled long before the Dongola Expedition. Abbas had complained about the efficiency of the army; Kitchener had endured a certain amount of petulant behaviour, then had resigned as sirdar. Abbas, realising he had gone too far, begged Kitchener to withdraw his resignation. Kitchener did. Undoubtedly Kitchener had been annoyed by the foolish young man, but the upshot of it was that he could now do what he wanted when he wanted without having to keep an eye open to see if anyone was being offended or insulted.

On 16 March 1896 Kitchener sent a small column to occupy Akasha, some forty miles south, to act as the first staging post. It was fortfied, then linked up by a railway constructed of materials which no one but Kitchener would have deemed still usable. The Dervishes were known to be in a force at Firket, a mere ten miles away, but left the invaders unmolested while Kitchener brought up ten battalions with supporting cavalry and infantry. In June Kitchener advanced, routed 3000 Dervishes, killing 800. The Egyptians performed even better than had been hoped.

Two days later the army was in Suarda, another twenty-five miles forward. This was good progress, but already signs of the main problem were becoming evident. Everything the army needed would have to be transported. There would never be a chance of capturing war material, or of living off the country. As far as the first cataract (at Aswan), Thomas Cook's river steamers had handled the army's supplies, but from that point onwards supplies had to go overland. There had formerly been a railway between Wadi Halfa and Firket, but not much of it remained now. Winston Churchill, who was accompanying the expedition, noted one grim relic. A railway line had been torn up to make a gallows; at the foot of it was a heap of bleached bones.

After Firket obstacles increased rapidly. There were 7000 men at Firket and a further 2000 at Suarda. Then, with the autumn floods, came cholera. At that time the cause was not known; it was suspected that it was a wind-born germ rather than water-borne. Cholera, as the men remembered from the Crimea, could wipe out an army within a few days. It is terrifying because an apparently healthy man can become ill, turn to a virtual skeleton and be dead

76

within a few hours. Here it killed nearly 300 men. Then, as some-times happens, it suddenly ceased.

It was followed by violent sandstorms, and those in turn by floods. Twelve miles of the new railway were washed away. This trail of calamities made it seem as if the army must now retreat, and try again later. But Kitchener refused to be deflected. Fortunately the Dervishes left them alone, waiting no doubt for a time when the expedition would be more vulnerable. Dongola was occupied without difficulty on 23 September. Nobody paid much attention to the fact that this had been the original objective; everyone now assumed the expedition would continue till it reached Khartoum. Advance posts were therefore established at Korti and Merawi. But Kitchener was not going to hurry. The whole of 1897 was spent in building a railway from Wadi Halfa to Abu Hamed. The Nile makes two enormous loops between Egypt and Khartoum. One is between Korti and Metemmeh, which was crossed in the abortive Gordon relief expedition, the other between Wadi Halfa and Abu Hamed. The arguments for short-circuiting the latter were overwhelming; the direct distance is 230 miles overland instead of the five hundred miles of river which include the three worst cataracts. However, the difficulties of building a railway in such inhospitable country were daunting.

The genius behind the construction of the railway was a Sapper lieutenant named E.P.C. (Percy) Girouard. He is generally assumed to have been French, but in fact was a French Canadian who had joined the British Army after attending the Canadian military college at Kingston, Ontario. He had spent three years working on the Canadian Pacific Railway, so was no stranger to the problems of bridging inhospitable wastes, but he had never encountered prob-lems to equal those he met in the Sudan. Kitchener did not interfere; it was said that once he tried to do so, but was so sharply rebuked by Girouard that he never repeated the experiment. Girouard's genius as a construction engineer did not stop at laying the rails; it extended to ordering and obtaining all necessary equipment, down to the last spike and lamp. Even so, he was economical enough to suit Kit-chener's exacting requirements. In later life he became governor of Kenya.

One fact which made the project possible is often overlooked. Railway building, and particularly locomotives, need water. It has been said that Kitchener ordered the sinking of two wells and by remarkable good luck water was found in each. The story is only partly true. Whether Kitchener was a water dowser himself is not known, but he certainly knew the value of dowsing. He would have learnt something of it at Woolwich, where until recently it was taught to young subalterns. Dowsing seems so bizarre that it is sometimes thought of as a superstition. There is, however, nothing ethereal about dowsing. If people have the gift for it, and about six out of every ten do, it works. With the railway builders were two sapper subalterns, both of whom died later and neither of whose name is known, who discovered the presence of water by divining. Kitchener was informed, and the wells were dug. They were the only two in the entire 230 miles.[1]

When the railway had reached halfway it was obviously unsafe to go further until Abu Hamed had been captured. A foray by a strong force of Dervishes could have been a devastating setback. In consequence, a brigade commanded by Brigadier-General Hunter pushed ahead, covered 132 miles in eight days and defeated the Abu Hamed garrison. Resistance was less than had been expected.

Even better news followed. Scouts reported that the Dervishes had evacuated Berber. The Emir had not received reinforcements he had been promised and had decided that he would be in a better defensive position if he moved back to Shendi.

The move took Kitchener by surprise. He had not expected the way ahead to be so clear, and suspected an ambush. There was always a possibility that a force of Dervishes might come across the desert in a wide sweep and cut the railway near the Wadi Halfa. If that happened the plight of those nearer Abu Hamed or in Berber itself would be desperate. There was no doubt that the Dervishes were capable of such tactics. Earlier they had raided Egyptian frontier posts with impunity by first making caches of water in the desert, then conducting a brisk raid, drawing a pursuit after them as they retreated, refreshing themselves at the point where they had left the water, and galloping off into the desert knowing that their pursuers had insufficient water to continue the chase.

Kitchener's problem now was to decide whether he was being lured on to disaster, or whether the Dervishes' retreat was genuine. His knowledge of the Arab mind suggested to him that the enemy would be unlikely to give up such a prestigious town unless it was essential. He therefore decided to go forward, aware that it was a decision that could easily be proved wrong. Wars are not won, as Kitchener knew, by taking risks. Battles should only be offered when a commander has good reason to believe that he will be the winner. Kitchener had planned a careful war of attrition against the Dervishes. Too many mistakes had already been made in the Sudan; he

[1] A similar miracle was performed for Patton's army in North Africa in 1942. The dowser was an American captain, Ralph Harris.

had made one of them himself at Suakin, when he had lost a battle and been wounded. But Berber was a rich prize and a key to further success. He decided to occupy it, thus showing he had an instinct for the right gamble.

He had another, different type of gamble to make at the same time. So far his Egyptian troops had served him far better than even he could have expected. But they were now a long way from their base. They could no longer feel they were protecting their homeland. They had beaten equal numbers and even superior numbers, but he had considerable doubts about how well they would stand up to massive numbers of Dervishes, fighting on ground of their own choosing with a secure base at their rear. The final battle would no doubt be at Khartoum. Common sense told him the Egyptians could not be expected to beat off the Dervishes' attacks unaided. Morale might crack, a battalion might give way, and all would be lost. What was needed was a stiffening of British troops who would stand up to whatever the Dervishes threw against them. And with one part of the field held solid while the bodies of Dervishes piled up in front of the Gatlings, the Egyptians could be rallied too. There were already British troops in Egypt and the War Office, with what appeared to be a warning to Kitchener that he was not necessarily as highly esteemed in their eyes as he was in his own, had sent his predecessor, Sir Francis Grenfell, to command them. Kitchener knew that news of his unpopularity in the Army had seeped through to the highest levels. Nevertheless it was essential that this campaign should be won and that, even if Grenfell came up with the British troops and took overall command, it would be a lesser setback than being defeated at Khartoum. With partial credit for a victory which he had largely engineered, his career could continue to flourish; with a setback it would be in ruins. He resigned himself to seeing Grenfell in command, and taking the credit for the victory he himself had made possible.

Then came an even worse setback. Baring told him that, in spite of all the cheese-paring, the campaign had already cost too much and would have to be held in abeyance for several years while the Egyptian treasury settled its debts and saved enough money for further ventures. Success had suddenly turned into a nightmare of uncertainty. Kitchener had been without leave for three years and he felt that he was near breaking point. Furthermore, the treasury decided it could not afford to pay for a garrison in Kassala, which the Italians were now leaving. The Dervishes would certainly move in and use it as a base from which to harass Kitchener's extended line of communication. There was only one course of action likely to bring Baring and his economists to their senses. He sent in his resignation.

Baring was now on the point of the sword. If Kitchener resigned, no one of similar calibre could be found to replace him. He neither accepted, nor argued about, the resignation. He asked Kitchener to come to Cairo, which Kitchener willingly did, then talked to him as a friend. For the sake of keeping him he would somehow find the money to pay for a garrison at Kassala; that would remove an immediate threat. As for financing further armies, that would have to wait. Kitchener had to be satisfied; he realised that the matter was not entirely in Baring's hands. But in December 1897 Wingate, who was now Director of Intelligence, gave him the ominous news that an army of Dervishes, estimated at 100,000, was about to advance on Berber. This was, of course, the nightmare situation that Kitchener had been dreading. He himself was at the end of a long line of communication and was about to be attacked by an enormous force of fanatical Dervishes. There was not a British soldier in sight. Baring promptly passed the news to London. The Prime Minister, Lord Salisbury, and his cabinet, were suitably impressed. This was no time for a change of horses, or rather of commanders. A brigade of British troops (consisting in those days of four battalions, rather than the three of to-day) was sent forward under Colonel Gatacre. Kitchener was left in overall command. Money was found to push the railhead as far as the town of Atbara, where the river Atbara joins the Nile. There Kitchener awaited the inevitable onslaught.

To his surprise it did not come. Wingate's spies told him that the Khalifa had assembled a vast army at Omdurman, outside Khartoum, and that it was ready to march. But, as often happens with temperamental warriors, there were fierce arguments about who was entitled to the privilege of being in the van and being killed first. The Khalifa's brother Yakub was the most senior and experienced commander but the Khalifa's son Osman was the most hot-headed. The Khalifa did what many a wise man had done before him. He made no decision and waited to see if time would produce a solution. The dispute was a stroke of luck for Kitchener for it gave time for reinforcements to reach him and enabled his force to be strengthened considerably. But the Khalifa could not wait for ever while his subordinates came to their senses. Something must be done to stop Kitchener's steady progress; he therefore ordered Mahmoud, a young, brave emir, to attack the invading column before it came any further. Mahmoud was happy to accept the task. He had been waiting for months at Metemmeh with a picked force. The Khalifa was sure that Kitchener would repeat the tactics of the Gordon relief expedition and make a dash across the desert from Korti to Metemmeh; Mahmoud would give him a surprise. His army numbered

20,000, so Kitchener's 14,000 were not badly outclassed. The Dervishes' leader decided his best tactics would be to march across the desert ahead of the column, across the Atbara river and then come in behind Kitchener to attack Berber. In this way he would avoid crossing barren desert and his men would arrive fresh to the battle.

Kitchener, by a combination of spies and intuition, guessed what Mahmoud was planning, and before the Dervishes could reach the Atbara he had moved thirty-five miles further south. This meant that Mahmoud had to make a wider sweep to reach the Atbara, and what was worse was that much of it was over barren, waterless desert, precisely the sort of country he was trying to avoid. Kitchener, of course, was thinking as a cavalry tactician would think. If an opponent is trying to make a flanking movement, or even merely cross the route ahead, a swift dash forward will either catch him in the flank or push him so far off course as he tries to avoid entanglement that the whole of his ingenious manoeuvre is thrown into disarray. There are, of course, risks in swift moves forward, but usually an opponent is so concerned at the threat to his flank that he gives little thought to making an effective counter-stroke.

The situation is best appreciated if the two rivers are seen as creating a huge letter 'Y' as they join. Mahmoud had been on the right fork (which is the Nile) and had crossed ahead of Kitchener to the Atbara (the left fork), planning to outflank his opponent by moving down the stem of the Y. However, as soon as he crossed the Atbara he realised that his plan had miscarried. He now found himself on the far side of the Atbara, but with over fifty miles of desert to cover if he was to reach his original objective. His tactical plan was in complete disarray. He could not go further because his huge force, with its many followers, had already used up most of its supplies; he could not, and dare not, retreat and try to explain to the Khalifa that he had not, unfortunately, managed to check Kitchener's advance. He therefore dug himself in in a strong defensive position, with the Atbara at his back and thick thorn scrub on each flank. To this he added a zareba, a hedged enclosure, of thorn bushes. He assumed rightly that Kitchener would not be likely to try to march past him, and so leave him firmly established in a position to harass the rear of the invading column; there would have to be a fight and Mahmoud calculated that he might win it. Had he known that a British brigade was rapidly coming up river, he might have changed his mind and given himself some room for manoeuvre.

Kitchener did not relish the idea of a bloody fight to the death in Mahmoud's stronghold, and therefore made several attempts, by cavalry reconnaissance, to lure the Dervishes out of their trenches.

By 4 April he had closed up and he was only twelve miles from their position. Gatacre's brigade had now arrived, having accomplished the remarkable feat of marching 134 miles in six and a half days. What made this achievement all the more extraordinary was that the issue boots in which the soldiers marched were so badly made that the stitches burst and the soles fell off. Many of the men finished the march barefoot. (Boots have improved gradually since those days, without ever being entirely satisfactory. In the Falklands War, in 1982, the much publicised new army issue boot was found to be more of a step backwards than an improvement.) G. W. Steevens made such scathing remarks about the boots that questions were asked in the House of Commons. The War Office stated firmly that the boots were very good boots but had been tried too severely. Steevens retorted that it was not much of an argument to say that the boots were very good boots but no good for the purpose intended. He himself had marched the distance in riveted boots and they had stood up to it. There were equally alarming stories about swords and bayonets which were made of such poor quality material that they bent when used. (When Kitchener became Secretary of State for war some sixteen years later he bore in mind the necessity of what is now called 'quality control'.)

Both sides now tried to find out the other's intentions. If Mahmoud was planning to move out into the eastern Sudan, there was no point in having a bloody battle to dislodge him from his fortified position. But if he intended to stay until the Khalifa sent a relief force, it might be wise to deal with him promptly. Kitchener had been criticised for being indecisive at this point. It is true that he did not attack Mahmoud's position until the 8th and that, in the four days between the arrival of Gatacre's brigade on the 4th and the 8th, he sent a message to Baring in Cairo. Both Kitchener and General Hunter had considerable doubts about the wisdom of hurling troops onto a strong position held by people who would prefer to die rather than abandon it. Furthermore, Kitchener would be throwing away his principal advantage. His greatest asset was his superiority in small arms and, if the Dervishes were prepared to come out into the open and charge, he could produce great havoc with rifle and machine-gun fire. If, however, they stayed in position, the advantage of Kitchener's superiority in small arms would be much reduced. Gatacre was in favour of attacking, perhaps because he was unaware that attacking a fortified position is normally understood to need three-to-one numerical superiority at least. In this instance it was the *attackers* who were outnumbered.

In any case, Kitchener could not attack until Gatacre's brigade had been reshod: over two hundred had been unable to complete the march; this did not include the ones who had carried on barefoot. At the very least, two days would be needed to deal with foot and footwear problems. After that it was a question of whether Mahmoud could be tempted out, could be starved out, or should be driven out. Kitchener's telegram to Baring gave him an excuse for waiting when his hot-headed brigade commander was urging immediate, and possibly disastrous, action. His asking Baring's advice was the nineteenth-century equivalent of the twentieth-century aphorism, 'When in doubt never commit yourself, always committee yourself.' Baring's reply suggested caution, as Kitchener had known it would; whatever course of action he now took would be justified. But the temperature around the zareba was now 117° F (47° C) *in the shade*. This would be more difficult for British troops than it would be for their opponents. The moment of apparent indecision was over, but it had not really been indecision at all. He had been waiting to see if the enemy might make the first move. The telegram from Baring covered whatever course of action he wished to pursue. He decided now he should attack.

The battle was fought in classic style. First there was an artillery bombardment, then an advance while the Dervishes, extremely well-disciplined, held their fire. Then, as the attackers came to 200 yards' range, the Dervish marksmen opened up and cut holes in the British lines. The charge was sounded: the British soldiers reached the zareba, pulled it apart, and hurled themselves on to the Dervishes in the trenches behind. There was fighting everywhere, and then in fifteen minutes it was all over. Unlike later battles which would drag on for days, sometimes months, the fighting in this campaign was short, sharp, and decisive.

Contemporary accounts described incidents in the battle as follows:

Headed by their officers, the Camerons rush through the gaps. Captain Findlay was the first of the British Brigade to cross the zareba, but ere he had gone many yards he was mortally wounded, being shot in the chest and stomach, besides being wounded by a spear. 'Go on, my company, and give it them!' he called out and a quarter of an hour after he was dead. The Seaforths rush into the zareba, followed closely on the heels of the Camerons, then the Lincolns and the Warwicks get through, and the whole of the British Brigade presses on. The scene inside the zareba is indescribable. One sees trench after trench of Dervishes, all firing point blank as fast as they can load, while the British and native troops dash forward clearing the trenches with bullet and bayonet. . . .

It soon became not so much a question of clearing the trenches as of killing every Dervish separately. The latter never lost an opportunity. Major Urquhart of the Camerons, one of the first to enter the zareba, was shot from behind by a Dervish, who, concealed amongst a heap of dead and dying, was waiting his chance to kill.

Sergeant-Major Mackay, of the Seaforths, had an experience which is probably unique. When jumping the palisade, a Dervish spearman made a drive at him in mid-air, as he was, so to speak, 'on the wing'. Fortunately the spear only tore the Sergeant-Major's kilt, and he finished his assailant with pistol and claymore.

Colonel Verner of the Lincolns, a man of such gigantic stature that he could hardly be missed even by an imperfect marksman, had bad luck. One bullet cut his helmet strap, one grazed his cheek, whilst a third hit him in the mouth, gouging away his upper lip and taking off his moustache. The gallant officer refused to retire, and, with bandaged head, continued with his men to the end.

Mahmoud had taken no chances with potential waverers:

The coolness and pluck with which the enemy contained themselves during the bombardment proved that the Dervish was truly brave, not merely when fired with enthusiasm in a fanatical rush but when face to face with death, without hope of escaping or of killing his foe. Many unfortunate blacks were found chained by both hands and legs in the trenches, with a gun in their hands and with their faces to their foes—some with forked sticks behind their backs.'

Casualties were given as 568 to Kitchener's force, 125 being British. Two thousand Dervish bodies were counted in the trenches, and a thousand behind. Two thousand were taken prisoner. Osman Digna escaped with a number of his followers.

Atbara was the first battle in which Kitchener had held overall command. A fair criticism is that he could have continued the preliminary bombardment for longer than the hour and a half which he allotted to it. It was performing the useful tasks of inflicting casualties and breaking down defences. It was, of course, using up ammunition which might be needed if the Khalifa suddenly came to

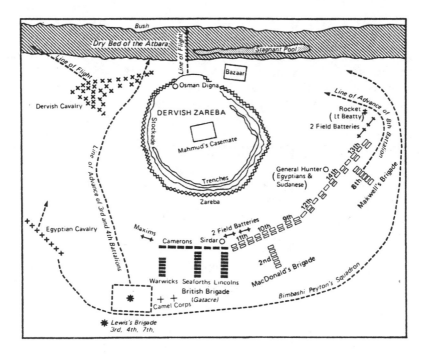

The battle of Atbara

the aid of his hard-pressed subordinate (and Kitchener was always careful about conserving ammunition); but it seems that Kitchener's principal reason was that he did not want to keep his infantry waiting too long before he committed them to battle. Choosing the right moment to launch infantry into an attack is not easy. If they are sent in too early, many of the defences are still intact; on the other hand, if the bombardment goes on too long, infantrymen may easily pass the peak of their keyed-up enthusiasm and be less effective than if they had gone in earlier.

Atbara was a very small battle by modern standards, but it was a vital one for the campaign. Mahmoud's command included one quarter of the Khalifa's entire fighting strength. Had those 20,000 men been available at Omdurman five months later the outcome of that critical battle might well have been different. But the Khalifa, though a good tactician, was a poor strategist. On the battlefield itself he handled his troops skilfully: in the wider area of the whole campaign he missed opportunity after opportunity. In consequence, the outcome of Omdurman, which concluded the campaign, was decided at Atbara.

Mahmoud was captured, interrogated by Wingate, and then

85

humiliated. He was taken to Berber and forced to follow the cavalry in the victory procession. He had fetters on his ankles, and a halter round his neck, sometimes he was left to walk, at others made to run. When he stumbled, Sudanese guards flicked at him with whips. The crowd jeered and threw rubbish at him. It was brutal, savage and, above all, degrading. Kitchener knew exactly what he was doing. It was essential that all the people in the rear areas should realise that Kitchener and his army were the victors, now and in the future. Any loyalty or sympathy for the Dervishes must be ruthlessly expunged by a demonstration that the great all-powerful Khalifa, successor to the Mahdi, could not save one of his most renowned generals from public disgrace. Furthermore, Kitchener's own troops expected such a demonstration, and would have been at least sullen, probably enraged, had it been denied them.

In the event it may not have been quite so successful a demonstration as had been anticipated, for Mahmoud regarded himself as the centre of attraction, walked with head erect, and showed no resentment either at his treatment or at being called a 'Kab' (dog). After the parade he was interned at Wadi Halfa where he warned his captors ominously that they would get a surprise they would not like at Omdurman.

Kitchener was not cruel or vindictive but he knew better than anyone the people he was fighting against and the people who, at the moment, were supporting him. It is said that he had turned a blind eye to reports that Egyptian labourers on the railway had been flogged, hanged, or had their hands cut off. It was Sudanese Islamic law and the victims would not have expected otherwise. Cutting off hands and feet, or both, was a well-established punishment for thieving or evading taxation in the Sudan.[1] Father Ohrwalder, a missionary who had been captured by the Mahdi at El Obeid, and in consequence spent ten years in captivity, left interesting accounts of Mahdism and the Khalifa. As a missionary he was treated better than the other captives, for the Mahdists always hoped to convert him. Even so, he lived in appalling conditions. He felt that Gordon had been entirely mistaken not to try to evacuate the Egyptian garrison from Khartoum when he first arrived there in February 1884. He said that Gordon had also made a great mistake by allowing the families of the Dervish warriors who were ranged against him to remain in Khartoum; they had appealed to him to let them remain, saying that otherwise they would starve. No mercy

[1] In 1985 it was announced that Iran is using a new machine which cuts off fingers 'painlessly' (*Daily Telegraph*, 8 Feb 1985).

was shown to the garrison or the inhabitants in return when Khartoum fell; then all the soldiers who had not already joined the Dervishes were slaughtered, as also were 4000 of the townspeople, including women and children. Of Gordon he said, 'He was entirely deceived if he believed that by the exercise of kindness and humanity he was likely to win over those people [the Dervishes] on his side: on the contrary they ridiculed his generosity and only thought it a sign of weakness. The Sudanese respect and regard only those whom they fear.'

Although Kitchener admired Gordon, he was not likely to repeat his idol's mistakes. In spite of his brusque manner and unbending severity, Kitchener had nothing sadistic in his make-up. On suitable occasions he liked to be kind. However, the Sudan campaign was not an occasion when kindness at any level was likely to do anything but delay or even jeopardise the desired result. In the army itself everyone knew that failure, even from an unavoidable cause, was a crime. If a horse went lame and a message was delayed, or if a man was sick, this was accepted, but was not treated as an excuse for failure. Kitchener drove himself no less hard than he drove his subordinates and would not tolerate the smallest degree of weakness or failure in himself either.

Chapter 7

War without End

Victory at Atbara could not be followed up promptly. The next battle would be much larger and would mean the end of the Khalifa's regime or an appalling disaster for Kitchener's force. More supplies would be needed; this meant that the continuation of the railway up to Atbara was essential. Equally important was the rise in the level of the Nile, which would not occur until August, for that would permit the river craft, including gunboats, to get themselves over the cataracts. So for the moment the army could take a well-earned rest, except that 'rest' in military terms invariably means training harder than ever for the next assignment. A well-known feature of military psychology is to make any time not spent fighting be less congenially occupied than exposing oneself to immediate destruction. But there was some genuine leave and Kitchener himself took a month of it. He returned to Cairo in June and had long talks with Baring. (Baring had been elevated to the peerage in 1892 and was now Lord Cromer, but for reasons of clarity we have continued to refer to him as Baring.)

Kitchener was apparently full of confidence, and felt he had more than enough troops for his purpose. He had, however, made arrangements for his force to be joined by another British infantry brigade, a cavalry regiment, some additional artillery, and (having learnt by experience) a considerable increase in field medical support. He returned in July and moved with his strenghened army to Wadi Hamed which was only sixty miles from Khartoum. Surprisingly, his moves were not harassed. The Khalifa had decided to meet him on ground of his own choosing, the plains of Omdurman. This, the Khalifa reasoned, would give his warriors a better opportunity to destroy the invader than to passively await a siege of the town itself. On 24 August 1898 Kitchener began the approach march and the Khalifa, well-informed by his spies, began to make his necessary dispositions.

Kitchener had approximately 25,000 men at his disposal, which was less than half the strength of the Khalifa's army. However, the numerical difference was more than cancelled out by Kitchener's advantage in artillery and automatic weapons. Ten gunboats and five transport steamers accompanied the expedition; these carried thirty-six guns and twenty-four maxims. The guns included a four-inch howitzer, eight twelve-pounder quick-firers, several six-pounders, and three 9 cm. Krupps. On land there were another forty-four, including two forty-four-pounder field guns, and a further twenty-four maxims. These could be expected to be very effective if they did not overheat, jam, or develop any other of the ailments which quick-firing weapons can develop at the least opportune moment.

One advantage which this superior weaponry gave was that it could destroy much of the town of Omdurman itself, which was of flimsy construction. (It had been a village outside Khartoum until the Mahdi had made it his capital.) Kitchener advised the Khalifa by special messenger to evacuate all women and children from the town, as he was about to destroy it with artillery 'in order to save the country from your devilish doings and iniquity'. The Khalifa ignored this piece of plain-spoken advice. Kitchener had sufficient ammunition to continue the bombardment for two months if necessary, so it was no idle threat.

Kitchener's land force was made up of two British brigades, totalling just over 8,000, and a division of Egyptians and Sudanese, totalling 17,000. On 1 September he took up position around Egeiga, a village on the Nile. This was six miles from Omdurman. The white tomb of the Mahdi at Omdurman had been visible for some twenty-five miles. It is said that the first person to see it on the approach march was Major Stavely Gordon, nephew of the murdered general. Jubilant though the army had been at the thought of a successful ending to the campaign, the brittle humour which normally prevails on these occasions was soon subdued by oppressive heat followed by torrential rain. The second brigade, which Kitchener had prudently kept in Cairo so that it could be fed there rather than up-country, now showed all the effects which could be expected from rushing unacclimatised troops into exceptionally harsh country. Marching over loose sand was a new experience, and caused many to fall out.

On the same day the cavalry units which were screening and reconnoitring the front of the position suddenly noted movement on the horizon. What had been thought to be a blur of thorn bushes shimmering in the heat was now realised to be Dervishes advancing in thousands. The man chosen to take the message of the Dervish approach to Kitchener was Winston Churchill, then a subaltern in the 4th Hussars. Churchill was pleased to have the distinction of bearing such important news, but not extremely happy about the reception he would receive from Kitchener, whom he suspected, rightly, might not be too pleased with him.

In his book *My Early Life* Churchill describes his earlier contacts with Kitchener. These had not had satisfactory results, and Churchill adopts a tone of injured surprise in his account of them. He recalls that when he had first joined the Army and wished to go on active service everyone had been very encouraging. Alas, attitudes had changed. 'I now perceived there were many ill-informed and ill-disposed people who did not take a favourable view of my activities.' He found people hostile and jealous, wondering aloud how young Churchill had managed to get himself active service in three campaigns, write for the newspapers at the time, and even criticise his senior officers. Some of his critics were 'openly abusive', as he put it. Although he adopts a mocking tone when describing the reactions his methods and success had brought, the reader feels that he is only semi-serious; he was driven by relentless ambition, and did not see why anyone should get in his way. Kitchener, of course, had taken much the same attitude to his own career prospects but did not perhaps care to recall later the way he had played off the Foreign Office against the War Office, had used official reports to proffer his own views, and had pulled every possible string to get himself out of Cyprus and into the Egyptian Army. Furthermore, Kitchener had assisted himself greatly by striking up a strong friendship with the Prime Minister, Lord Salisbury.

Needless to say, the fact that Churchill had also made friends with the ageing Lord Salisbury and had exploited his own aristocratic connections to the full in attempting to further his career had not been unnoticed by Kitchener, whose efforts to obtain the support of influential families had been much more difficult. Churchill's career looked like being remarkably similar to Kitchener's own, with the possible difference that Churchill had begun from a much more favourable position, worked less strenuously, and was even less scrupulous. Kitchener had risen to fame on a basis of solid achievement, and had had few people to support him in the early stages; Churchill, although not lacking in dash and courage, was hoping to rise by more political methods.

At the beginning of the campaign he had written to the War Office asking to be given a post in the Expeditionary Force; his request was refused and he learnt through various sources that Kitchener had vetoed the appointment. Churchill therefore arranged for his mother to write to Kitchener. Kitchener replied with the utmost politeness that he already had more than enough officers for the campaign . . . but that if at some future time opportunity occurred, he would be pleased, etc., etc..

After some heart-searching, Churchill then decided that the only way was through Lord Salisbury, whom he now approached. A telegram went off to say that Lord Salisbury would not dream of trying to interfere with the commander-in-chief's wishes but he would be greatly pleased 'on personal grounds' if young Churchill could be accepted. Back came a telegram from Kitchener saying somewhat sharply that he had no vacancies for officers and that if he had there were plenty of people he would choose before Churchill.

Churchill then tried an old family friend, Lady Jeune, wife of a judge. She informed Churchill that she had heard Sir Evelyn Wood, at a dinner, expressing dissatisfaction at the way Kitchener had picked over the officers recommended by the War Office, rejecting a large number. Wood was not happy to see any field commander behaving in such an autocratic manner to the War Office. Churchill thereupon asked her to tell Sir Evelyn Wood that Kitchener had even turned down one of Lord Salisbury's recommendations, mentioning his name. She did. Two days later Churchill was told he had been attached as a supernumerary lieutenant to the 21st Lancers (although he was himself in the 4th Hussars). On the day he received this message Churchill went to the son of the proprietor of the *Morning Post* and suggested that he should write a series of letters describing the campaign, at a fee of £15 a column.

Small wonder that Churchill, knowing that Kitchener would be well aware of how he had been outwitted and overruled, felt that their first meeting might not be entirely amicable. He rode up at an angle, drew his horse close, and saluted:

'He turned his grave face on me. The heavy moustache, the queer rolling look of the eyes, the sunburnt and almost purple cheeks and jowl made a vivid manifestation upon the senses.

' "Sir," I said. "I have come from the 21st Lancers with a report." He made a slight nod as a signal for me to continue.' Kitchener listened in silence, paused and then replied, 'You say the Dervish Army is advancing. How long do you think I have got?' Churchill replied immediately: 'You have got at least an hour, probably an hour and a half, sir, even if they come on at their present rate.' Churchill did not know whether his estimate was accepted or rejected. He was then dismissed with a nod.

It was hardly surprising that Kitchener was sunburnt, nor perhaps that he looked almost purple. Although Churchill does not mention it, he must have announced his identity, saying, 'Lieutenant Churchill, sir. I have come ....' To have been brought vital news by this scheming young upstart, who was also a detested journalist, at the most critical moment of the campaign was enough to turn anyone purple, but Kitchener clearly mastered his feelings; he even asked a question of this novice in the interests of the battle he was about to fight. The encounter does him great credit; he might have exploded, thinking that Churchill had engineered this piece of showmanship too. Instead, he concentrated entirely on the task ahead.

There seems, however, to be no doubt that exposure to the desert sun, and the strains of the long campaign, were beginning to give Kitchener a mesmeric look. The ride across the desert when he had hurried back from the Araba expedition in 1883 had left a lasting effect on his face, giving him an impassive, stern immobility. Damage to his eyes caused him to stare in that penetrating yet unseeing way that often goes with imperfect eyesight. But he had no time for more than a momentary surge of irritation. There was a battle to be won.

It was now midday. His army had begun making its preparations for the coming night, and was therefore deployed in a wide defensive arc. The approach of the Dervishes had taken Kitchener by surprise. He had expected to meet them on the plains the next day, in their own defensive position, where they had said they would fight. But if they were coming out to meet him, and might begin a battle which could go on past nightfall, he would face a set of problems which would not be easy to solve. In order to see how much of the Khalifa's army had been committed, he ascended a 300-foot hill named Jebel Surgham, which gave him a good view towards Omdurman. To his surprise it seemed that the whole Dervish army was approaching, not merely a cavalry reconnaissance. So, far from being the attacker, he now looked like being the defender of a hastily constructed camp with its back to the river. But suddenly the Dervishes wheeled and turned back. The Khalifa had clearly decided that attacking fortified positions was not the best use for his troops. Kitchener reflected that he must have been goaded into taking some form of action by the relentless bombardment from the gunboats, which were using lyddite-filled, high explosive shells. These had not only made great gaps in the city walls but had also knocked holes in the dome over the Mahdi's tomb. Clearly the Khalifa could not timidly stand by while such sacrilegious acts were taking place, but a closer look at Kitchener's camp had convinced him that he would be better off fighting in a position of his own choosing.

Kitchener, of course, had no means of knowing what was in the Khalifa's mind, and therefore decided to put some of his own ideas into it. The approach of the Dervish army, followed by an apparent withdrawal, looked ominous. If it had not retreated far, it might now be deploying for a night attack. A night attack on the Egeiga position could be disastrous. In the darkness the Dervishes would be able to infiltrate deep into the defensive positions where neither field nor machine-gunners would be able to distinguish their proper targets; the entire battle might become a hand-to-hand combat, fought in the dark, between heavily outnumbered and physically outclassed British troops and some of the most athletic warriors the world has seen. Defeat was not merely a possibility, but a probability. The only defence was to make the Khalifa think that Kitchener's army was itself about to make a night attack. This was done by sending local villagers into the Dervish lines with information, for which they knew they would be rewarded, that Kitchener had already announced that intention to his troops. Such news would presumably be welcomed by the Khalifa, who would then make his own preparations. Whether in fact a night attack had been the Khalifa's original intention was never discovered, but even if it had been, the fact that search lights from the gunboats were being used to sweep over the ground immediately in front of the Egeiga position would have been an additional deterrent.

The attack on the Egeiga camp eventually came soon after dawn. It was made by a force of some 10,000 Dervishes commanded by Osman Azrak. It came towards the left and centre of Kitchener's position and was cut down by concentrated rifle, machine-gun and shell fire before it had reached closer than 300 yards from its objective. It lasted from 6.45 a.m. to 8 a.m. Osman Azrak himself was killed, as were 2000 of his followers. When the emirs realised that their efforts were achieving nothing except the slaughter of their own men, the remainder of the force withdrew. This attack was succeeded by another wave of Dervishes, this time on the extreme right. It was led by the Khalifa's son Osman Sheikh-Ed-Din. It began well but faltered under the same sort of concentrated fire which had stopped the previous attack. But this, Kitchener realised, as he assessed the position, accounted for only half the Khalifa's strength. If either of the first attacks had met with success, the remainder would undoubtedly have been seen by now, following up in a wild unstoppable thrust. But they had not, and more cunning tactics were being employed. In fact, the larger part of the uncommitted reserve was lying concealed behind the Jebel Surgham, the rocky hill from which Kitchener had observed the

Dervish army the day before, but which now lay well behind the Dervish lines.

It was an interesting stalemate, though no stalemate was likely to last long with Dervish armies burning to avenge the damage to Mahdi's tomb. But having beaten off two attacks, Kitchener now had to advance if he was to reach Omdurman by nightfall and avoid fighting in the streets in the darkness. The Khalifa was waiting for him to make that move, to come away from the entrenched position around Egeiga and out of the protective range of some of the covering guns. But the Khalifa underrated Kitchener's reading of the battle. Kitchener had made up his mind that, with half of the Khalifa's army repulsed and thousands already dead, the expeditionary force could deal with any further threat. Although Kitchener did not know exactly where the Khalifa had positioned his main force, he realised grimly that he would soon be in no doubt. Victory would be decided by an interesting equation. Either the small-arms fire would cut the Dervishes to pieces before they reached Kitchener's column, or there would be so many of them that they would reach the machine-gunners and riflemen and ride over and through them. There was still movement in the heaps of Dervish dead, and the Egyptian soldiers began firing wildly at them. They were probably aware that a wounded Dervish is often even more dangerous than an unhurt Dervish because his final desperate ambition is to kill one more of the enemy before he himself dies. Kitchener seems to have regarded the matter differently and was reported to have called out in annoyance: 'Cease fire, cease fire. Oh, what a dreadful waste of ammunition.'

Although it was obvious that the main body of the Dervishes must lie somewhere between this point and Omdurman, it was essential to know exactly where they were positioned and what their probable intentions were. To this end, Kitchener sent out cavalry in the form of the 21st Lancers, commanded by Colonel Martin, to conduct a reconnaissance, initially along the plain between the Jebel Surgham and the river. Although the main body was likely to be on the far side of the Jebel, it was possible that there was a substantial number of Dervishes on the nearer side and, if so, these might be expected to come in on Kitchener's left flank as he moved forward.

The 21st Lancers had had an interrupted career since the regiment was originally created in 1759. It had been disbanded three times when it became surplus to military requirements, and had even been named the 3rd Bengal European Cavalry for a short period. It became the 21st Hussars in 1861 and had only been the 21st Lancers since 1897. Whatever the feats of its antecedents, it was technically a new regiment and thus very anxious to show that it lacked nothing in cavalry spirit, not least perhaps because there were several attached officers, including Winston Churchill, with it on that day. They would doubtless comment on its performance later when they rejoined their own units.

On spotting a small number of Dervishes half-concealed in a khor (a dried-up watercourse), Martin therefore ordered the 320-strong regiment to charge and scatter them. To his surprise, when he reached the top of the khor some 2000 Dervishes rose to their feet and confronted them. The 21st were now too committed to be able to swerve to the flanks, so they simply rode through the Dervishes, reformed 300 yards on the other side, turned, and made a second, flanking charge. It was a magnificent performance, though it had absolutely no effect on the battle. The regiment had twenty-one killed and forty wounded; the Dervishes may have lost more; after this brisk and bloody engagement the remaining Dervishes moved off to join the Khalifa's main army. The encounter had lasted three minutes. One of those killed was Lt R. S. Grenfell, nephew of Sir Francis Grenfell. He belonged to the 12th Lancers but had been attached to the 21st for this campaign and given the troop which, if Churchill had not been delayed, would have been his. Three Victoria Crosses were awarded. (In the nineteenth century VCs were given out far more liberally than in later wars when a man who earned one was likely to have it conferred posthumously.)

But even before the 21st had had a chance to report back, Kitchener had set the rest of his force on the move. While doing so he executed the somewhat delicate manoeuvre of changing the position of two brigades while they were actually on the march. He had misgivings about Lewis's all-Egyptian brigade, which in view of the Khalifa's tactics might now receive the full weight of the Dervish attack, and therefore exchanged its position with Macdonald's, which included three battalions of Sudanese troops. While this was taking place the Khalifa observed that Macdonald's brigade was separated by about half a mile from the rest of the column and promptly launched his Baggara cavalry at it.

In the following two hours the fate of the expedition once more hung in the balance. If Mahmoud had not been obliterated at the Atbara, if Osman Sheikh-Ed-Din had held his attack a little longer, the Dervishes would have been too numerous. They were not, as they have so often been depicted in films, an undisciplined body of savages armed with spears: they were first-class cavalry and infantry, mostly armed with rifles which they could fire accurately, and precise and accurate in their tactical moves, because the only factor which could stop them was death or an order from their superiors.

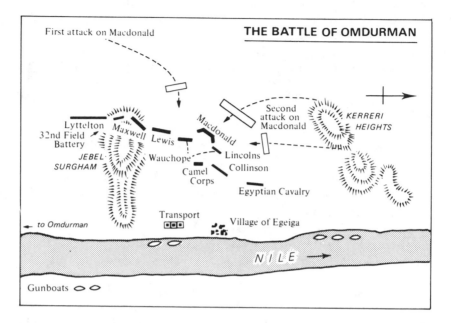

First attack on Macdonald

THE BATTLE OF OMDURMAN

Second attack on Macdonald

KERRERI HEIGHTS

Lyttelton
32nd Field Battery
Maxwell
Lewis
Macdonald
Lincolns
JEBEL SURGHAM
Wauchope
Camel Corps
Collinson
Egyptian Cavalry

← to Omdurman

Transport
Village of Egeiga

NILE →

Gunboats

The attack on Macdonald's brigade was described by an eye-witness:

> The Baggara cavalry on this occasion showed remarkable reckless daring. They evidently intended to break through our lines and divert our fire, so as to give the Dervish infantry an opening. To carry this out was hopeless, for it meant riding to certain death, but they galloped forward in loose open order, their ranks presenting one long ridge of flashing swords. Every soldier in the Sirdar's army watched breathlessly this daring feat. Nearer and nearer they came until the foremost horseman emerged almost within 200 yards of Macdonald's lines. A continuous stream of bullets from our lines was emptying the saddles but they came on until not a single horseman was left. One Baggara succeeded in getting within thirty yards of the lines before he fell. The whole of the Dervish cavalry had been annihilated. There is no instance in history of a more superb devotion to a cause, or a greater contempt for death.

This, however, was but the prelude to a display of equally reckless courage on the part of the Dervish infantry in their last despairing effort. The latter, though they had seen the fate of the cavalry, swept like a great white-crested wave towards our ranks,

96

without the slightest pause or hesitation. Hundreds planted their banners in the ground and gathered round them only to drop lifeless at the foot, as the price of their devotion. The carnage was fearful, as the dauntless fanatics hurled themselves to inevitable death. Most noticeable of all was the Emir Yacoub, who bore forward the great black banner of the Khalifa (his brother) surrounded by his relations and devoted followers. Although decimated by the hail of bullets before and around them, they surged forward until only a mere handful of men remained, and these, never faltering, rushed onwards until they dropped dead beneath it.

With attacks like this coming in from all sides, there was no time for Kitchener to use correct military channels and the chain of command—even if he had wished to. He conducted the battle himself, ignoring his staff and issuing orders direct to brigade, even battalion. As each Dervish attack came in, Kitchener switched his troops to present the strongest possible front to it. It must have been infuriating and frustrating to the brigade commanders, who were handling their commands extremely well, to find that Kitchener had issued an order to one part of the brigade to continue or to delay a move. But there was no time for sulking in one's tent like some latter-day Achilles; they were all fighting for their lives and knew it. Furthermore, Kitchener was infinitely more experienced at fighting the Dervishes than anyone else on the field was. He had learned the hard way, coming from failure at Suakin to modest success in later battles. But the fact that he was indisputably the best commander on the field would not have made him take direct command unless he felt it was vitally necessary. It was not a unique performance. In moments of desperate crisis other commanders have done likewise: Auchinleck in the Alamein battle of July 1942, Patton in Europe, MacArthur in the Pacific. But it is always a crisis move, as Kitchener knew, for the confusion which results from sudden switches on the battlefield is aptly summed up by the army as: order, counter-order = disorder!

By 11.30 the Dervishes who had survived the battle were ordered to retreat; they included some who had already arrived at that decision independently. 'He who fights and runs away, lives to fight another day' may have been the thought in their minds, but they reckoned without Kitchener. When he judged this part of the battle to have been won, he gave the order for the brigades to re-form and then march forward to Omdurman. This took them away from the battlefield. At 12 noon they were halted and given an hour and a half for rest and recuperation. There was probably little rest: most of the time would be taken up with checking equipment and making sure everything was in order for what the immediate future might hold.

Kitchener rode at the head of the column as it entered Omdurman. He was quite indifferent to the risks he took then and later in occupying exposed positions. The town appeared to be empty apart from an old man, an emir, who came forward on a donkey, dismounted, flung himself at Kitchener's feet, then rose and gave him the keys of the town. Kitchener took the keys and spoke to him. He told him that there would be no massacre of old people, women and children, whom he knew were in the town, provided all arms were handed over promptly, and there was no resistance of any kind. The announcement of this unusual clemency travelled rapidly. Within minutes inhabitants who fell into that category appeared everywhere.

Kitchener inspected the town carefully and thoroughly. Most of the army followed him into the city and occupied it. There were, in fact, a few Dervishes within the walls and some of these injudiciously opened fire on the incoming soldiers. In the inevitable retaliation a number of civilians and children were killed, alongside the would-be urban guerrillas. Kitchener, busying himself with inspecting everything, was nearly killed by a shell fired by one of the gunboats which thought it was being helpful. It killed his companion, the Hon. Hubert Howard, who was there as special correspondent for *The Times* and the *New York Herald*. The journalists in the party may have wished it had been otherwise and that Kitchener, not Howard, had been killed. With rare exceptions, such as Howard, G. W. Steevens, and Bennet Burleigh, Kitchener regarded journalists as detestable, a dangerous liability to Intelligence, and despicable as well. The day before the battle several had waited patiently outside his tent for several hours in the baking sun. When he finally emerged, they asked him whether he had any news for them. His reply was, 'Get out of my way, you drunken swabs.'

He stayed in Omdurman till well after dark, then went out to a cleaner-smelling bivouac in the desert. He must have been totally exhausted, but showed little sign of it. His last remark before he went to sleep had an Old Testament ring to it. He said he thanked the Lord of Hosts who had brought him victory that day at such a small cost in British blood. The cost had indeed been low. Only forty-eight of his force had been killed, of whom twenty-three were British (including three officers), and 434 had been wounded. Against this they found, on a careful count, 11,000 dead Dervishes. A further 16,000 Dervishes, many of them wounded, had been taken prisoner.

It now seemed as if the battle must have been one-sided and easy; those who took part knew differently.

One of Kitchener's telegrams to Lord Cromer mentioned that he now had 300,000 woman cooks and concubines on his hands and that he had no use for the services of either, nor any means of supplying them with food. This light-hearted statement has been interpreted as showing that Kitchener was not as other conquerors or he would have wished to choose the best half-dozen concubines for himself. This does not allow for the fact that former Dervish concubines might not have been a very easily acquired taste.

The Khalifa had gone. He had left the battlefield as Kitchener was marching towards Omdurman in the afternoon and gone into the town with a view to organising further resistance. Nobody showed much enthusiasm for joining an already defeated leader, so he went to the Mahdi's tomb and prayed, then left. He was followed by those remnants of his army which had not been killed, wounded, or taken prisoner, and remained at liberty deep in Kordofan for fourteen months. Brutal tyrant though he had been, no one ever tried to betray him. Like Prince Charles after 1745 (who moved freely and safely among starving peasants with an enormous price on his head) he was safe because he represented Sudanese independence from foreign conquerors, and perhaps the right of his own people to dominate others. He was eventually tracked down by Reginald Wingate, future governor-general of the Sudan, and killed in a skirmish.

In the next three days Kitchener personally supervised the evacuation of the wounded on to the Nile steamers and also arranged a memorial service to Gordon which took place outside the old palace in Khartoum, now in ruins. Gordon's favourite hymn had been 'Abide with Me', and after this had been sung Kitchener was seen to be sobbing audibly with tears running down his cheeks. He recovered himself sufficiently to tell General Hunter to dismiss the parade, and then displayed a side to his character which no one had suspected. In a quiet and hesitant voice he explained how much it meant to him to have avenged Gordon who had done so much for Britain, whose government had then abandoned him to his fate.

Two days later, in a somewhat different manner, he ordered that the battered remains of the Mahdi's tomb should be completely destroyed, and that the Mahdi's bones should be thrown into the Nile. Gordon's nephew, referred to earlier, was allotted the macabre task of disposing of the remains, but Kitchener, according to Churchill, decided to retain the Mahdi's skull himself. Subsequently Churchill wrote: 'Being now free from military discipline, I was able to write what I thought about Lord Kitchener without fear, favour or affection and I certainly did so. I had been scandalised by his desecration of the Mahdi's tomb and the barbarous manner in which he had carried of the Mahdi's head in a Kerosene can as a trophy.'

This statement can scarcely have endeared Churchill to the man he was to work with some twelve years later as a close colleague. When Sir Reginald Wingate took the Khalifa's skull as a personal trophy later, he was more discreet about it: he was said to have drunk champagne out of it for the rest of his life on each anniversary of the battle of Omdurman. Using the skull of a defeated, tiresome adversary represents a long tradition among barbaric—and allegedly more civilised—generals.

Not surprisingly the press, with which Kitchener was unpopular even before the injuries which he was alleged to have inflicted on them in this campaign, rose to the occasion. The *Manchester Guardian* was particularly eloquent. Many years later Malcolm Muggeridge, who once worked for the paper, noted that the *Guardian*'s indignation about events was always in inverse proportion to their distance from Manchester. Conditions in factories in Madras were denounced vigorously: complaints about the standards of hygiene and comfort in their own staff canteen were brushed aside as mere frivolity. More time was given by Parliament to discussing Kitchener's subsequent behaviour than was allotted to giving him credit for winning all his battles. The senior ranks of the Army were further embittered by the manner in which he had overruled subordinate commanders on the campaign and in the final battle. However, the soldiers, British, Sudanese, and Egyptian, whom he had commanded, thought the world of him; the general public loved him as they love generals who win battles instead of making excuses for losing them. And Queen Victoria was very touched by the way he had looked after the wounded and held a service at the scene of Gordon's death.

But there was still work to be done, much work. He thought better of his plan to keep the Mahdi's skull and had it buried secretly in a Moslem cemetery at Wadi Halfa. He explained that it had been necessary to demolish the Mahdi's tomb because shell-fire had made it unsafe and it could easily collapse and injure innocent worshippers. Gradually the indignant protests died down and Parliament, not without considerable dissension, voted him £30,000. He was raised to the peerage and took as his title Lord Kitchener of Khartoum and Aspall. Aspall, of course, had been his mother's home in Suffolk. He was also awarded the GCB (Grand

Cross of the Bath). But these rewards did not come till later. Immediately after Omdurman he had other pressing duties, which were to test his skills as a diplomat.

In August 1898, while in the final stages of the campaign against the Dervishes, he had received sealed orders, to be opened immediately after the defeat of the Khalifa. He opened them on the day after the capture of Omdurman; they originated from the Foriegn Office and instructed him to take an expedition up river immediately to deal with a crisis caused by French action in the Upper Nile region.

It had come to the notice of the Foreign Office that a French expedition, led by a Major Marchand, which had set out from French Equatorial Africa in June 1896, had now reached the Upper Nile and was said to be at the small, though important, town of Fashoda. The journey through such inhospitable regions might have been enough to daunt anyone, but Marchand had accomplished it. Admiration for his feat was tempered by the fact that the whole of the Nile valley had been claimed as a British sphere of influence some three years earlier; and the campaign against the Khalifa had been undertaken on that understanding. It was as well for Marchand that Kitchener had caused the Dervishes to concentrate at Omdurman at the time of the Frenchmen's arrival: uninterrupted, the Khalifa would have made short work of the unwanted visitors.

Confirmation of Marchand's presence at Fashoda was brought to Kitchener in an unexpected form. The Khalifa had already sent a steamer and a small flotilla to deal with the intruders, but these had not managed to bring them to book. The steamer therefore returned to Khartoum to ask for reinforcements and further instructions. It arrived on 5 September and its captain was surprised to find Kitchener in command, instead of the Khalifa. He cannot have been looking forward to an interview in which he reported failure, and was doubtless relieved to find the change of command. Marchand's party numbered 128, i.e. himself, seven French officers, and one hundred and twenty native soldiers from Senegal. (One account says that these were the original numbers, and that casualties had reduced them to eighty.)

Kitchener thereupon set off on 10 September with an overwhelming force. It comprised a company of Cameron Highlanders, two battalions of Sudanese, a Mountain battery, and an adequate supply of maxims.

It was Kitchener's first diplomatic mission and it was one of extreme delicacy. A false move, even a careless word, could lead to fighting which would not be limited to Fashoda. The national pride of two countries was at stake. When Marchand had set out, the only ruler who might be said to exercise any sway in the Upper Nile region was the Khalifa, and it was likely that the French did not regard his claims very seriously. Britain, on the contrary, was working in conjunction with the Egyptian government, which had claimed suzerainty over the region for many years and, prior to the Madhi's arrival, given practical demonstrations of their presence. France and Britain already had a long history of conducting wars against each other in Europe and thousands of miles overseas at the same time: this looked as if it might become another of them. What happened next depended entirely on Kitchener's diplomatic skills, and diplomacy was an art in which he had no training, little experience except at Zanzibar, and no special aptitude. However, the hour brings forth the man.

He began by anchoring twelve miles downstream from Fashoda, and from there he addressed a letter to Marchand as 'The Chief of the European Mission at Fashoda'.

He informed Marchand that he had defeated the Khalifa, liberated the country, and arrived here with a considerable force. (There were, of course, substantial forces of Dervishes in the area, and Marchand must have been aware that his own position was none too secure.)

Marchand replied immediately, congratulating Kitchener on his victory, and begging to inform him that a treaty which he had signed twelve days previously with the Mudir of the region had put the territory in that area under French protection 'subject to', as he put it delicately, 'ratification by the French government'. This, of course, neatly transferred the responsibility for what happened next to the intellectuals of the quai d'Orsay.

With these preliminaries accomplished, and having then made sure that negotiations would not begin with a burst of gunfire, Kitchener took his force up river. He observed that the French flag was flying over the government buildings which the Egyptians had occupied before the Mahdi had dislodged them some fifteen years before. All Kitchener's ships were flying Egyptian flags and Kitchener had put on the uniform of an Egyptian general, complete with tarboosh (a form of fez). He greeted Marchand and invited him to lunch on his gunboat. Fortunately he and Marchand took an immediate liking to each other, a process which was greatly assisted by the fact that Kitchener spoke fluent French, and from his schooldays, his former home at Dinan, and his experience with the French Army, had learnt how the French expect their friends to behave. Both men were well aware that there were great issues at stake, but maintained a friendly tone even at the most critical points of their discussion. Kitchener informed Marchand that the French presence was a direct violation of the rights of both Egypt and Great Britain, and that the French flag should not have been raised in an area which lay under the jurisdiction of the Khedive. (The fact that Britain and Egypt had abandoned the Sudan for thirteen years was not mentioned.)

Marchand replied that he was a soldier and therefore had to obey the orders he had been given: they left him no option. Kitchener then said that his orders left *him* no option either, and that he had the necessary force to implement them, which Marchand manifestly had not. He would hate to have to take matters to this extreme and informed Marchand that he would be very happy to convey Marchand and his party down river to Cairo in comfort. Marchand could not see his way to accepting this kind offer and, furthermore, pointed out that, if Kitchener used force to dislodge him, he and all his force would die rather than leave their posts, an event which would, of course, lead to war between their two countries. He added that he could leave only if he received orders from his government to do so. He thought these might be forthcoming but would take some time and he suggested to Kitchener that he should be patient.

The conversation took a sharper turn when Kitchener asked if Marchand had been authorised by the French government to stop Egypt from putting up its flag and re-asserting its authority over the region. Marchand replied that if Kitchener wished to hoist the Egyptian flag he was in no position to stop him. Kitchener then informed him that he proposed to do so immediately, but that he would not interfere with the French flag in any way: whatever flag was eventually left in sole possession of the flagpoles was a matter for governments, not for themselves, and that it would be duly decided by diplomatic means he did not doubt. The Egyptian flag was then hoisted and greeted with a twenty-one-gun salute.

Kitchener departed soon after and established another post further up river. He confessed he was astonished at Marchand's courage and resolution at accomplishing so much with such a small and badly equipped force. He sent him a present of wine and foodstuffs accompanied by a note saying that 'all transport of munitions of war on the Nile is absolutely prohibited'. He then went to the Mudir with whom Marchand had made his treaty and extracted from him a written statement denying that he had ever made a treaty with Marchand. He may well have known that the treaty which Marchand had made was a verbal one, but whether this was so or not, the denial by the other party that a treaty existed would be a considerable disadvantage in any hard bargaining the

French might be expecting to do. However, the French, only too well aware of the growing power of Germany, which had inflicted such a crushing defeat on them less than thirty years earlier, were determined neither to engage in a distant war nor to alienate Great Britain, who might perhaps become an ally against the might of Germany. In consequence they recognised the Egyptian claim. Britain had even more reason to be relieved at this peaceful outcome as it was now clear that she was soon to be engaged in a difficult war with a tenacious foe in a huge country many miles from her own shores.

Kitchener returned to a hero's welcome and to receive his peerage, at the award of which he seemed surprised. He wrote to his cousin Emma, who sent him a letter of congratulation, 'Dear Cousin Emma, Many thanks for your congratulations. I certainly did not expect a peerage and fear I shall make a very poor peer ....'

His reception by the public was so enthusiastic that he felt overwhelmed. He was given the Freedom of the City of London, accompanied by a Sword of Honour with an eighteen-carat gold hilt, a blade damascened with gold, and gold bands on the scabbard. The ceremony took place on 3 November 1898; the same evening the French Ambassador called upon the Prime Minister to inform him that Major Marchand had been ordered to leave Fashoda. As Lord Salisbury had just told Kitchener that he was to be Governor-General of the Sudan, as well as Commander-in-Chief of the Egyptian Army, this news must have come as some relief to the new governor-general, as he could scarcely have welcomed further military diversions in the deep Sudan at that moment.

In the circumstances it is a pity he could not have read the letter General Joffre wrote on hearing of his death in 1916: '*C'est sous le drapeau de la France que ce grand Anglais avait fait ses premières armes. C'est pour la gloire commune de la France et de la Grande Bretagne, pour la victoire du droit et de la civilisation qu'il est tombé, en soldat. Sa mort m'a frappé comme celle d'un ami personnel, et d'un des meilleurs amis de mon pays.*'

But even while honours of every description, including honorary degrees and freedom of cities, were being heaped on Kitchener, his thoughts were never far removed from his responsibilities in the country of which he was to be governor-general. In late November he launched an appeal for £100,000 to establish a college at Khartoum in memory of Gordon.[1] Through it he hoped that Gordon's

[1] There was already in existence a Gordon Boys' School, founded in his memory in 1885, which flourishes today at Chobham, Surrey. This was also funded by public subscription and was a typical English boarding school, for boys from impoverished backgrounds.

wishes for the future well-being of the Sudan would be achieved. The appeal was oversubscribed within a month. His critics suggested that Kitchener's interest in having an efficient secondary school built at Khartoum was practical rather than idealistic, and that he required the college less as a tribute to Gordon's memory than as a source of educated junior administrators. Basic education would be catered for by the establishment of primary schools throughout the land; higher administrators by attracting the cream of British university graduates to what would become perhaps the most prestigious part of the overseas civil service: the Sudan Political. As this last attracted so many outstanding athletes, the Sudan later came to be known as 'the country of the blacks ruled by blues'. Undoubtedly Kitchener's educational aims *were* practical rather than emotional. He was no product of an English public school who might have pined to found a Sudanese version of his alma mater in a distant land, maintaining links with the establishment on which it was modelled and becoming known as the Rugby or Wellington or Cheltenham of the Sudan. He did not believe in the cultural virtue of cricket or rugby football and had probably never played either game in his life.

Sad to say, after a mere six months Baring informed Lord Salisbury that Kitchener had already become bored with Gordon College, even though it looked like fulfilling its purpose. Had Kitchener survived the First World War, he might have become less bored than outraged at the developments in his college as it progressed to university status and en route displayed some of the characteristics for which new universities are known, or even notorious.

Cromer was hoping for much from Kitchener and had already tried to influence his colleague's approach to his work. He wrote a private letter from which the following extract is taken:

I want to add something privately to the official and semi-official instructions I am sending you. I am—as I feel sure you are aware—anxious that your civil should be as successful as your military administration. I have been at this sort of work for some forty years and know something about it. I think therefore you will not mind my speaking frankly to you.

In the first place, pray encourage your subordinates to speak up and to tell you when they do not agree with you. They are all much too inclined to be frightened of you.

In the second place, the main thing in civil and political life is to get a sense of *proportion* into one's head, and not to bother too much about insisting on every particular view as regards non-essentials.

I commend these principles to you. Whatever success I have attained is largely due to strict adherence to them. I learnt them from my two old chiefs, Sir Henry Storks and Lord Northbrook, who taught me most of all I know.

In the third place, *pray* keep me informed and consult me fully. A secretive system will not work so well in civil as in military matters. The latter are far less complex and in some respects less difficult than the former. Remember that previous consultation and full information do not necessarily involve centralisation: indeed the very reverse is the case. Excuse me for stating my views so frankly.

Kitchener, it seems, accepted the advice in the spirit it was intended and saw it less as a criticism than the advice of a friend. Both men knew that Cromer's analysis of Kitchener's methods was correct. A second letter, written a fortnight later, also contained useful advice, but was less likely to be acted on:

I am sending you officially the Sudan agreement, as also a general letter of introduction. The latter is couched in very wide terms. It is impossible to enter into great detail. Generally what I want is to control the big questions, but to leave all the detail and execution to be managed locally.

In the word 'big' I of course include all such measures, for instance, as involve any serious interference with the water supply of the Nile, or any large concession to Europeans or others.

It was unlikely that Kitchener would leave administrative details to others to supervise. Work, in his mind, was like justice: it not only had to be done but had to be seen to be done. Nothing in his experience had suggested that work could be delegated without sudden, unannounced, and careful inspection of the results or lack of them. He sent instructions to the mudirs in the various districts giving them instructions on how they should organise and administer the areas of their responsibilities. With them he struck an original but important note: 'The people should be taught that the truth is always expected and will be equally well received whether pleasant or the reverse. By listening to outspoken opinions, when respectfully expressed, and checking liars and flatterers, we may hope in time to effect some improvement in this respect in the country.'

A lesser man would not have known where to begin in administering the million square miles of the Sudan. Much of it was still inhabited by wandering bands of Dervish, some quite large; the one which included the Khalifa probably numbered 6000 and was by no means unique. Much of the country was unmapped, and even the parts which were had a bewildering variety of names. Some place names changed from one generation or even one owner to another. On the map which Kitchener used to fight the battle of Omdurman the village of Egeiga was named El Gemuaia. Even when place names had not changed, they might be spelt in several different ways.

But above all the problem of the Sudan lay in the fact that a predominantly Christian overlordship had now become responsible for a completely Moslem population. If that overlordship was to produce a constructive result it must secure the co-operation and goodwill of the people administered. In the event it did, but it was due less to Kitchener, who was soon to leave the country, than to Reginald Wingate, who succeeded him as governor-general.

By the time Kitchener left the Sudan in late 1899, he had completed his victory and received his rewards. He had destroyed a powerful enemy; he had been rather less successful in making genuine friends, though the ones which he had made were of the highest worth. But perhaps his most important achievement was that he had made possible one of the most interesting developments of the twentieth century—government by trusteeship. On 19 July 1899 a treaty establishing an Anglo-Egyptian Condominium of the Sudan had been signed. Its purpose was to protect, instruct, and assist a backward country to a point at which it could govern itself and take over the administration of its assets. The Condominium lasted till 1953. It served as an example for all the mandates, or 'mandated territories' created from former German and Turkish colonies after the First World War, when major powers were given exactly the same responsibilities in a variety of territories. After the Second World War the mandates transferred from the League of Nations to the United Nations and became trust territories. Most are now fully independent.

For proving that government on the principles of trusteeship can be successful Kitchener, by that first year in the Sudan, undoubtedly deserves credit. Credit for his other achievements has been plentiful; but for establishing the notion of stable trusteeship his contribution seems to have been unnoticed.

Chapter 8

A Difficult Enemy

In the summer of 1899, Kitchener took two months' leave in England and used it to enhance his future prospects. He stayed with various influential people, not least Lord Salisbury. There were two areas where developments looked like producing an appointment to Kitchener's liking, and which he would be well qualified to fill. One was India, where he could be the military representative on the Council of the Viceroy, Lord Curzon; the second was South Africa, where a war seemed extremely likely. If war did come in South Africa, Field-Marshal Lord Roberts, who was at that time commander-in-chief in Ireland, might well be asked to take charge of the expeditionary force. Kitchener went to the Curragh to see him and enquire about the possibilities of being given a senior appointment on his staff if that happened. He dreaded the thought of being left in the Sudan inspecting irrigation schemes or the establishment of village schools, when there was fighting to be done elsewhere.

On the social side his fortunes were mixed. He became a personal friend of the Duke of York who, in 1910, would become King George V.[1] The two rode together in Rotten Row and often dined together. It was rumoured that both men drank heavily when they dined together and, if this is true, it shows that Kitchener had come a long way from the occasional whisky and soda which he used to drink in the mess. He also became very friendly with Lord and Lady Cranborne: Cranborne was Salisbury's son. But his efforts to persuade a 'suitable' woman to marry him proved a failure, for Lady Helen Vane-Tempest-Stuart now refused him. He shrugged off his rejection. He had followed everyone's advice about seeking a wife who would not only be a great comfort to him but a considerable asset to his career, but here he had met defeat. He bore no resentment. He

---

[1] After Kitchener's death his walking stick was presented to George V, who used it daily. Letter from Lord Slamfordham to Sir G. Arthur.

had managed his life and career satisfactorily enough before and no doubt could continue to do so. Nobody was to blame.

Roberts was not initially made commander-in-chief in South Africa. At sixty-seven he was thought to be too old for such an onerous appointment, but the first general to be appointed to the difficult position was a man named Buller, and after a disastrous beginning to the campaign Buller was replaced by Roberts. Salisbury had considerable misgivings about Roberts' appointment, on the ground of his age rather than his popularity and competence (which were not in doubt), and agreed only on the condition that Kitchener should accompany him as his chief of staff.

The situation in South Africa presented problems even more varied and complex than those of the Sudan campaign. At the time of the Boer War (1899–1902) the country extended over an area of half a million square miles. Most of the land was an average of 6,000 feet above sea level, and the terrain was often extremely rugged. The war which would take place there was not so much a war in which two opposing sides confronted each other and fought for lands which the other side held, but a war in which the combatants disputed much the same territory. Within that area which both sides felt was their own by right, if not by possession, were certain towns and districts which were clearly under the control of one side or the other. To understand this remarkable state of affairs one needs to look back briefly into a very long and haphazard history.

The Cape of Good Hope, at the southern tip, had been discovered by European voyagers such as Bartholomew Diaz and Vasco da Gama in the late fifteenth century, but the interior looked inhospitable and dangerous and they made no attempt to settle. However, an English privateer, James Lancaster, visited the Cape several times at the end of the next century and in 1620 landed and claimed it for Britain, although the British government under James II refused to accept it. But in 1652 members of the Dutch East India Company made a small settlement which soon attracted a variety of other peoples, mainly refugees such as French Huguenots. The settlement expanded and soon clashed violently with the Hottentots who, because they were there, assumed that the country belonged to them. Later the immigrants met the Bushmen who were culturally still in the Stone Age and did not distinguish between Boer herds and wild cattle. In retaliation for the slaughter of their herds the settlers, mainly Dutch Boers (farmers) who came to be called Afrikaners, hunted and killed the Bushmen like animals. By the end of the eighteenth century the Boers were meeting more formidable opponents as they pushed inland looking for farmland: a branch of the

109

Bantus, known as the Xosa. The Boers had already developed a military organisation, which they called a commando and which elected its own officers and made punitive attacks on Hottentots or anyone else who raided lonely farms, but although the frontier Boers found the Xosa increasingly troublesome, their problems aroused no sympathetic response in the Dutch government at Cape Town which was interested only in sea trade and a quiet life.

When, in the Napoleonic Wars, France overran Holland, Britain arranged with the Dutch government in exile that the British Navy should take over the Cape. In 1802 the British restored the Cape to the Dutch, but in the second phase of the wars from 1806 to 1815, occupied it once more. When the war was concluded, the Treaty of Paris provided that Britain should retain the Cape and pay the Dutch six million pounds compensation. South Africa, like Alaska and Florida, was therefore originally a colony by purchase.

During the next fifteen years the relationship between the Boer farmers and the British overlords gradually deteriorated. The British government gave lukewarm support to safeguarding the frontier areas, despite the extreme danger to settlers when the Bantu were on the march, and the last straw came when, in 1834, Britain abolished slavery within the British Empire. Compensation was paid for freed slaves, but money was not what the Boers wanted. They wanted labour. They needed Bantus on their farms working, not burning their homes and stealing their cattle, and eventually they decided that, risky though it was, they must break away and move up country to a place where they could be free of the British, make their own laws, and provide for their own safety.

In consequence, 'the Great Trek' of 3000 Boers took place in the late 1830s. The Afrikaners crossed the Orange River to form the Orange Free State and they crossed the Vaal River to form the Transvaal. One party reached Zululand where, in a murderous battle, it defeated Dingaan's warriors and proclaimed the Boer Natal Republic.

As the years passed, the Boers had sporadic clashes with the Bantu and learnt much in the process. They became hard men and hunters; they could shoot straight from the saddle of a moving horse and, although outnumbered, they could beat the Bantu at their own game. They learnt fieldcraft the hard way and when their successors used these inherited skills against the British at the end of the century the British learnt the hard way too.

This turbulent situation on the frontiers was a nuisance and embarrassment to the British government in London, which felt it had some responsibility for those territories but deplored the idea of spending money on them. As a way out, the British government signed a treaty in 1852 (the Sand River Convention) with the Transvaal Boers, guaranteeing them their independence, and in 1854 a similar treaty with the Boers of the Orange River Colony, enabling them to form the Orange Free State. It seemed at the time that the South African situation had been settled once for all, quite painlessly. Then in 1867 diamonds in quantity were discovered along the Vaal River. Within months there were 40,000 prospectors digging there. The diamond fields were called Kimberley, after the British Colonial Secretary at the time. It was a name which would become familiar to many outside Africa when the war came.

The area in which the diamond fields lay was named Griqualand West, and was the home of some five hundred Griquas who were mainly of mixed Dutch and Hottentot ancestry. Their chief thought that in spite of the Sand River Convention they were still under British protection. The Afrikaners thought otherwise, but agreed to abide by the decision of an impartial arbitrator. When the arbitrator judged the area was British, the Afrikaners made no formal complaint but decided that such unfortunate developments must not occur if other mineral wealth was discovered.

That event occurred in 1884 when gold was discovered on the Witwatersrand (Ridge of the White Water) in the Transvaal. Three years earlier the Afrikaners had fought an indecisive war of independence, known as the First Boer War, against the British and been granted formal independence at the end of it by Gladstone, always ready for an excuse to shed responsibility for colonies. The Afrikaners now had a forceful leader named Paul Kruger who, as a boy, had travelled on the Great Trek, who was said to have read only one book in his life—the Bible—and whose attitudes were determined from the Old Testament rather than the New. He believed that he was the instrument of God for Boer independence. But he did not believe in rights for other people in Boer areas. Although the Boers in the Transvaal were soon outnumbered by engineers, technicians, and others with essential skills from many different nations, he would not allow the establishment of schools or courts where any language other than Afrikaans would be spoken. As the immigrants (known as Uitlanders) paid 90% of the taxes collected, they felt they should also have some rights. Kruger did not agree, and in case there should be trouble spent a good proportion of the revenue in importing arms.

War between the two sides became inevitable when Dr Starr Jameson, a doctor with the British South Africa Company, took a small force from the area which would later become Zimbabwe, and

111

tried to seize power in the Transvaal. The date was 1 January 1896 and the force, which was badly organised as well as being too small, was quickly rounded up by the Transvaal Boers.

Attempts were still made to arrange a reconciliation between Boers and British, but Kruger felt he might have some outside support (notably from Germany) when war came, and was content to collect money and arms and be prepared. Thus 187,000 rifles were imported through Mozambique in 1897, though rather more significant than numbers was the quality of the arms which were now coming into Boer hands. Kruger had no illusions about his task or needs, still less his ambition, which was to have a Boer Republic of South Africa. The British government, realising that war was not merely inevitable but imminent, began reinforcing the garrison in South Africa.

On 9 October 1899 Kruger, being unwilling to see the balance of power tilted in Britain's favour, issued an ultimatum which demanded the withdrawal of all British troops from the frontiers of the Boer Republic and the evacuation of all British troops landed in South Africa since the previous June. He also demanded that all troops en route to South Africa by sea should be turned round and sent home. If these requirements were not met, war would be declared. On 11 October the ultimatum expired, the Boer forces invaded both the Cape Colony and Natal. Kruger had 50,000 well-armed men at his disposal to confront 20,000 British. The British forces, in what seemed to be an unfortunate but unbreakable tradition, took the field with inadequate, obsolete arms. They were totally unprepared for mobile warfare over a terrain as large as France and Germany combined. None of the British generals concerned in the opening stages had any concept of the difficulties of the forthcoming campaign. The Boer farmers were natural soldiers from the outset, and fought with an intelligence and resourcefulness which Britain had not encountered since the Napoleonic Wars. Furthermore they had a dedication to their cause which made them far more dangerous than any conscript army could be. Their main handicap was numbers, for at the best they only managed to put 90,000 troops in the field; yet it took 450,000 British and colonial troops to beat them. They had large reserves of ammunition and, though short of artillery, were first-class marksmen. An additional factor was that they were using the new smokeless powder and thus proved extremely difficult for British forces to locate.

For the British commander, General Sir Redvers Buller, VC, the war was not so much a problem as an insoluble puzzle. The two main bases, Capetown and Durban, were separated by a thousand miles.

112

There were no accurate or reliable maps, there were very few roads and bridges—those bridges there were were mainly for railways—and the fords (known as 'drifts) had steep sides which made those crossing them extremely vulnerable.

The Boer advance into Natal was checked at Talana Hill, but the British troops in this area were too far forward and exposed. Their commander, Sir George White, therefore withdrew into Ladysmith, hoping that the Boers would besiege him and be diverted from invading Natal. Unfortunately Ladysmith was not a particularly good position for successful defence, and although the siege immobilised a certain number of Boers it was far more damaging to the British. Meanwhile, the Boers had also closed in around Mafeking and Kimberley. Thus, after the opening round of the war, the disastrous position was that three British garrisons were locked in by Boers, who had ample time to prepare defences against any relieving forces. The single course for hope was that the Boers, by tying down a number of their own troops in sieges, had made it impossible for them to drive forward to Capetown, where in one great battle they might have ended the war successfully.

Attempts to relieve the beleagured towns led to the famous 'Black Week' of 9 to 17 December 1899. Gatacre was defeated at Stormberg with heavy losses. Methuen had an even greater disaster at Magersfontein, a position which the Boers had prepared carefully for this sort of contingency, and Buller was hopelessly out-generalled by Botha at Colenso. As it now seemed possible that Britain might lose the war, and lose it very quickly, the home government realised that drastic changes of command were needed. The first was that Buller was removed from his post as commander-in-chief, although he was retained to complete his assignment of relieving Ladysmith—a compromise which led to further difficulties. Buller, who had won his VC twenty-one years earlier, had no relish for the task of storming the Boer positions outside the town, and would have preferred campaigning in a different manner in a different area. He was an officer with exceptional regard for the welfare and safety of his troops and heartily disliked the thought of incurring heavy losses in trying to relieve a town which need never have been besieged. However, there was no avoiding the military requirement. In a badly mismanaged engagement Boers and British met at Spion Kop on 24 January 1900. After sustaining heavy casualties, the British force eventually retired without achieving its objectives. But unknown to them, the Boers had also decided to withdraw, and the way to Ladysmith lay open here while Buller now tried, with no success, to break through further west.

However, in February Roberts arrived on the Kimberley front and took command. Salisbury had made it clear that if Roberts were appointed Kitchener must be there too as his chief of staff. It was an unusual appointment, for the chief of staff in the modern sense did not exist: a more appropriate name for the post would have been second-in-command. Kitchener had been at Khartoum on 18 December when he received his new orders, but by making surprising speed he managed to join Roberts at Gibraltar where the latter was on the *Dunottar Castle*. Each man had made his own chillingly realistic appreciation of the difficulties which lay ahead. 'Black Week', followed by Spion Kop, had shown that there was something very wrong with British forces in South Africa. Intelligence reports revealed that the Boer artillery, although outnumbered by British guns, had greater range and power, and the Boer small arms were not only more efficient but infinitely better handled. And for beginning a cavalry war Britain was desperately short of mounted troops. Kitchener wrote: 'Our artillery has turned out useless as I expected. When you think all our field guns were originally 12 pdrs; they were then bored out to make them 15 pdrs, which naturally only allows their being fired with reduced charges. We are hopelessly behind the age, owing to our Artillery officers' dislike of anything new. I wired from Cairo what guns we ought to have but of course the official reply was against doing anything. My God! I can scarcely credit their taking the fearful responsibility of sending us into the field practically unarmed with artillery.'

Roberts decided that his best plan would be to take his force from the Cape across the plains of the Orange Free State to Bloemfontein and then, having captured that Boer stronghold, to press on to Pretoria in the Transvaal. In his 30,000-strong force he had the best of the cavalry, commanded by Sir John French. The Boer commander, Cronje, did not believe that Roberts would dare to move away from the safety of the railway line and thus did not bother to strengthen the besieging screen around Kimberley. As the British force moved forward with French's cavalry in the lead, Cronje realised too late what was happening, and sent reinforcements to bar their road. But they were too little and too late. French, in a spirited cavalry charge, went right through the Boers and relieved Kimberley that night. The date was February 15th. The situation now looked much more favourable to the British but, not for the last time in this difficult war, optimistic predictions were to be reduced to nothing by swift Boer counter-strokes. On the day of the relief of Kimberley, Christian de Wet, the name which would become as familiar to Kitchener as his own shadow, fell on the supply train which was following Roberts' army. Roberts had the choice of turning back and saving the convoy or pressing on with troops on half-rations. He chose the latter.

Undoubtedly Roberts and Kitchener saw eye to eye over the strategy of this campaign. From his experience in the Sudan, Kitchener had brought two convictions. One was that if troops were busy and making headway they can survive on rations which would produce a mutiny in peace-time. Second, and perhaps even more important, the practice of doggedly clinging to the safety line, whether in the Sudan where it was the Nile, or out here the railway, robs an attacker of all initiative. In the Kimberley area Roberts and Kitchener were fortunate in that they were confronting a Boer general who was conservative and cautious in outlook. After the relief of Kimberley Cronje had to decide between making a swift and certain escape without his ox-wagon supply train, or a possible, though risky, departure with all his force intact. He chose the latter and nearly succeeded, but on 16 February the dust raised by his forces was spotted by Kitchener as he stood on a kopje, scanning the countryside through binoculars. British infantry followed up, and Cronje fought a series of rearguard actions and held them off. On the 17th Cronje had reached the Modder River and was ready to cross it just to the east of the Paardeburg Drift. However, before he put his oxen to the strenuous task of hauling wagons through the drift he knew he had to give them a little time to rest and graze. So he halted.

This then became Kitchener's battle. Some say it was his greatest triumph: others that he mismanaged it. But no one denies that it was a victory, and it has been suggested that it marked the turning point of the war. Command had fallen to Kitchener at this vital moment because Roberts was ill.

Cronje, once he realised the British were on his trail, abandoned part of his supply train in order to make better speed. Kitchener was therefore presented with wagons, Mauser rifles, ammunition, shells, explosives, food, coffee, sugar, tobacco, even some champagne. It was an unexpected bonus, and of the utmost value. The War Office had failed to provide even necessities. As he had said just before this in a letter to his friend Ralli: 'Not a single emergency ration so the men have to fight all day on empty stomachs. I am afraid I distrust the old red-tape heads of departments. They are very polite and after a bit present me with a volume of their printed regulations generally dated about 1870 and intended for Aldershot manoeuvres, and are quite hurt when I do not agree to follow their printed rot.' Happily there was now no shortage of supplies.

But Cronje was by no means at the end of his tether. He had 5000 tough, well-mounted men, and he knew that there were another 3000 from the Free State in the vicinity, and a further 1000 under De Wet not far away. Still others were making all possible haste to reach him and help. He decided that his best plan would be to cross slightly above Paardeburg at Vendutie Drift. For the moment his forces were in a huge defensive laager or encampment; he saw no reason why he should not hold off the British attack until his reinforcements arrived, then cross with all his train at leisure. This would be decidedly better than abandoning most of the train and hastening through the drift. But just as he was moving into a more favourable position near the Vendutie Drift he was caught by a burst of brisk fire from French's brigade, which had set out from Kimberley at 4.30 that morning. French had less than 1000 men, and they were nearly dropping with fatigue after their long rides of the past few days, but they had twelve field guns with them and with these began to lob shells into the heart of Cronje's position. Two British infantry brigades also came up, but they too were far from their best after long marches. In the meantime Cronje dared not cross, under threat of fire from French's guns, but at the same time could be confident that, if he waited, reinforcements would soon besiege his besiegers.

Roberts, realising that Kitchener had the experience and ability to win this battle on his own, gave him full authority to do so without reference to himself. He had now put 20,000 men under Kitchener's command, scattered over a wide area and with very limited means of keeping in touch with each other and their commander. He had with him only his personal staff, and it included no signallers, gallopers (fast-riding horsemen for taking messages), or orderlies for local communication. Not since medieval times had a commander gone on to a major battlefield so ill-equipped.

By the afternoon of the 18th the ring around Cronje was complete but the position of the besiegers was by no means comfortable; Boer attacks from De Wet's and Steyn's forces inflicted heavy casualties, though not enough to enable Cronje to break out. Casualties sustained by the British amounted to eighty-five officers and 1185 other ranks. Although these were light enough in relation to the numbers involved and the need to get a quick result, they were high enough for Kitchener to be criticised for his tactics. Those tactics had been to increase the pressure on Cronje's laager, to make it impossible for him either to cross or to break out, and to try to force a surrender before the other Boer forces could break through to relieve him. However, after the first few attacks on the laager it was obvious that Kitchener lacked the resources to achieve a swift victory. Therefore he decided to concentrate on holding off the would-be relievers and

116

allow starvation, casualties and disease to effect Cronje's surrender. Subsequent analysis of the battle established that the attacks by Kitchener's forces had been badly co-ordinated. In view of the deficiencies in his staff it is surprising that there was any co-ordination at all. This was not a battle, like Omdurman, where a commander could see the whole field and gallop from place to place issuing orders.

Eventually, on 27 February, Cronje surrendered with 4000 men. By this time the besiegers were in little better case than the besieged. Both were short of rations and both had had to rely on the Modder River for drinking water. The Modder, by the 27th, was so contaminated with bodies of dead men and animals that it was the perfect breeding site for typhoid. Casualties from disease were soon to exceed those caused by fighting, and disease, mainly typhoid, proved to be one of the most stubborn features of the campaign.

Paardeburg was both a victory and a defeat. It was a victory in that it caused the Boers heavy losses in men and material, but in the delay it caused to the British forces, preventing Roberts' bold dash to reach Pretoria from being successful, it was a considerable setback. However, there were grounds for claiming it as the turning point of the war. The Cape colony was now freed from Boer attacks, and Boer planning had been frustrated. In consequence, Boer morale was lowered while that of the British, which desperately needed a stimulus, had now received a shot in the arm.

Three years later Kitchener, who was then in India, wrote to Sir Ian Hamilton about the battle:

I am quite willing to accept the full responsibility for the battle of Paardeburg. As a matter of fact, putting aside local South African ranks, I was the senior officer in the Army present.

On arrival on the ground my first business was to get into communication with General French on the north side of the river. This was done at once, and I explained to him the situation. He told me that he could hold the enemy from any attempt to escape north, and that he could deal with any unimportant snipers who had come up from the east to help Cronje, but that his horses and men were too done up to take any part in the attack on the enemy. I fully recognised the justice of this and made my plans with the force at my disposal.

The river Modder, at Koedersrand Drift, which was the scene of the fight, runs approximately from east to west through open country sloping to the river, but with steep banks twenty-five to thirty feet high. The river is very winding, and the banks are covered with scrub, whilst close to the river are some trees of considerable size. Cronje's wagons were huddled together in a confused mass, immediately on the north side of the Drift, where there was some open ground clear of scrub, and where the river makes a loop or bend to the north. All his men and animals were hidden in the river bed. I had four brigades of infantry and the Mounted Infantry at my disposal, besides a few mounted troops such as Kitchener's Horse. [Kitchener's Horse was a volunteer regiment from Capetown but at this time had had little experience or training.]

Kitchener went on to describe his dispositions; artillery and one brigade to the south, French's cavalry to the north, Smith-Dorrien's brigade plus a battery of artillery over the river and on to the north bank. An attack was to be launched towards the laager using two brigades from Colville's division, and the brigades under Smith-Dorrien and MacDonald.

The Mounted Infantry was briefed to creep as close to the laager as possible and then, when the Boers were engaged with the other attacks, to try to rush the Boer position and capture their wagons. (Mounted Infantry uses horses as transport, and dismounts to fight; it is not cavalry, and is not used as such.)

Kitchener continued:

The attack from the west commenced, and shortly afterwards from my central position I saw that Stephenson's brigade, which had been sent round east out of range to get on to the river opposite the Mounted Infantry and support them, was facing east, and apparently doing nothing. I sent my ADC to find out the meaning of this, and later my senior staff officer, Colonel Hubert Hamilton. My ADC brought me back word that the brigade were carrying out my order to support the Mounted Infantry who were facing east, apparently about to advance against the small body of snipers on the eastern ridge, which General French had told me of, and for which he was responsible. About the same time I received a message from Colonel Hannay [commanding the Mounted Infantry] that he could not get on. I sent him a strongly worded message that he must at once carry out my original instructions, and pay no attention to the snipers on the east, otherwise he would be too late to take advantage of the attack from the west which was then rapidly developing. I also pointed out that by his action General Stephenson's brigade was being led quite wrongly, and could give no assistance to the western attack. I also sent orders to the brigade to get into the position assigned to them on the river facing west.

This was done, but it was too late to assist the western attack, and Colonel Hannay nobly sacrificed his life in a futile attack on the laager.

The fact that Kitchener's irate instructions had caused Colonel Hannay to engage in what was described as 'a futile attack' throws some light on Kitchener's unpopularity with certain elements of the Army. Hannay was clearly in an impossible position, and his death would be blamed, not unfairly, on Kitchener's botched plan. The Mounted Infantry would not forget.

Under our heavy artillery fire from both banks, it was certainly, to my mind, extraordinary that the Boers were able to hold the western attack in check, and had their rear been threatened at the right moment I think they would have hardly succeeded in maintaining their position. This, however, was not done owing to the above circumstances, and their resistance proved that when cornered in a hole like a badger they are hard to draw out and can show their teeth.

Lord Roberts never expressed or implied any censure on me for the battle. He regretted, with me, that it had not been more successful, but he knew full well that, had the action not taken place, he would never have been able to send the telegram that Cronje and 4000 men had surrendered; for with 4000 mounted men it was quite easy for Cronje to break through either French or myself during the next night before reinforcements came up, and with small loss, as we have seen the Boers do so successfully when barbed wire blockhouses were round them.

The action of Paardeburg, however, only left Cronje with twenty horses all told. During the attack we captured all his trek oxen, every other animal being killed, and, thus rendered immobile, the Boers were at Lord Roberts' mercy, and could not escape.

Instead of penitently acknowledging my error, as one writer considers I should, I maintain it was the only course to pursue, and that had I allowed Cronje to escape after all the exertions I had called for and received from the army, I should be most rightly censured and have lost the confidence of the troops.

It was in no frenzy, but with the most deliberate view of my responsibility in the matter that I decided on the attack, which I maintain is very erroneously described as a frontal attack. As a matter of fact it was an all-round attack, as the artillery from the north and south outflanked and enfiladed in every way the position taken up by the enemy to resist the attacks from east and west.'

119

The press, with its established fondness for criticising Kitchener's methods had seized upon the heavy casualty figures of 18 February and blamed them on Kitchener's tactics. In retrospect, these tactics seem to have been the only ones possible. Kitchener had caught up with Cronje just when the Boer general was at his most vulnerable (at a river crossing point), had surrounded him with his own forces, both exhausted and outnumbered, and had held off Boer relief attempts with the greatest difficulty. If he could have broken into the laager and caused Cronje to surrender a few days earlier, Roberts' plan to reach Pretoria quickly *might* have succeeded. It seems that Kitchener's attacks on the Boer laager on the 18th were an entirely justifiable expedient. It was the fact that they did not achieve their immediate objective though sustaining heavy casualties (compared with his previous battles) which caused the bitter criticism, not the tactic itself. However, it might well be argued that any general who brings about the surrender of 4000 of the enemy, along with one of their best leaders, can scarcely be called a failure. Kitchener was, as he discovered, facing an enemy with a different motivation from his previous opponents. The Dervishes had been ready, even anxious, to die in battle, and made little attempt to avoid doing so. The Boers, on the other hand, were sophisticated campaigners. They would have approved of the words of General Patton nearly half a century later. 'Patriotism does not mean dying for your country; it's making some poor bastard die for his.' As Kitchener was soon to realise, the Boer soldier would be as dangerous on the verge of defeat as he could be on the eve of victory. The Boers had been fighting losing battles for so long against the British that they had developed a means of robbing the winner of the fruits of victory. And, as the Boers had learnt, if a victor finds that all his efforts produce no lasting results, but only an outward show of success, he will soon tire and abandon his original objectives.

Kitchener, though the architect of victory at Paardeburg, was not there for the final surrender. Roberts, having recovered from his indisposition, arrived on the 19th and decided to bring about Cronje's surrender by siege methods. It seems, however, that the presence of the commander-in-chief on the spot did not alter Kitchener's conviction that he was still in charge. He is reported as having gone to Brigadier Smith-Dorrien and urged him to make a further attack in spite of Roberts' orders. In the event the attack never took place, but Kitchener could well have been dismissed for what can only be described as a headstrong and insubordinate act. The incident came to nothing because Kitchener was sent forward on the 22nd to organise the communications which would be needed for the next stage in Roberts' plan. The principal communications were the railway line and bridges into the Orange Free State. As Percy Girouard, builder of the Sudan railway and now a lt-colonel, was already there, there was little for Kitchener to do: previous experience had taught him that interfering with Girouard's ideas would be pointless and unproductive. The fact that Girouard was the best man for the job and could be left in charge proved opportune, for Kitchener was urgently needed for another assignment at the same time. To the surprise and concern of the British authorities, the Dutch in the Cape colony had suddenly risen in rebellion. This rising, if not dealt with promptly, could cause a serious threat to Roberts' communications with the Cape: a particular danger was to the railway junction at De Aar, through which all the army's supplies were routed. Kitchener's solution was to organise a series of flying columns to swoop on rebel centres and break up any newly formed commando units they found. By 25 March the threat had been removed, but not without anxious moments. Meanwhile Roberts was pressing forward to Bloemfontein. He had a brisk encounter with De Wet at Poplar Grove near the Modder, and another at Driefontein, but his momentum was not seriously checked. On 13 March he entered Bloemfontein. When the British generals Clements and Gatacre crossed into the Orange Free State a few days later, Kruger and Steyn, their opponents, fled to the north. Within a few months of his arrival Roberts had transformed the war in South Africa from frustration and defeat to victory and exhilaration. Nobody at that time—except perhaps Kitchener—could have believed that the war still had over two years to run.

Kitchener was, in fact, a worried man in the spring of 1900. In his letters the reader finds sentences such as: 'Our great difficulty is transport, and this is greatly increased by the large number of mounted troops we have, entailing enormous supplies of forage' . . . . 'It is quite astonishing the way [the enemy] keep under cover, and with smokeless powder it is almost impossible to see even where they are firing from, and their guns are sometimes invisible' . . . . 'We shall require some time at Bloemfontein to reorganise: a great deal has to be done.'

The cavalry was a subject of constant concern. So far in this war it had proved considerably less enduring than had been hoped. The climate, the terrain, and the lack of grazing had all contributed to a disappointing performance. Kitchener's remedy was to apply the methods he had used in the Sudan. Only the minimum of equipment would be carried: there would be no spares. Some transport was necessary for essential stores like ammunition, and therefore every wagon must be as serviceable as regular maintenance and greasing could make it. Two officers who tried to lighten the burden of campaigning by taking a few luxuries with them were promptly and publicly court-martialled for disobedience. They must have thought it absurdly unjust. In the earlier Sudan campaign, officers had occasionally received hampers containing such exotic luxuries as Brand's Essence, sardines, cocoa, and an occasional bottle of wine. But here there was to be nothing. 'It was all that Sapper's idea,' they complained. 'He really had no conception of what a man needed to take his mind off the rigours of active service.' But they did not express these views in Kitchener's hearing.

Much to everyone's surprise, the next phase of the campaign went without a major hitch. Roberts' force, numbering nearly 100,000, advanced in four main columns. The worst obstacles were the dogged attacks by De Wet and an outbreak of cholera in Bloemfontein. The Boers made no effort to make a determined stand. They even abandoned the siege of Mafeking. Not surprisingly the relief of Mafeking was celebrated with great enthusiasm. Baden-Powell, its defender who later founded the Boy Scout movement, had bluffed the Boers into believing that his garrison consisted of much more than the thousand police and armed townsmen it contained. The siege had been conducted with an almost knightly courtesy. The Boers refrained from shelling the town on Sundays. However, when Baden-Powell used the respite to organise games of cricket, the Boers were so scandalised at the idea of playing games on Sunday that they threatened to open fire if such sacrilegious behaviour did not immediately cease.

Roberts' force reached Johannesburg on 31 May and Pretoria on 3 June. There was no resistance in Pretoria. Kruger had already left for Mozambique en route for Europe with as many boxes of gold as he could carry. Unfortunately De Wet had not been caught by the advancing forces and it was from him rather than Kruger that future trouble would come. Four days after the capitulation of Pretoria De Wet calmly seized a station on the line between that town and Bloemfontein and blocked all communications for a week. Kitchener was told to settle accounts with him once and for all.

There was very little cavalry for the purpose, for it was all up with Roberts, but Kitchener collected some untrained yeomanry and some experienced infantry and set off to capture the Boer guerrilla leader. But De Wet was a worthy opponent. Having destroyed most of the British stores he had captured, he abandoned the railway and set off west. Then, before anyone realised where he was, he came back to the railway, twelve miles north of his former position, and nearly captured Kitchener. De Wet, who by this time was known to his opponent by the almost affectionate abbreviation of 'Chris', was well aware that by now British forces were closing round him. All his escape routes were thought to have been blocked—until he slipped through a pass which was not, and disappeared for the time being.

Up country Roberts was pushing forward to Mozambique. He sent a message to Botha, requesting to meet him and discuss terms for a Boer surrender. Botha first agreed to the meeting, then refused. (An unusual feature of this war was that opposing commanders often sent letters to each other, generally commenting on some behaviour that was thought to be unsportsmanlike and requesting the other to desist from it.) Roberts' aim was to prevent the Boers escaping into Mozambique, which was Portuguese territory, but his forces advanced too slowly for that to happen. Kruger went on to Holland; Steyn and Botha took refuge in the Northern Transvaal. Buller, who had done little of note since relieving Ladysmith the previous February, came into his own when the Boers tried to make a final stand at Bergendal, on 27 August; he displayed energy and resolution which had been sadly lacking earlier in the war.

This period, which was thought by most people to be the end of the war, turned out to be merely the end of the first and easiest part of it. All the principal Boer leaders were still at large, and becoming more daring and experienced every month. Roberts went home in November, after handing over his command to Kitchener. Buller had already left. Roberts had crowned his military career with a brilliant campaign long after normal retiring age, but unfortunately added to the impression that the war was over by referring to the remaining Boers as 'a few marauding bands'. His remarks fell on receptive ears at the War Office and the Secretary of State, St John Brodrick, promptly wrote to Kitchener pointing out that a substantial reduction in British forces and expenditure should now be possible. He pointed out that the Army had 230,000 men in the field, whereas the Boers were reported to be down to 8000. The home establishment had been stripped almost bare to provide troops for South Africa and the war had already cost eighty million pounds. At the time his letter was being drafted, Kitchener was writing one himself, requesting an increase in expenditure. The Boers, in his estimate, still had 70,000 men available, of which some 20,000 were in the field and operating in very small groups. In the 1980s we have learnt to appreciate how formidable small guerrilla groups can be. They are at their best when they have no fixed base, and, by capturing the principal town of the Boer Republic the British had removed any restriction on Boer deployment and mobility. A guerrilla is also at his best when the government he is opposing is trying to restore normal peaceful conditions. To counter his activities very large numbers of police and troops were required. In Malaya in the 1950s some 200,000 troops and police were needed to eradicate guerrilla activities by some 5000 Communists insurgents. There are few countries today which have not experienced the problem of the urban and rural guerrilla; all those which have realise the enormous difficulty and expense of eradicating them.

Kitchener, who had an admiration and a liking for brave soldiers whatever their nationality, had understood the guerrilla threat from the beginning. He realised that, however long the war lasted, it was highly unlikely that British troops would ever become, man for man, a match for the Boers at this form of warfare. Certain regiments might do so, and certainly the Australians and Canadians looked very promising, but the Boer, he reasoned, would never be beaten by a series of running battles in the field. The only method likely to prove successful was the denial of supplies. If there is nothing to eat and no forage for a horse, the bravest and most resourceful guerrilla must eventually die or surrender.

Therefore, some fifty years before the same plan was used in Malaya, Kitchener decided on the blockhouse system. The procedure was that an area would be stripped of supplies, which would then be collected and put under armed guard. Farms were to be burnt, and with them any supplies useful to the guerrilla which the army was unable to remove. But before the process could begin, the women and children living on those farms must be collected up and put in secure camps, which were given the unfortunate name of concentration camps. By October 1901 80,000 Boer dependants were living in those camps, some peacefully, others giving as much trouble as they could. Meanwhile the vast countryside was divided up into sections, each cordoned off with barbed wire and plentifully covered with defensive points known as blockhouses. The theory was that by denying the guerrillas bases in the shape of farms, which could also be both intelligence agencies and supply depots, they would gradually be eliminated. The method would be slow and difficult, but was the only way. With hindsight it has been pointed out that once the guerrillas had lost their homesteads and their families there was nothing to check their mobility, and their morale would be sustained by the thought of the sufferings of their wives and children.

There was no shortage of information about those sufferings, though rather less about the share of responsibility for it. Confining some 80,000 country people in camps and allowing them to organise their own administration and hygiene was not wise. The Boer families who had farmed on the veld had no experience of living at close quarters, of the need for camp discipline, for proper sanitation, and mutual assistance. Living in camp requires close adherence to hygienic behaviour. All waste products must be disposed of well away from cooking areas; the camp must be kept spotlessly clean or foodstuffs and water supplies will be contaminated and vermin and disease will flourish. Typhoid and cholera had already been seen in South Africa; and they took a devastating toll in the camps. Commissions, largely of women, visited the camps (having been given War Office facilities to do so), but did little to alleviate the trouble. Not all the camps were bad, but there were enough examples to feed a press campaign in which Kitchener was naturally seen as a prime cause of all the hardship. Immediately after the war Boers and British in South Africa became reconciled by a generous peace treaty but when, after the Second World War, the British element appeared to the Afrikaners as being too progressive with native emancipation, old hatreds were revived. In the late 1940s there were Afrikaner leaders who spoke bitterly of seeing cartloads of dead leave the camps in which they themselves had been confined while children. Before South Africa was granted dominion status in 1910, the franchise had been arranged to give the rural areas better representation than the urban areas. In consequence, the most dour element of the Afrikaners was able to win an election and implement a policy of apartheid (separation) which denied the rapidly increasing black population political power or opportunity. But nobody has so far blamed the policy of apartheid on Kitchener's method of winning the war in 1901 and 1902. At that time the black population, much smaller than it is today, simply looked on in wonder at their white masters tearing each other to pieces. At the same time both Boer and British regarded with misgivings this war in which an already outnumbered white population was weakening itself while disregarding a potentially dangerous element which had already shown what it was capable of on many occasions, most notably in the Zulu Wars.

In the circumstances there was surprisingly little residual bitterness. The farms which were destroyed had been built with much labour and were a symbol of the owner's ability to conquer the wilderness. Now it would all have to be begun again. At first the Boers jeered at the attempts to fence them in with blockhouses, but as these and the British mobile column became more efficient the joke became less obvious. At first the blockhouses were a mile and a half apart, then, as more were built, the distance fell to four hundred

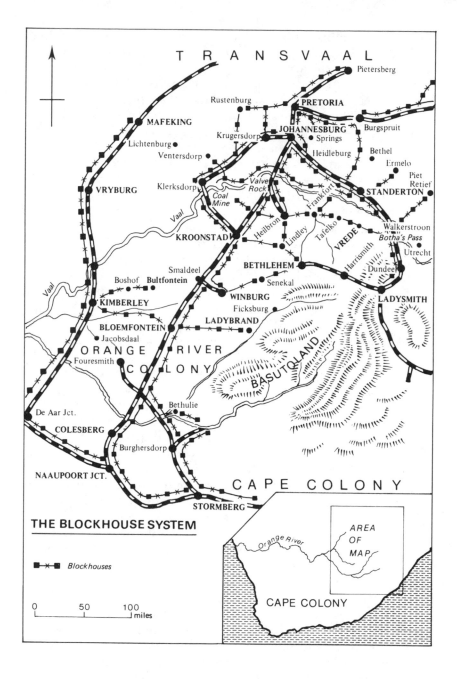

THE BLOCKHOUSE SYSTEM

Blockhouses

0   50   100
└──┴────┴────┘ miles

126

yards. Eventually there were 8,000 of them, all linked to each other with barbed wire. As Kitchener cordoned off areas he used up to sixty mobile columns at a time to try to capture Boer leaders. Prisoners were an embarrassment to both sides. The British deported several thousand to islands such as St Helena. When British soldiers fell into Boer hands, they were merely disarmed and stripped of boots and trousers before being set free again. Kitchener could not but approve of this humanitarian approach in moral terms, but he found it damaging in the military sense for it made the war more like a game of chess than a serious campaign. Wherever possible he court-martialled soldiers whom he suspected of giving up when the fighting became uncomfortable. It was a war of strange contradictions. On the one hand, the soldiers in the field developed a liking and respect for each other; on the other hand, although the civilians in the camps blamed the British authorities for the disease which killed several thousand of them, they also approved of the educational oppotunities which were provided.

For Kitchener the war caused endless strain and frustration. He was harassed by the War Office for needing so many men and so much money to complete a campaign of which everyone was heartily tired. He was frustrated by the lack of combatant spirit in his own troops: once in a blockhouse, the soldiers were inclined to devote less of their energies to patrolling than to producing a neat little homestead with a garden and a few animals and chickens. He was exasperated by the failure to capture enough Boers to break their resistance: they were as capable of cutting barbed wire as the British were of setting it up.

Some of his troubles were of his own making. He had always found it easier to take decisions himself than to delegate, and, although he was an ardent letter-writer, his office administration was chaotic, with papers of varying importance littered everywhere. He also had a habit of trying to combine movements where no effective combination was possible. And, to cap this, there was the awareness of the fact that his popularity at home was slipping from him. Emily Hobhouse, who had been allowed to visit the camps officially, blamed him for the conditions in them. She made a second visit without permission and had to be arrested and deported after leading violent demonstrations. Lloyd George excelled himself in his denunciation of Kitchener, whom he compared to Herod, and the remainder of the Liberal party divided their energies between condemning him for incompetence and reviling him for ruthlessness.

Not the least frustrating aspect of the war was the fact that the Boers were also divided about continuing it. Botha and the Transvaalers wanted peace: Steyn, De Wet and the Orange Free Staters were equally adamant that if they persevered long enough the British would tire and go home. De Wet was not only uncompromising; he seemed to prove his words by deeds. He was a master of offensive defence. He raided camps, captured stores, received surrenders and contemptuously set prisoners free. But in time even De Wet began to lose the goodwill of his own side.

Eventually a meeting was arranged between Boers and British in April 1902. The ensuing talks lasted six weeks. Kitchener, who might have been thought to have been at the end of his resources, drew on reserves of patience and diplomacy that even he was probably unaware he possessed. The vital need was to make the Boer leaders feel they were partners in establishing peace, not defeated leaders being granted terms. The fact that the war had begun with Boer invasion of British territory was never mentioned; the fact that the Boers could never win now, however long they dragged out the struggle, was not even hinted at. Kitchener listened. A generous peace treaty was eventually drafted, only to be rejected by Steyn and De Wet. Then, suddenly, De Wet changed his mind. On 31 May peace was signed.

Two people came to know Kitchener very well during his years of strain in South Africa. One was Frank Maxwell, who became his ADC in December 1900. Maxwell was a cheerful young man of twenty-nine, whose military life had been full of incident, mainly in India. He had been awarded a Victoria Cross for exceptional courage in an action in South Africa the previous March. In December 1900 Maxwell, like many others, had decided that the war was virtually over and was expecting to leave South Africa. Kitchener, who needed an ADC at that time, decided Maxwell was probably the right man for him. He asked Maxwell if he would care to join him, and Maxwell agreed. The new ADC described the occasion in a letter to his mother:

My dearest Mother,
The telegram which I'm just sending off will surprise you rather. As I left Bobs' house with his mails K. of K. called me, and asked me to be his ADC. Why or wherefore I don't know, as we ain't acquainted. However, point blanked with this, I had to say 'Yes'.

In a letter to his father on 14 December 1900, Maxwell wrote:

My dear Father,
K. seems to have pretty well knocked De Wet's scheme of entering the colony on the head—for the present anyway. He has

now with his usual tactics, split up into several parties, and is being hunted north, east and west, jinking about like the best of pig. No doubt he has a concentration in view somewhere. . . .

Later in the same letter he wrote:

Clements, some forty miles from here was attacked by a large force of 2500 under Delarey and another. We don't know much about it yet, except that he has had very heavy casualties, including four officers killed and a large number wounded. Four companies of Northumberland Fusiliers belonging to, but detached from his force, are supposed to have been taken . . . .

I think it must have been 'raining' somewhere, because it certainly poured yesterday for down by Rouxville 150 of Brabant's Horse were killed, wounded or taken—probably mostly the latter, as this corps has been recently recruited, and I know had nearly 75 per cent of the regiment raw men. Hang this wretched surrendering though I suppose sitting in an armchair it is easy enough to be brave; but it does seem to happen a bit often, doesn't it? . . .

In a letter written to his mother on 27 February 1901, he described Kitchener's meeting with Botha.

Middleburg

My dearest Mother,
Mrs Botha having brought a letter from Louis last week in which he said he would like to meet Lord K, we lost little time over the business, and left next morning, although there would be little chance of Botha being able to get here till a good deal later.

Arrived here, a letter was sent from out outposts to a Boer laager seven or eight miles away. That was on Saturday night: today, Wednesday, a letter has come from Botha to say he will be here tomorrow morning. K., with his usual impatience, was beginning to fidget but is now quiet again.

28th February
Botha has come and gone. He arrived at 10 a.m. and left at 5 p.m., having brought four others of his staff with him. He was at once closeted with K. and they remained so till 1 o'clock for lunch. His four companions lay remarkably heavy on our chests after the first hour or two but were quite good fellows, especially three of them, and could speak English well. Much chaff was bandied and we got quite funny and witty at times.

Louis [Botha] is a great big fellow running to fat a bit, but has a very nice expression indeed, and must be the good fellow one has always heard him to be. He is very quiet, shy and reserved. His secretary, De Wet, (No relations to "Chris") is quite different, being decidedly vif and all there. He was educated at Cambridge, and is quite a good fellow

Yet even with this friendly exchange at the top, the war still had another year to run.

In the middle of March 1901 Maxwell wrote a letter to his father in which he says:

I think I have told you that K. is a lover of animals—in a quite odd sort of way very often. The other morning we found him darting about his room in his early morning attire (touzled hair, short dressing gown, etc) trying to catch a couple of young starlings that had fallen down his chimney. We caught them after a heated chase, and deposited the poor little beggars in the wire pigeon house in the garden. Then there was much fuss all day about their food; and the good man would leave his important duties every half hour to see if I had given them meat, or procured succulent worms, and bustle in and say they were starving. It was no use pointing out that they hadn't learnt to eat by themselves yet, or that the pigeons wolfed any food put in for the infants. The poor parents were in great distress, flying round and round the cage, but at length got bold and fed the little things through the wire, which interested the Commander-in-Chief so much that the operations in South Africa received no attention most of the remainder of the day.

Next morning he complained to me that there was a third youngster outside, who he was sure was occupying an undue share of papa and mamma's attention, to the detriment of the babies inside, and I must try to catch it (Quite an easy job to execute on a strong-on-the-wing young bird in an open garden). He clamoured for this possibility to such an extent that I thought the time had arrived for some remedy other than protestations of inability, which are in all things and at all times quite lost on K. of K. So, sneaking out of breakfast early, I whipped out a four foot high sham stork that stands in the hall, and put it in the cage, and then lost myself in case of accidents. The joke came off A.1. He was fairly drawn, laughed much, said I was an impertinent beast, and hasn't murmured a word about catching any third birds. I tried this morning to induce him to let the surviving youngster out (one died last night), pointing out to him that the parents were becoming callous, and that he would die also, as he couldn't eat himself; and then the young ass of a bird gave away the show by paddling up to a fat worm placed there for his delectation and swallowing the whole length without a wink. So my case and his own chance of freedom were lost by the rash act, and his precocious capacity for teaching himself to eat in such a short time has been the ruin of this poor little starling's prospects in life. Besides who can say what far-reaching results his capture may have, if the C.-in-C. of some 200,000 men *at war* spends half his day watching it 'fluffing worms', and chirping at it through the wires.

Maxwell certainly understood Kitchener, and was able to tease him. Kitchener, who nicknamed Maxwell 'Brat', is shown in these letters to be far from the humourless martinet he has so often been made out to be.[1]

On 3 May 1901 Maxwell wrote to his father again:

My dear Father,
  We are now High Commissioner of South Africa, as well as Commander-in-Chief, and draw about £300 a month more, which isn't so bad. In talking at or to K. we always say 'We made a speech', 'We drew so much pay', 'We are this and that'. The object of this is that we shall participate in the emolument or credit, and he has to be frequently told that he doesn't take the hint in the right spirit and shell out.

(This is somewhat incoherent: presumably he means that Kitchener has to be reminded of his responsibilities frequently.) On 24 May there was trouble again:

My dear Father,
  Lord K. went to Pietersburg three days ago, Hamilton and I staying behind. Unfortunately no sooner was K. gone than the starling bird, now in a large roomy cage by itself, broke loose after being fed by a Highlander orderly and took to the garden. Hamilton (the Military Secretary) who takes life terribly seriously, was completely floored by this catastrophe, and very wrath with my evident satisfaction. Having brooded over it all day, he thought the matter should be broken to the Chief while he was away so that the shock would be less when he came back. I was told to send him a wire that would break the sad news cheerfully, and accordingly the following wire was sent:
  'C.-in-C.'s humming bird, after being fed by a Highlander this morning, broke cover and took to the open. Diligent search instituted; biped still at large. Military Secretary desolate; ADC in tears. Army sympathises.'

[1] By the 1914–1918 war Maxwell had become a general, but he was killed at Ypres on 21 September 1917.

He returned yesterday, having apparently recovered from the first spasm of grief, and seemed to take the matter stoically. However, having rushed through the accumulation of two days' telegrams, he was out in the garden, and having gathered a small army of staff officers, menials and orderlies, was hunting the poor bird till lunch. The pursuit continued after the meal and was only knocked off by him personally when it was time for him to go out riding. By that time he was in a fine mess, having repeatedly fallen prone in wet flower beds in his efforts to grab the starling. However, in the end the poor bird was captured at 7 p.m. in a neighbouring house's chimney, but minus its tail. And now it is hopping about in the cage as before. Everybody tries to make out it is much happier than outside—perhaps it is. If so, he showed extraordinary disinclination to get back to it, in spite of every inducement. K., as he gave up the pursuit to go into lunch, remarked breathlessly: 'I've never been so fond of that bird since it's been loose'. In fact, lately, he has spent what little leisure he has had in spouting Hindustani, instead of chirping at the bird.

At the time, the fact that Kitchener was learning Hindustani, even while on an exacting and exhausting campaign, meant little to Maxwell. Although he knew him well, Maxwell did not realise that Kitchener was already preparing himself for his probable new job as commander-in-chief, India.

To his father on 13 September Maxwell wrote:

K. is not the purposely rough-mannered, impolite person those who have never seen him suppose. He is awfully shy, and until he knows any one, his manners—except to ladies—are certainly not engaging. He really feels nice things but to put tongue to them, except in very intimate society, he would rather die. I suppose most Englishmen loathe any sort of gush, display or sentiment. K. is unfortunately endowed with ten times most people's share of this virtue, with the result it is almost a vice in him.

In October Kitchener went to Johannesburg for a conference with the Prime Minister of South Africa and various other leading figures in the government. Maxwell wrote: 'They had a great meeting, the Chief dressing them down like anything, and rubbing it into them hot and strong. The Chief believes in short discussions, and makes them hot while they last, and absolutely refused to continue after lunch.

'After lunch I bore K. off to a photographer, where he was taken in various fancy attitudes. He simply hates being photographed ordinarily but was like a lamb over this.'

In December Kitchener went on a tour of the 'concentration' camps, mainly to talk to the captured Boer leaders. Everyone apparently agreed with Kitchener that the Boers in the field should now come in and talk peace; however, the Boers knew that if they went out to their fellow-countrymen who were still fighting and tried to persuade them to give up, they would probably be shot for their pains. 'K. said he didn't wish them to risk their lives, and didn't really see the necessity of anyone going, because he thought there were *other means* of communication with the Boers outside this method.'

His speeches were very well received. Maxwell said: 'There is no doubt about it, the Boer has an unqualified partiality for K. of K.—I suppose because they know he is quite straight in his dealings with them, and because they know he is a *strong* man.'

Even when he had already been his ADC for well over a year, Maxwell still found Kitchener absorbingly interesting:

Next morning [2 March 1902] up at 4.30–5 and till 7 a.m. busy preparing the scheme for a new drive. K. is an extraordinary person. He sleeps and dreams on schemes all night, and in the morning, in pyjamas and dishevelled head, gets you to work with scale and pencil and maps, and in two hours plans are more or less complete, and orders more or less drafted. Then, being a quick-change artist, he is off and has shaved, dressed and is ready to ride out to columns while you are but washing your teeth.

Everything is at high pressure; at 7.15 we were off at a gallop, and visited two small columns and two large ones. . . .

But Kitchener was extremely vulnerable, as Maxwell noted. When Delaney defeated Methuen's column in the Western Transvaal, capturing Methuen himself, the blow was as heavy as it was unexpected.

It floored poor K. more than anything else during the campaign and he didn't appear at five meals.

On the morning of his recovery, however, when I hobbled (being a bit lame from a fall) into breakfast, where he was alone, he said 'How's your leg?' I said all right, knowing he expected me to ask how he was. But, as I was perfectly aware he wasn't ill, I sat tight and said nuffink. Not getting any enquiry about himself (in which case he would probably have said 'All right') he volunteered the remark that 'his nerves had all gone to pieces' and when I told him it was quite the most natural result of practically forty-eight hours of starvation he very practically agreed by eating a very sound, for him, breakfast. And that was the end of the slump in his spirits and he is, and has been, as right as possible since.

Kitchener remained firm but fair with the Boer leaders to the end. Maxwell wrote: 'They are all immensley impressed with the Chief, who handles them splendidly. One of them said "I can see right through Lord Kitchener", meaning by this he was so straight.... Louis brought his little son here, ten years old, and has not taken K.'s advice and sent him to school in Natal. He is a nice little creature, and told me he never wanted to leave Pretoria ....'

After the peace treaty, Maxwell returned to England with Kitchener. There he was designated 'Special Staff Officer'. In December he and Kitchener sailed to India together where Maxwell served a further two years. In India Kitchener became much more sociable, but his skill at polo did not impress his ADC. 'We went at it hammer and tongs and had great fun, old K. playing up like a man on a rather slow nag. With him playing they beat us....'

Maxwell's letters say very little of his time in India as Kitchener's ADC but there is a revealing passage in one written on 16 December 1903.

K. has had rather a bad four or five days, though he is now all right and out of bed. He got a stitch or something from always lying in one position, which made him very uncomfortable. He couldn't read, nor play bridge, and lay and moped all day. He never allows anyone to do anything for him and has steadily from the first refused to be read aloud to. However, he has caved in in this regard at last, and found he rather likes it. Three days ago I found him at about 5 p.m., looking grievously sorry for himself and without a kick in him. Following is the dialogue, accurately described, which ensued.

'Bridge to-night, sir?' in the most objectionably cheerful voice. Answer from bed, hardly audible, 'Oh dear, no.' 'That's a pity; aren't you feeling up to the mark?' Reply, a groan. 'Here's the paper, would you like to read it?' Deep sigh, and 'I can't possibly.' 'All right, I'll just read you out some of it, shall I?' 'No, don't bother.' And so the paper was read through, accompanied by heavy sighs from the bed.

That finished, dialogue begins again. 'Paper is finished; what book are you reading, sir?' Feebly, 'I don't know.' 'Oh, yes: I expect it's this one, is it?' 'No, I don't think so.' 'Which one then?' No answer. 'Oh, I know, you were reading "Gough's Life". How far have you got in it?' 'I don't know', and a groan. 'All right then, as you haven't finished it, I'll read the last chapter, which will make certain of not going over the same ground.' Then, however, seeing there was no way out of it, he let out where he was in the book, and was soon got to work. Moans, frequent at first, gave way to short exclamations on anything that interested him in the book and he never suggested a stop till more than two hours afterwards, when I had to go and change for dinner.[1]

Kitchener was now fifty-three. The outdoor man of action was trying to adjust to being the indoor man of contemplation. He could win physical battles with weapons: mental battles with people who were his equals or superiors intellectually built up tremendous frustration. Although he possessed remarkable and realistic foresight, his mind had no inner reserves on which he could draw when his patience was tried. This book is not a psychological study of Kitchener, for the writer has no qualifications in that field, but it does appear that Kitchener became greatly disturbed when he felt he might be losing control. He loved animals and birds but he liked them to be obedient. The pet bear which he had kept in Cyprus had proved too independent; after it has disgraced itself by getting first into his bath and then into his bed, it was dismissed from his entourage. The starlings intrigued him, but he wished to see them in a cage and under control. There is no account of his having a great affection for his horse, or even for a camel. Large animals did not appeal to him. He was, however, exceptionally fond of, and tolerant towards, dogs. In the years before his death he had four black cocker spaniels, which he named 'Shot', 'Bang', 'Miss', and Damn': a collection perhaps related to the fact that he was an indifferent shot. In one of his letters, Kitchener gratefully accepts an invitation to shoot partridges, but doubts whether they will suffer very much from his presence.[2] Of the four spaniels the least well-disciplined was 'Miss', and strangers were occasionally surprised to hear a distinguished-looking gentleman shouting, 'Miss, come here, Miss' when there was apparently no 'Miss' in sight. Calling the dog 'Damn' must also have surprised passers-by. One needs to be very sure of one's self to give bizarre names to one's dogs.

The spaniels became like a family to him. While he was in India he had decided on the purchase of a house into which he could eventually retire; as he pointed out to his friends and accountant: 'I need somewhere for my dogs to live.'

The welfare of human beings, however, rarely seemed to have as

[1] *Letters of Frank Maxwell, VC* (London, 1921).
[2] Letter in the possession of Mr Richard Probert.

much importance for Kitchener. Up until the end of the South African campaign he had assumed that all other men—and women—were as tough and enduring as he was himself. His personal safety was cared for by a unit named 'the Commander-in-Chief's Bodyguard'. The exact strength of this formation is not available, but it was probably a regiment which also performed other duties too. It included detachments from other countries. One of its officers was R. W. Warner, who wrote: 'At the Intombi river where the Bodyguard stayed 14 days there was absolutely nothing to eat but mealie meal and mutton. There was no salt or sugar and the men suffered from scurvy and sores.' One might wonder at a commander-in-chief being so uninterested in the welfare of the unit which was responsible for his own safety that it could be allowed to develop scurvy from inadequate rations. The writer added, 'But it is not the hardship and the cold but the messing about and the humbuggery that I cannot stand.' He himself had emigrated to South Africa just before the war. He noted that the army's policy of attracting labour from farms to military depots by offering high wages to the 'Kaffirs' was upsetting the labour market. The British farmers were unable to compete. The average wage for a native labourer was from two to three pounds a week, whereas a British soldier received less than a fifth of that sum. Warner never mentioned Kitchener in his letters home, although one might have expected to hear the Commander-in-Chief's reaction to the following: 'The Rhodesian Contingent of the Bodyguard have had a bad cut up. There were 120 men; of these 50 were killed and wounded and the remainder made prisoners. Colonel Laing, a captain and two lieutenants were amongst those killed. There were no scouts, no flankers or rearguard, the whole company were marching in sections and just as they were crossing a drift the Boers opened fire from a slight ridge on the other side of the river. One fellow was hit in nine places, eight of the bullets being explosive.' Kitchener may well have thought it served them right, if they couldn't protect their own lives they were hardly in a position to safeguard his.

Another view of Kitchener came from W. R. Birdwood, later to become Field-Marshal Lord Birdwood of Anzac and Totnes, and Master of Peterhouse, Cambridge. Birdwood was posted to Kitchener's staff in 1900:

Kitchener was then 50 and I was 35. All his life he was a curiously shy man, except with those he got to know intimately, and I am convinced that this shyness of his was the main cause of the reputation he acquired for being abrupt and brusque. Once this

136

initial reticence had worn off he was entirely approachable; and I found, too, that, having once given you his confidence he trusted you completely—perhaps almost embarrassingly, for he might give you only the roughest idea of what he wanted done, and then leave you to work out the details for yourself. If you failed him, he tried someone else.

A few days after taking up my appointment I was dining with Lady Roberts, and Kitchener too was a guest. In the course of conversation Lady Roberts happened to mention my wife, whom she had known in India. Kitchener jumped out of his chair with a shout, 'What! His *wife*? That fellow married—God Lord!'

Lady Roberts at once bridled up. 'Yes, Lord Kitchener—married; and, let me tell you, like all good officers, better for being so!'

Lord Kitchener thereupon collapsed, murmuring, 'Oh, I'm glad you think so!'

Neither Lady Roberts nor Birdwood can have known the real reason for Kitchener's outburst. As we have seen, for the Sudan campaign he had selected officers who were neither married nor engaged. He had no objection to officers being married, but he preferred not to have them on his staff as they would presumably have distractions which would prevent them giving all their time to their duties. Birdwood was already employed on a task of reorganisation which meant full-time attention to work in the office. Had Kitchener been aware that Birdwood was married he would not have appointed him, but he could hardly explain himself in the face of Lady Roberts' rebuke.

Birdwood went on to say:

Yet I am bound to say that, far from ever resenting my marriage, he became in after years the best of friends to my wife and family. He insisted on providing my son with his first uniform when he joined the Service, seventeen years later, and when our second girl was born he stood godfather to her. So far from being a stern and unsympathetic man of the kind repellent to children, I well remember how, when our son was a small boy of about five, we were at a garden party at Viceregal Lodge in Simla, when suddenly there was a large crash. This frightened Chris, who at once ran up to Lord Kitchener, seizing his hand and standing close to him for protection—a gesture which obviously pleased him enormously at the time. A year or two later, when asked by his cousin, Edith Monins, which had been the proudest moment of his life, he replied, not with one of the expected references to his campaigns or career but with the remark: 'I think when little Chris ran across and put his hand in mine with such complete confidence.'

But Birdwood was not uncritical of Kitchener in other ways. He himself was appalled at the losses of horses in South Africa, most of which died because they were ridden too hard before they had had time to get acclimatised (12,000 a month were imported). Birdwood used to plead with Kitchener to allow more time for horses to become acclimatised, but had no success. 'Kitchener,' he said, 'was the most persevering man in the world but also one of the most impatient; and once he had ordered a movement to take place, he was never happy till it was well on the way.' Kitchener raised no objection to criticisms from his staff: he simply brushed them aside. On the other hand he was profoundly embarrassed if anyone tried to thank him for some gesture. On the day Birdwood was promoted to lieutenant-colonel (on Kitchener's recommendation) the two were out riding together. Kitchener suddenly asked. 'Have you seen Orders this morning?' Birdwood answered, 'No', wondering if he had missed something important and was being rebuked. 'Well,' replied Kitchener, 'you'd better look at them when you get back.' In some trepidation Birdwood did so, and discovered his promotion listed there. He reflected that Kitchener was much too shy to have told him and would have been embarrassed by his thanks for the recommendation.

Underlying this story is the Army's attitude to Orders. 'Orders' are the duplicated sheets of paper which are posted daily in every Army unit. They are often described as 'Routine Orders', to distinguish them from special or emergency announcements. They may be Army Orders, Battalion Orders, or even Company Orders. The one thing they have in common is that few people ever bother to read them, on the basis that most of the information contained in them is unpalatable, such as numbers required for guard mountings, church parades, disciplinary offences, etc. There is an Army saying: 'There's no better way of keeping a secret than putting it in Routine Orders.' But Orders do, on rare occasions, contain good news such as promotions. Birdwood probably spent the rest of his ride with Kitchener wondering what offence he had committed or whether there was some vital information on which he should be commenting.

According to Birdwood, very few women were allowed to enter the Transvaal but there was one who was, with Kitchener's full approval. This was Lady Tullibardine, wife of the Marquis of Tullibardine, who had taken a very active part in the Sudan campaign as a captain in the Royal Horse Guards (now the Blues and Royals). However, Lady Tullibardine won Kitchener's approval not because of her sound qualities but, extraordinarily, on account of her abilities as a recruiting officer for the regiment her husband had raised to serve in South Africa, the Scottish Horse, and also for other regiments too.

Chapter 9

Indian Interlude

Six days after the signing of the Treaty of Vereeniging of 31 May 1902, which ended the South African war, Kitchener was informed he had been created a viscount,[1] and was awarded £50,000 by Parliament.[2] He also received the Order of Merit. Once again he was spectacularly received and fêted. It seems that at this time his thoughts turned once more to marriage, for he was said to have spent a lot of time with the very rich (English) widow of a German baron. However, this romance also faded swiftly and irretrievably.

The fact that Kitchener had no direct heir, nor now seemed likely to have one, created problems over the succession. He enquired therefore whether Toby, the son of his elder brother, Colonel Henry Chevallier Kitchener, could inherit the title. He was told that this was not possible, but that King Edward VII was prepared to allow it to pass to Colonel Chevallier Kitchener himself. If that happened, Toby would inherit in due course. However, Toby, who was a commander in the Royal Navy, died before his father, and the title eventually went to the colonel's grandson.

The move to India was not without its problems. Brodrick, the Secretary of State for War, who had learnt to respect Kitchener in the early days of the South African campaign, now wished him to reform the British Army at home. Kitchener had already been very critical of the Army in remarks made to the Royal Commission on the South African War and Brodrick therefore felt that he would be the ideal man to shake up the entire organisation of the British Army. In view of the growth of German power and the fact that large armies of conscripts were being trained in Europe, an army which had been so easily defeated in the early stages of the South African War certainly needed careful examination. Hindsight suggests that

[1] Many people thought, and said, he should have become an earl.
[2] £50,000 represents about £1¾ million at today's values.

140

it might have been better for the country if Kitchener had stayed in Britain.

His decision to go to India and undertake Army reforms there was taken because he knew that such a task would prove much more congenial overseas. At home he would have to argue his case amongst obstructive, self-seeking politicians. Kitchener himself could hardly be described as oblivious to opportunities for personal advancment, but the blatant selfishness and intrigue of people whom he regarded as political lightweights appalled him. Nor was there any issue in British politics at the time which attracted him. He had no desire to be mixed up with the Irish aspiration for self-government and he was quite unable to understand why women should be so anxious to have a vote, or indeed any other rights. On top of everything else, the English climate, after all those years abroad, brought out unexpected aches and pains.

In the circumstances, Curzon's persuasive arguments that Kitchener should become Commander-in-Chief in India and have free rein to effect all necessary reforms was tempting. Had Kitchener guessed how seriously he would clash with the quarrelsome, headstrong Viceroy (as he soon found Curzon to be), he might have hesitated longer before accepting. Curzon had been appointed Viceroy of India in 1899, after considerable experience as Under-Secretary of State for India in Salisbury's government of 1891, and was also a Privy Councillor. Undoubtedly he knew more about India than Kitchener did. However, Curzon, who was forty-four was far from diplomatic in his approach and, in addition, even more ambitious than Kitchener. At the height of their subsequent quarrel, in 1905, he was forced to resign. However, Curzon should not be judged entirely on his experiences with Kitchener. He became a successful Foreign Secretary after the end of the First World War and also earned lasting gratitude for his work in purchasing ancient castles which he patiently restored at enormous personal expense. Without his interest, Tattershall Castle in Lincolnshire would now be a ruin, if not actually demolished, and Bodiam Castle in Sussex, one of the most beautiful castles in the world, would be very different from its present state.

As Curzon was well aware, the army in India was in urgent need of reform. Since the end of the Indian Mutiny in 1857 there had been no clear directive on what the Indian Army's priorities should be. They were, of course, abundantly clear to Kitchener. Throughout his military life Kitchener had seen many indications that Russia was intent upon expansion. The decaying Turkish Empire afforded obvious opportunities, and Kitchener was by no means sure that

Britain's relationship with that country was accorded the importance it deserved. But even more sinister was the constant Russian
pressure on Afghanistan, to the north-west of India. There was
always trouble on the frontier and much of it was ascribed to Russian
influence. That view may well have been unduly alarmist, but the
fact remained that Afghanistan was the gateway to India from
Russia. The obsessions of British nineteenth-century politicians and
generals with the Russian threat to Afghanistan now seem rather less
absurd than they were long thought to be, with Russia having
actually occupied that country.

It was Kitchener's reputation as a successful general which
enabled him to make reforms rapidly. He saw the task of the Indian
Army not as acting as a safeguard against another mutiny but as a
means of defending the country from an external aggressor and, if
the need arose, of supplying units for tasks overseas. He therefore
created a central command of corps and divisions. Battalions would
no longer be stationed in isolated places, where they had originally
been placed to guard against potential trouble, but would be com-
ponents of brigades, which would in turn form part of divisions, two
or more of which would make up a corps.

The fighting ability of regiments varied considerbly. Those in the
north, like the Gurkhas, Guides and Punjabis to name but a few,
were clearly of much greater value than some in the south. Fourteen
of these latter were now disbanded and re-formed with fresh recruits
from more martial sources. As many of the disbanded and re-formed
regiments had a poor military record, it was obviously unwise to
preserve their former names, so the whole numbering and naming
system had to be reorganised. There were mutterings about this, for
some of the older regiments which had not been allowed to retain
their proud titles felt they were being reduced in prestige. Ultimately, by a reduction of unnecessary garrisons, Kitchener was able
to form an Indian Army of nine divisions. Five of these were then
deployed from Peshawar to Lucknow, the other four in Poona,
Secunderabad and Mhow. Each division consisted of one British
and two Indian brigades. There had been a proposal to have mixed
brigades of one British and two Indian battalions but this would
have placed an enormous burden on the system of distributing
rations. The strength of feeling amongst certain peoples against
different forms of food is rarely appreciated and understood outside
the territories in which they live. However, in India the lesson had
been well and truly learnt from the experience of the Mutiny, which
had been triggered off by the belief that cartridges for the Enfield rifle
(which had to be bitten before being inserted) had been greased with

a mixture of beef and pork fat, and were therefore 'unclean'. The cow was sacred to Hindus; Moslems abominated pork. The mere presence of any British personnel in Indian cookhouses was believed to contaminate all the food there. Such convictions made any form of communal messing impossible

Careful avoidance of taboos of religion and caste created one set of problems, long-standing traditions produced another. It was essential to retain friendly relations with the Amir of Afghanistan, who controlled an army of over 100,000. If Britain supplied the Amir with the modern weapons he coveted, he would remain friendly and would thus form an effective barrier against the Russians. If the British did not supply him with arms, his army would be less efficient, and he himself less friendly. An even more daunting possibility was that, after the British had supplied his army with modern arms, he might be deposed by insurgents using those very arms for the purpose. His successor, almost certainly, would be in league with the Russians, and might well have ambitions in the direction of invading India.

On a lesser scale there was a continuing problem with the frontier tribes. These lived in the mountainous country between India and Afghanistan, and numbered 300,000. Fortunately they possessed insufficient modern rifles to equip more than one man in three. (This led to some of the most accomplished thieving the world has ever known, in which tribesmen would enter guarded British compounds at night and steal rifles which had been chained to their owners.) At times, frontier tribes would raid towns in India, of which Quetta and Peshawar were tempting targets. However, most of their martial ardour was usually directed more locally. There was bitter rivalry between tribes, between neighbouring valleys and even within families themselves. General C. R. Ballard pointed out that in the Pushtu language the word 'dushman' means either cousin or enemy because it is inconceivable that a cousin could be anything but an enemy. Peaceful co-existence had no attractions. Birdwood tells a story of a British officer who encountered a Pathan soldier in one of the most uncomfortable sectors of the Western Front in 1916. Shell holes and corpses were on all sides. The officer said, 'What a terrible war this is.' 'Yes,' said the Pathan, 'but it is better than no war at all.'

The policy of the Indian government towards the frontier tribes was cautious. Experience had shown that any form of positive approach, however friendly, was likely to have unpredictable, and often unwelcome, results. In consequence, policy in the frontier areas was considered to be the prerogative of the Viceroy rather than of the commander-in-chief. The proviso seemed nonsense to Kitchener, who considered that military and political policies on the frontier should be identical and that both should be under control of the military authorities. From the beginning he acted as if his was the sole authority: he toured the whole frontier, travelling in considerable discomfort, and inevitably earned the respect of the warlike tribesmen; they admired warriors, particularly warriors with a reputation for winning battles. Curzon, though disapproving, could do little to restrain the commander-in-chief whom he had requested under the impression he would be able to 'manage' him.

Curzon's belief in his ability to control the most eminent military figurehead lay in what was known as the 'Dual Control' system, of which Kitchener seems to have been unaware until he arrived in India. 'Dual Control' meant that whereas the commander-in-chief's responsibility was to train the army to the required pitch of fighting efficiency, all other military matters were the responsibility of the Viceroy through the Military Member of the Viceregal Council. The Viceregal Council bore a close resemblance to the Cabinet at home; members represented various departments, such as Trade, Finance, or Railways. In previous decades, when communications were less developed, the Military Member had performed an essential function in organising and controlling all the supply and non-combatant services; this freed the C-in-C from routine chores. The Military Member was always a major-general of the Indian Army; his office was known as the Military Department.

In practice, the presence of the Military Member on the Viceroy's Council meant that a major-general was able to make policy suggestions to the Viceroy which were then presented to the commander-in-chief as virtual directives. Equally, information from the commander-in-chief would go first to the Military Member, who would add his comments to it before passing it on to the Viceroy. The Viceroy, with his background of Eton, Balliol and Parliament, knew nothing of military matters and in fact had a general contempt for them; although he was well aware that Kitchener had a forceful personality, he had been anxious to acquire him, for he had full confidence that he would be able to control his new commander-in-chief as easily as he had done the last one, Sir Power Palmer. In fact, so supine had the previous C-in-C been that the Military Department had been able to make considerable inroads into matters such as training and discipline.

Kitchener, of course, decided immediately that the existing system was unworkable, but realised that change would take a little time. Not the least of the problems was the fact that the present system was enshrined in the Constitution. Thus, whereas the Military Member attended *all* meetings of the Viceroy's Council, the commander-in-chief was expected only to attend those in which military matters of special interest to him were under review. It was clear, however, that Curzon would be immensely sensitive to any attack on what he considered his prerogative. He had already displayed an interesting example of pettiness. His title was Lord Curzon of Kedleston, but he signed himself 'Curzon'.[1] When Kitchener arrived, he signed himself 'Kitchener of Khartoum'. Curzon wrote, pointing out that to use the full signature would occupy more time and space than was necessary: 'Kitchener' alone should suffice. Kitchener immediately agreed, noting as he did that a man who could exhibit such petty jealousy over a title taken from a profession he despised would be a tiresome colleague in more serious matters.

India affected Kitchener in several different ways. For the first time in his life he was not able to rule in an autocratic manner. Since the days of the Palestine Exploration Fund he had been accustomed to getting his own way. In Egypt, Cromer had influenced Kitchener, but could never be said to have controlled him. Kitchener had always known that he was so important that the mere threat of resignation would bring opponents to heel. But in India, at a stage when he might have expected to be supreme, he found he was having to share power. Even more galling was the fact that he was being manipulated by people of inferior rank and knowledge. The Military Member, Sir Edmund Elles, was a mere major-general, whereas he himself could expect to be a field-marshal within a few years. In his own way the Military Member, perhaps because he was so conscientious and able, looked like being even more tiresome than the Viceroy.

All this built up frustration in Kitchener. When bouts of malaria were added to his other troubles, he suffered from the periods of depression which often follow malaria. On 15 November 1903, he had a serious fall when out riding alone near his country house, Wildflower Hall, near Simla. His horse shied, he was thrown, and both the bones in his left leg were broken just above the ankle. Unfortunately the doctors who attended him seem to have been either incompetent or so overawed by the importance of their patient that they set the leg badly: in consequence he was left with a slight limp to add to his other physical disabilities. As may be imagined, he was not what is known as 'a good patient'.

But the habit of unceasing toil also seemed to be deserting him, partly perhaps because he felt that much of what he was doing was

---

[1] A few years later he was signing as 'Curzon of Kedleston' again.

futile. Most of the work he would normally have kept for himself was now delegated to his staff. This was, of course, normal and sensible procedure; the principal function of a commander-in-chief is to ensure that subordinates are carrying out their duties properly, and he does this by making constant inspections. In the Army, as Kitchener doubtless knew very well, C-in-C's inspections are treated more as theatrical performances than examinations of the proper working of the system. For the majority of, though not all, inspections in the army, due warning is given. Anything to which the inspecting officer might take exception is carefully altered, amended, adjusted, or removed. After the inspection is over the unit maintains its usual standard of efficiency until a short time before the next visitation is due. Then, as the appointed date comes closer, a frenzy of preparation begins once more.

Kitchener now began to enjoy ceremonial occasions. His two principal residences were Snowdon at Simla, and Treasury Gate just outside Calcutta. He decided these must be worthy of the post of commander-in-chief. He therefore built a panelled hall and new dining room, drawing room and library at Snowdon. The library ceiling was an exact copy of the one at Hatfield, where he had stayed so often with Lord Salisbury; the gardens were attractively laid out and planted with orchids and other flowers. At Treasury Gate the changes were even more dramatic; the building was virtually gutted and given a new interior. His servants were all dressed in 'white liveries with red bibs and belts, and a good deal of gold embroidery', he told Lady Salisbury in a letter. He was a compulsive letter writer—mostly to women. He wrote to Queen Victoria, to Lady Salisbury, to Lord Roberts, to his friend Pandelli Ralli, to his sisters, to his brothers. He seemed to take a delight in airing his troubles to his two chief confidantes, Lady Salisbury (even before Lord Salisbury's death in 1903) and Margot Asquith. Had he been brought up at an English public school, he might have pondered on whether he was 'sneaking' as he made statements which he hoped would eventually be to the detriment of Curzon. At his formal dinner parties, which up to a hundred might attend, guests would be served off gold plates, and the food was equally luxurious. It was at this time that he began contemplating retirement. He planned to end his days in a house which, though not so magnificent as his formal residences had been, would be a model of good taste. His search for suitable furnishings became even keener.

According to Birdwood, Kitchener never learnt Urdu. Urdu is a derivation from Hindi to which words from other languages, such as Persian, have been added; it was used by the Indian Army because it

146

was widely understood. It might be more accurate to say that Kitchener never *spoke* Urdu. For conversations with Indians he used Birdwood as an interpreter, and he also had as an Indian ADC, Abdullah Khan, who spoke good English. It seems possible that Kitchener preferred to converse through an interpreter because the lengthy process gave him more time to compose his replies. It seems unlikely that a linguist of his ability would not have acquired a good knowledge of the language of the country in which he was living. (There are, of course, some 225 languages spoken in the Indian sub-continent, but a knowledge of one or two suffices.)

'He enjoyed his Calcutta life,' wrote Birdwood. 'He had a mail phaeton with a lovely pair of horses, with which he won prizes at the Calcutta Shows. Fortunately, on such occasions his coachman drove, for much as Kitchener loved his horses and riding, he was one of the worst whips I have ever been sentenced to sit beside. Why we were none of us killed, I have no idea. In the "Lie Book" which was kept at Viceregal Lodge, there was an entry: "His Excellency the Commander-in-Chief stated that he knew where he was driving".'

Birdwood elaborated on Kitchener's driving habits later. He held the reins, and often a cigar and a glove in his left hand, galloped furiously on either side of the road, and seemed indifferent to the fact that pedestrians often had to flee for their lives.

But more significant than Kitchener's somewhat eccentric behaviour was his ultimate achievement. Birdwood said, 'I shudder to think what would have happened on the outbreak of war in 1914 had not Kitchener's reforms been in force. In that year I was Secretary to Government, so all communications and mobilisation orders passed through my hands. Sir Beauchamp Duff was Commander-in-Chief, and, under his cool direction, mobilisation was carried out with wonderful smoothness. We were able to despatch two cavalry and two infantry divisions to France, two divisions to Mesopotamia, and a force of nearly the same strength to Egypt, each brigade and its staff proceeding complete from its peacetime station, all without a hitch. Under the pre-Kitchener situation, nothing short of chaos must have resulted from such an effort.'

The full value of Kitchener's reorganisation which made the despatch of those divisions possible can only be realised by noting the effect those divisions had when they reached their destinations. The troops sent to Egypt repulsed a Turkish invasion of that country (they included a young officer named Claude Auchinleck, of the Punjabis, who would become a field-marshal in the next World War), the troops sent to Mesopotamia protected the Allied oil supplies in the Persian Gulf when they were in danger of being lost, and the divisions sent to France supplemented the woefully inadequate British Expeditionary Force.

Kitchener also increased the number of Gurkha battalions from sixteen to twenty. With his experience of the Sudan Campaign, and South Africa fresh in his mind, he pressed for an extension of the existing railway system, so that, if the need arose, troops could be transferred to the north-west frontier rapidly. On the frontier itself he decided that the best policy might be that of leaving well alone. When he eventually left India an article by a respected journalist said: 'His reforms were wise, but perhaps his greatest wisdom was shown in what he left undone.' In theory, the political officers in the north-West Frontier Province were administering their districts by fining or warning unruly tribes; in practice, money payments were usually the other way and the potentially unruly were bribed into co-operative submission by benefits of one kind or another.

During the first year of his appointment Kitchener was too occupied with the thought of necessary army reforms to brood too much on the frustration of having to work with Curzon. But in the summer of 1903 he decided to make a test case. He had drafted an Army Order and sent this to the Military Department to be printed and issued. When the Military Member saw it he made a small amendment. This touched Kitchener in two ways: he regarded the action of an officer of lower rank altering his wording as impudence, and he resented the fact that the alteration implied that his own grasp of English syntax was in any way deficient. There was, of course, some truth in the latter belief. He had not had the classical education which had been the experience of most of his peers. Confronted by the polished erudition of Curzon, for example, he felt a sense of inferiority. He decided that this was a moment for action. He informed Curzon that unless he issued a reprimand to the Military Member he, Kitchener, would resign. He rested his case on the point of whether the Military Member had the authority to override the commander-in-chief. He was, doubtless, well aware that on many occasions officers have altered their senior's instructions for the purpose of clarifying, or even preventing the latter from making fools of themselves, but he allowed no such thoughts to come into his mind at this juncture. Curzon, then on quite friendly terms with Kitchener in spite of their clashes on official matters, agreed to concur with his commander-in-chief's wish. Kitchener therefore withdrew the threat of resignation. He was in a stronger position than he realised at that moment. Curzon had no wish to damage his own reputation of being a suave and able diplomat (as he, if not others, saw himself) and realised that to have his commander-in-chief resigning over a point in which he was clearly in the right would be a disaster. But their relationship now became distinctly cooler.

In April 1904 Curzon went back to England; he had not been well and a change of air was thought advisable. While in England he attended a meeting of the Imperial Defence Committee, where he was shown a paper from Kitchener addressed to the Committee which said that the system of dual control was the basic cause of any deficiencies in the Indian Army, and that the Military Member and his Department should be banished immediately. Curzon would have seen the paper at a later date, for his agreement was necessary if the proposal was to be adopted, but he was surprised and angry to find Kitchener by-passing him in this way. He settled the matter firmly to his own satisfaction by declaring that alterations to the Viceregal Council were constitutional matters, not defence prerogatives, and therefore could not be discussed at this moment. The Prime Minister, who was now A.J. Balfour, agreed with Curzon, and the matter of dual control was shelved for the time being. (A.J. Balfour later acquired the nickname 'Bloody Balfour' on account of his attitude towards Irish Home Rule, but he also negotiated the Anglo-French Entente of 1904, and the creation of the Jewish National Home in Palestine which led to the establishment of Israel. He was said to have a smile 'like moonlight shining on a tombstone'.)

Kitchener had accepted that, after Curzon's retirement at the end of 1904, he would be able to negotiate the abolition of the Military Department with a less obstinate successor, but when he learnt that Curzon's term of office as Viceroy had been extended for two more years he realised that urgent steps were necessary. Now that his proposal had been shelved, he submitted his resignation once again. At this point the Cabinet in London should have debated the matter and suggested a solution. But it did not. Instead, Balfour referred the matter to the Viceroy's Council. Perhaps he hoped that the long interval which would elapse before it could be discussed might bring an answer, but more probably he wished to stave off Kitchener's resignation, which would be politically embarrassing.

The Viceroy's Council eventually debated the matter in the spring of 1905. Kitchener had submitted his views in a paper; the Military Member submitted a defence of the system in another, and Curzon added to it. In his minute he paid a glowing tribute to Kitchener's military record and to his achievements in India, but he said that the commander-in-chief was now proposing to replace the Viceroy's constitutional military authority with a military autocracy headed by the commander-in-chief. To everyone's surprise, Kitchener took little part in the subsequent discussion. He had made all the necessary points in the paper he had submitted and saw nothing useful in repeating them or trying to elaborate on them in the Council. He was probably wary of being drawn into a public debate with such a skilled practitioner as Curzon. As Kitchener foresaw, his proposal was defeated.

But the situation was by no means resolved; if anything, positions were now much more deeply entrenched. Curzon felt that his point of view was adequately supported by the Constitution, which he was hardly likely to wish to change for Kitchener, whom he had now begun to detest. Kitchener's strongest card was his resignation, which was still possible. He was aware of the strength of his position. If he was forced to resign because an obsolete constitutional arrangement was making the reform of the Indian Army impossible, the repercussions would be considerable. Balfour's political position was under threat (he was to lose the next election in any case) and he did not wish to add to his embarrassments by having a popular and successful commander-in-chief resign because he was being prevented from completing the task he had been sent out to accomplish. A compromise solution was therefore put forward by Brodrick. It was so vaguely expressed that even those who had drafted it were not clear exactly what it meant; the gist of it was that the Military Member would no longer have the power to criticise or advise on the proposals of the comander-in-chief, but there was to be a member of the Council who would be in charge of military supply services. Kitchener now seemed to be in a compromising mood; doubtless he planned to make sure that the military supply member would be one of his own nominees and would give no trouble. Curzon, however, sent a message to the British Cabinet saying that he wished to nominate Sir Edmund Barrow for the appointment on Elles's retirement. His request was refused, and in consequence he tendered his resignation. This was accepted by the cabinet with such speed that it was suggested that they felt they must act before he changed his mind. He had little chance to do so, for four days Lord Minto was appointed to succeed him as Viceroy.

At this moment there was relief all round. Minto, the new Viceroy, was sixty-one, five years older than Kitchener, a keen sportsman, and had no fixed ideas about either India or Army reforms. It is, however, impossible not to feel some sympathy for Curzon at this point. It was said that the enormous power and prestige of his position had gone to his head, and that he was over-emotional. Possibly, the fact that he was a sick man himself and his wife was dying of cancer made him less than tactful when dealing with Kitchener, who was no less wedded to principles than he was

150

himself. For the last year of Curzon's term of office the two men had hardly been able to exchange a word in conversation, although correspondence had occurred normally. Curzon was not overawed by Kitchener, as a lesser man might have been, and he had no hesitation in accusing him of deception. Kitchener was no less forceful in his opinions. In his personal correspondence he stated quite clearly, 'Curzon is a liar.'[1]

Relief at the end of the dispute was probably greatest in the Cabinet, which at that moment was looking anxiously at the situation in the Far East. Japan had recently defeated Russia in a war in which the decisive factor had been sea battles. However it was felt that this by no means diminished the threat to India, and the resignation of the commander-in-chief might easily convince the Russians that this offered an opportunity to recover some of the prestige they had lost in the war with Japan. It is unlikely that Kitchener held that view after he had toured the frontier area; his view of the Russian threat was long-term rather than immediate.

Minto shared Kitchener's view that there was no need for alarm, but both were somewhat disconcerted when the views of the men on the spot were taken by the new Cabinet to justify a reduction in military expenditure in 1906. The Conservatives had been swept out of office the previous December and the Liberals who replaced them believed that considerable savings could be, and should be, made in military funding. For this reason they approved of Kitchener's economical approach to military expenditure; he was firmly opposed to extravagance but equally he was adamant on where the line should be drawn between sensible economies and cuts detrimental to the system. In particular he did not wish to preside over an inadequately paid and thus unhappy army. Service in the Indian Army had for many years been well-paid and therefore was a haven for officers without private incomes. In the British Army officers were expected to live a full social and sporting life, but this could not be managed without private means. Now, while the cost of living in India had risen, the purchasing power of the rupee had shrunk. Kitchener could not immediately revise the entire pay scale of the Indian Army for officers and men, but he made recommendations which were eventually accepted and in the meantime introduced a series of changes which made living less expensive for the military.

Even though the Army knew that Kitchener had everyone's best interests at heart, it did not give him the affection which it had lavished on Lord Roberts. The reason seems to have been that he

[1] Letter in possession of the Hon. Mrs Charles Kitchener.

151

was too shy to put others at their ease. He listened, and spoke little. He visited units, waved away ceremony, and stayed briefly. He learnt as much as he needed to know, and did all that was necessary. But there was little rapport. In the early days of his service he had enjoyed adventure, risk and responsibility. Now the time for the first two was past, and what he needed was something more intellectual and artistic than he found in everyday peace-time army life. He was at his best when at home, redesigning his official residence, supervising his gardeners, and showing off his acquisitions. It was said that when he was talking about his artistic possessions he was a totally different person. His passion for collecting became more marked than ever. It was also said that when he went on a shopping expedition dealers closed their premises until he had passed; they had no wish to be browbeaten into parting with their greatest treasures at less than cost to a buyer who knew as much, and sometimes more, about real values than they did.

In 1907 his tour of duty in India was extended, and he stayed on till 1909. Long before this second tour of duty began, the conflict between the commander-in-chief and the Military Supply Member had been happily resolved; when a series of military expenditure cuts were made by the Liberal government in 1907 and the post was abolished, Kitchener was sorry to see it go.

There was an extensive correspondence between Kitchener and his friend and accountant, Arthur Renshaw. Renshaw had advised him on the best ways of investing the huge sums which Parliament had granted Kitchener after his successful campaigns, and in consequence the commander-in-chief had a substantial private income in addition to his pay. Although in Kitchener's letters he often says he knows little about financial matters, his suggestions were invariably practical and wise. He had a quick eye for a short-term profit. He was an early investor in Japan and also suggested that Russian railways might offer a good return, although, as he explained, he was not particularly fond of that country.

In his book *Khaki and Gown*, Field-Marshal Lord Birdwood gives detailed accounts of the numerous tours which Kitchener made around his command. On one occasion an impressive parade included a man riding a rhinoceros. A typical item runs:

We spent two days riding and walking through the country of the Shinwaris and Malagoris. The tribesmen always presented the [Commander-in-] Chief with offerings of fine goats, which were invariably returned the next day that they might be kept with their flocks till the next visit—both parties knowing full well that there

A blockhouse in South Africa in 1901 showing the liberal use of barbed wire

At the peace conference which ended the South African War. Kitchener's ADC, Frank Maxwell (*second from right standing*), looks alert and somewhat suspicious

Col. Henderson.   Van Velden.   Major Watson.   Mr Fraser.   Major Maxwell   H. De Jager.
De Wet.   Genl Louis Botha.   Lord Kitchener   Col Hamilton

Kitchener and his personal staff, Simla 1909. His dogs form an untidy heap in
the foreground

Inspecting the militia in Tasmania in
1909

A painting by John Collier of Kitchener as a field-marshal in 1910

Broome Park, near Canterbury, which Kitchener bought for his retirement but never lived in

Kitchener with
General Joffre, 1914

Kitchener with Indian soldiers in France, 1915

Kitchener at Gallipoli in 1915, watching the Turkish trenches from thirty yards away. Kitchener (*second from right*) with his former ADC, now Brigadier-General Maxwell (*in foreground*)

Kitchener and H.H. Asquith talking to a French soldier in France in 1915

Kitchener and Lt-Col FitzGerald (his personal military secretary) walking through Whitehall

Two pictures showing that Kitchener was deep in thought, whether in uniform or out of it, in 1916

Kitchener talking to wounded soldiers at Broome Park in 1916. The soldiers were from the Army Nursing Home at Folkestone. One was blind in both eyes and Kitchener was 'especially kind' to him

Kitchener with Admiral Jellicoe being shown round the flagship *Iron Duke*
before joining the cruiser *Hampshire* on which he was drowned later that day:
5 June 1916

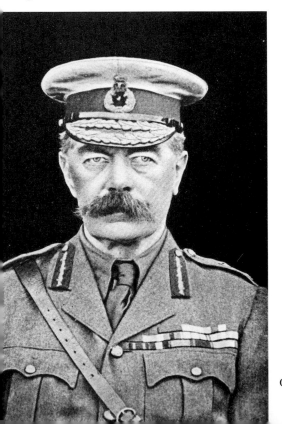

One of the last portraits to be made of Kitchener

was little likelihood of our return. But it would never have done to refuse the gifts outright.

In March 1907 Kitchener had a slight brush with the Duke of Connaught, who was at that time Inspector-General of Overseas Forces. When he arrived in Calcutta, the dress regulation for his reception was given as 'Full dress—white'. This, said Birdwood, 'was a new order of dress for Kitchener who, when inspecting troops in their white full dress, would, with his Staff, wear the white kit corresponding to the order known as "Staff in Blue".' When Birdwood was driving Kitchener to meet the inspector-general he suddenly noticed that Kitchener was wearing white gloves. This, Birdwood pointed out, was incorrect for hot-weather uniform. When Kitchener asked why, Birdwood told him that they made the wearer too hot in hot weather. Kitchener replied that it would be disgusting not to wear gloves. Birdwood said, 'Well, sir, as you are Commander-in-Chief, I can't tell you to take them off. I can only repeat that you are improperly dressed.'

Nor was that the end of the matter. Birdwood noticed that Kitchener was also wearing the broad crimson sash of the GCB. He was not so sure about the sash, but he felt that this was probably wrong too—with a white jacket. Kitchener was not pleased. 'It's my full dress,' he said. Birdwood, with misgivings agreed. Kitchener went on: 'And now I suppose you want me to take off all my medals and decorations! Please stop talking rot.'

When they arrived at Government House Kitchener observed that the Viceroy was not wearing his GCSI sash. (Knight Grand Commander of the Star of India) sash. He therefore persuaded Minto to send for it, and it was put on in some haste.

At lunch the following day the Duke turned to Kitchener and said: 'Kitchener, when I arrived yesterday you were wearing white gloves.' Kitchener looked sharply at Birdwood, who was strongly inclined to let out a yell of delight, and replied, 'Yes, I was in full dress uniform and, of course, wore white gloves.' To this, the Duke replied tartly, 'I know the dress regulations very well, Kitchener. Gloves are not worn with white uniform. However,' he continued, 'that is a minor matter. I arrived wearing no sash, and I found the Viceroy wearing the GCSI and you the GCB. That was *quite wrong*.'

Once more Kitchener protested that he was in full dress and that this was surely correct, but his explanations were swept aside. The Duke, apparently, had been so incensed by this unseemly irregularity that he had sent a wire to King Edward VII for a ruling on the matter. Within days a formal order arrived confirming the correctness of the Duke's statement. (The Duke was not one to miss a detail: while inspecting a parade of several thousand men later, he complained that one of the havildars, or Indian NCOs, was slightly out of step.)

Some years later the dress regulations were changed, though not at Kitchener's instigation. Kitchener would, of course, bear no resentment. Army regulations, whether of dress or anything else, have usually evolved rather than been invented, and even if apparently absurd must be rigidly observed. Everyone accepts that it is just as correct for the commander-in-chief to be rebuked for wearing white gloves when no white gloves should be worn as it is for a soldier to be rebuked for having his puttee wound a quarter of an inch wider than it should be. Kitchener may have huffed and puffed but he knew the rules.

The fussiness of many army rules is not really as absurd as it may seem to outsiders. The basis of army discipline is meticulous attention to orders, to cleanliness, and above all to weapons. A sloppy soldier may well have a dirty rifle and be inattentive to orders. By parade-ground drill he is made to pay attention to the most minute, finicky detail. Soldiers going into action will shave carefully before smearing their faces with black camouflage cream or even soot. The English archers at Agincourt in 1415 who defeated four times their number of Frenchmen had carefully kept their bow strings dry by putting these inside their hats.

Sir Francis Younghusband, who was a few years younger than Kitchener, was involved in a minor controversy in India of which the details are no longer available. Thereafter, he said, 'For many years he highly disapproved of me, probably because I did not see eye to eye with him in India and he could not tolerate anyone disagreeing with him. But the hatchet was completely buried one day just before the Great War, at Welbeck. The Duke of Portland was giving a big lunch at which Lord Kitchener was present and so was I. Before lunch Lord Kitchener was seen pushing his way through a crowd of distinguished guests, and everyone looked to see who he was aiming at. I was at the moment looking the other way, talking to a lady, when I heard a voice say, "How do you do, Younghusband?"

'I turned round and there was Lord Kitchener with his hand out. What he said is not the least concern to anyone else, but it buried the hatchet there and then.'

Younghusband felt that Kitchener had been at his best in Egypt. 'There he was undoubtedly a great man, a great administrator, leader and soldier.

'Kitchener had a powerful intuition possessed by few men, but by

154

many women. A woman will express a decided opinion on some subject, or concerning some person. She can give no reason for her verdict and perhaps has no special knowledge but she intuitively feels she is right and very often is. In the same way Lord Kitchener would order a thing to be done which might appear quite impossible; he could not perhaps explain how it was to be done, but intuitively he seemed to see the job accomplished, and it generally was. Whether his intuition was always rightly directed is another matter.'

An officer who had served under him in Egypt, Sir George Gorringe, confirmed that Kitchener possessed this unusual attribute. Kitchener sent him some task (Younghusband could not recall exactly what), but Gorringe after careful study considered it impossible. He therefore went back to Kitchener and instead of saying that he considered the task impossible simply asked for advice on how it should be done. Kitchener replied that he had no idea, but that Gorringe should get on with it forthwith. Eventually, the task was completed to Gorringe's surprise and everyone's satisfaction.

During his service in India Kitchener found himself in the unusual position of being popular with the press. Younghusband said: 'There is little doubt that Lord Kitchener at one time was a little spoilt by the press and public, and could brook no view or opinion, however sound, opposed to his own. He used openly to remark that apparently he could do no wrong, and that he meant to take advantage of this excellent state of affairs as long as it lasted. "But," he always added, "I know they will round on me some day as they did on Lord Roberts."'

Although Kitchener's health had not been particularly good in India, he had decided that he would like very much to stay on as Viceroy if the post were offered to him. Minto did not in fact retire till 1910, but Kitchener, who had rushed back from America to be in England at the right time, was never in the running for the appointment. Morley, the Secretary of State for India in the Liberal government, was too cautious to wish to appoint a military man to such a sensitive post.

While commander-in-chief, Kitchener had made every effort to reform not merely the system but also many of those living within it. Like officers before and after him, he made continuous efforts to see that the soldiers under his command did not destroy themselves by yielding to temptation. This was not merely moralising: alcohol and venereal disease can cause much damage to an army's efficiency. Kitchener stated that it was the responsibility of officers to give the young soldiers 'the utmost protection against himself that we can afford him'. However, giving that protection did not extend to

155

establishing licensed brothels, a practice which had been adopted in the past but which had by then been discontinued. He issued a memorandum to be given to every soldier:

> The climate and conditions of life in India are unfortunately such as to create temptations greater than those which exist in countries outside the tropics. The absence of home associations throws men more on their own resources and deprives them of many of those helps towards resisting temptation which surround them in England. During the cold weather there may be enough work, healthy exercise and amusement to keep men occupied, mentally and physically, but throughout the long months of great heat in the plains, time often hangs heavily on their hands, and with want of occupation comes the temptation to excessive indulgence.

The Army attempted to fill the long, hot hours by setting absurdly high cleaning standards. Boot studs and the metal tags on laces had to be polished, as were buckets, and even the polish tins when the paint had been scraped off. But there were limits even to these occupations.

> It is therefore all the more necessary that those who are serving their country in India should exert to the utmost those powers of self-restraint with which every man is provided in order that he may exercise a proper control over his appetites. They should avoid any excesses in liquor, on no account touch country spirits, take an active interest in their profession, and do their utmost towards making themselves really smart and efficient soldiers in every respect. They should take part in all healthy outdoor sports and games and always keep themselves in good training and physically fit. Both mind and body should be fully occupied, and a lively interest cultivated in their surroundings. In this way, work will be found easier, and life generally more pleasant.

The soldiers to whom this sound advice was addressed had to agree, if only because their attention was drawn to such principles at frequent intervals by their company officers, or their chaplains.

There was much more in the same vein:

> Above all things, men must remember that they should do credit to their regiments: for the good name of a regiment lies in the keeping of every man belonging to it, and necessarily suffers if the men become inefficient through venereal disease.

One cannot help thinking that at this stage the commander-in-chief was getting slightly out of touch with the mind of the average soldier. It has not been entirely unknown for certain regiments to take a guilty pride in having the highest VD statistics in the country.

It is therefore the duty of the soldier, not only to keep himself clear of disease but also by his good example to help his comrades to avoid temptation. The older men particularly should realise their responsibilities in this respect.

Remember the better influences of life. What would your mother, your sisters, and your friends at home think of you if they saw you in hospital, degraded by this cause?

It is clear from this memorandum that Kitchener had remained totally isolated from the home life of the average soldier. There were, of course, soldiers with loving mothers, sisters and friends at home, where all conduct was restrained and seemly, but a large proportion of soldiers came from considerably less ideal environments. Some had joined up when drunk, others because they were without jobs or money, others because they had been cajoled by recruiting sergeants who received a commission for each new recruit, others because it was an alternative to a prison sentence. In their pre-Army lives many of them would have been only too glad to give way to temptation if the required money and opportunity had presented themselves. Here and there the commander-in-chief's words might have fallen on receptive ears and evoked the right response, but experience, sadly, tells that he might have been delivering a lecture on higher mathematics for all the relation it seemed to have to their everyday lives. Of course it had to be said, and words to the same effect would be repeated many more times in the future. Baden-Powell, who after his experiences in the Boer War had founded the Boy Scout movement, was another who tried to inculcate an appropriate attitude. 'A Scout is clean in thought, word and deed,' he insisted, hoping that in time this would prove true.

Part of the problem in tropical or sub-tropical countries where the Army was stationed was that the local population often seemed to have acquired a partial immunity to venereal disease. Soldiers who contracted it were much more seriously afflicted.

But in case the good advice was not sufficient, the memorandum continued more severely, and gave graphic details of the final stages of syphilis.

Lord Kitchener would further point out that, although the military penalties incurred by those who contract venereal disease can only be regarded as of minor importance when referred to the more dreadful and far-reaching consequences above referred to [on marriage and family life], yet men should remember that they

157

exist and should know what they are.... Promotion may be affected, first-class service pay is affected ... guards and duties missed while in hospital have to be made good, so that the self-indulgence of those who contract the disease may not throw work on their comrades: on their return to duty they may find all indulgences, passes, etc., withheld and the canteen may be closed against them. Should men be invalided for venereal diseases, gratuities and pensions are likely to be affected.

Further, it must be remembered that it is impossible for long to conceal the existence of the disease, and that the attempt to do so is an offence which is very severely punished.

Of the penalties, the soldiers were well aware. Hard-won promotion would be lost at a stroke. Kitchener's admonitions were undoubtedly sound and uttered in a spirit of genuine conviction. They do, however, show how far he had managed to distance himself in thought from the average soldier, and perhaps from those who might have advised a slightly less pontifical approach. The average soldier received little money, and most of the more salubrious places of amusement were barred to him. 'Soldiers and dogs not admitted' was not merely a joke, and he had to find his amusements in the cheapest possible way. This drove him into the poorest districts of cities. These were, of course, out of bounds and he would be penalised if the military police caught him, but he went there just the same. If he contracted venereal disease, he considered it to be bad luck, not a divine retribution for his evil ways. Kitchener could see a long way into the future, and exercised wise judgement, but, as most of the officers, warrant officers and NCOs under his command could have told him, men who have had a few drinks are not deterred from going with a local prostitute by thoughts of the honour of the regiment, or the possibility of marriage in the remote future. The penalties for 'bad luck' might have given him pause. Enlightened views on the rehabilitation of offenders were not prevalent in the Indian Army of that time. The problem of VD has persisted long past Kitchener's day, in spite of strenuous endeavours inside and outside the Army to solve it. Most of the Second World War generals had something to say on the subject at one time or another. What makes Kitchener's speech interesting to us is that he believed that, if men are given the right advice, they will eventually follow it. He could lead men, he could even inspire them, but he had as little conception of what went on in their minds as they had of what went on in his.

Chapter 10

Egypt Once More

Remote as Kitchener was from the average soldier, and incomprehensible as many of his addresses to them were, it did not in any way affect their hero-worship of him. When he handed over his command in September 1909, men walked miles in their thousands to line the roads along which his car would pass. He had served the country well. It might have been better for Britain if he had left India in 1907, as he wished to do, and become British Ambassador to Turkey. Had he been able to do so, it is highly unlikely that Turkey would have become an ally of Germany in 1914. Turkey had mixed feelings about Britain. Through British manoeuvres, both Egypt and Greece had become independent of Turkish suzerainty, but when Russia had threatened Turkey later in the century, Britain had come to Turkey's aid. The Turks liked Kitchener, and Kitchener respected the fighting qualities of the Turks. Had Kitchener brought Turkey into the First World War on the Allied side in 1914, or even kept her neutral, there would have been no need for Gallipoli or the Mesopotamian and Palestinian campaigns. It was said that his failure to get the appointment was out of the jealousy it provoked in the Foreign Office.

One of Kitchener's most important achievements in India was the establishment of a Staff College at Quetta. Since the inception of the British Staff College at Camberley in the mid-nineteenth century, the value and prestige of attending its courses had increased steadily. Neither Kitchener nor Roberts had attended the Staff College, but both were keenly aware of its importance. At this time the course lasted two years and this meant that few officers of the Indian Army would go, for few were prepared to spend that amount of time in England, where they would not receive Indian Army pay.

Kitchener's proposal to establish a Staff College at Quetta, with a course identical to that at Camberley, was not received without criticism at home. It was felt that to have a sister college in India might very easily create rivalry between military doctrines. That view was dismissed, and was in any case found to be an unnecessary fear. Just before he left India Kitchener addressed the students at Quetta and told them how pleased he was with the way the college had developed. At the same time he suggested that they should 'take delight in learning' and not regard it as a tiresome burden. In retrospect the Staff College at Quetta has substantially fulfilled all its founder's aspirations.

Kitchener handed over his command in India to Sir Moore O'Creagh in 1909. The following day he was promoted Field-Marshal. As a reward for his services in India, he was also voted a world tour at public expense, and on 12 September he set off for China and Japan as the first stage. He was accompanied by his ADC, who was now Captain O.A.G. Fitzgerald of the 18th Bengal Lancers. Fitzgerald had been with him for four years, and had replaced Frank Maxwell when the latter had returned to England to attend the course at the Staff College. Fitzgerald was neither married nor ambitious, so he was happy to serve in an interesting post as long as he was required. Kitchener liked him and relied on him. In consequence Fitzgerald stayed on with Kitchener, and the two went down together when the *Hampshire* was sunk in June 1916. (Another of Kitchener's ADCs in the early days of India had been Victor Brooke, elder brother of Alan Brooke, later to become Field-Marshal Lord Alanbrooke.)

At this moment Kitchener found himself in something of a quandary. Edward VII was anxious that he should become High Commissioner in the Mediterranean as Field-Marshal Commanding-in-Chief. The post had previously been held by the Duke of Connaught, and was prestigious though not exacting. It did not appeal to Kitchener who felt he would have little to do and find little to interest him, but in view of Edward VII's strongly expressed wish, he had little option but to accept, hoping that an opportunity to relinquish the post might occur in the not too distant future. The opportunity came more quickly than he expected, in fact even before he had begun on his Mediterranean duties. Minto's retirement as Viceroy was announced and Kitchener, who had by now reached America in his world tour, hurried home to put himself in contention. His first step was to see Edward VII and request to be relieved from acceptance of the Mediterranean post. The King was not pleased, but gave his assent. He also confirmed that he would support Kitchener's bid for the post of Viceroy. Kitchener then approached the Prince of Wales, soon to be George V, and learnt that he too would support him. Kitchener did not delude himself that the battle was already won. There were plenty of people who would oppose him, and some of them had considerable influence. Nevertheless, the situation looked to be marginally in his favour, when a not unexpected blow fell.

Edward VII died on 6 May 1910. This was undoubtedly a setback, but Kitchener had had setbacks before and had overcome them. He tried to discourage his principal rival, Sir Charles Hardinge, the Permanent Secretary at the Foreign Office, by telling him that the post required a large private income, which he knew Hardinge had not got. Hardinge decided he could cope with that situation if the need arose and remained a candidate. However, the Prime Minister, H.H. Asquith, was prepared to support Kitchener's candidature and informed Morley (the Secretary of State for India) of his views. Morley's response was to threaten to resign if Kitchener was appointed. To this there could be only one answer. The Prime Minister felt he dare not let one of his principal ministers resign over the issue, and put the matter to the Cabinet for them to resolve.

Morley's successful stand on his Liberal principles proved in the long run to be in the best interests of all concerned, because it freed Kitchener to make his great contribution in the First World War. All of this, however, was far ahead. Morley wrote to Kitchener, informing him that he was not to become Viceroy, and declared he had 'never had a more disagreeable task in my life than the writing of this letter'. He went on to say that undoubtedly time would produce a suitable post for 'a man of supreme capacity and many proved successes'.

This was the first major failure in Kitchener's life, and the bitterest. He had known success in Palestine, Cyprus, Egypt, the Sudan, South Africa and India. He had even defeated no less adroit a politician as Curzon. But now the post which he saw as the accolade of his career, Viceroy of 'the brightest jewel in the Imperial Crown', had been snatched away from him and given to an inferior. He had no intention of taking the Mediterranean post, and in case there should be any doubts about that, confirmed his refusal. Wisely, he took himself off on a visit to Ireland, where he went back to the places he had once known so well. In time of crisis great and distinguished men often do well to revisit the scenes of their youth: the experience revives their sense of proportion.

There were, as Kitchener well realised, other interesting posts which might become available: Ambassador to Turkey was one, Consul-General in Egypt was another. Both posts lay in the province

161

of the Foreign Office, and Kitchener wondered whether Hardinge who, as its ex-head, still possessed considerable influence, would use it in favour of his defeated rival. Kitchener was aware that while there was a Liberal government in office (and there would be one for nearly the rest of his lifetime) he could not afford to neglect any possible supporters. He was not the type to relish this constant lobbying, as some contenders for office do, but he was a realist. He knew very well how the scales were balanced. As a known Conservative and a forthright military man, he was anathema to many Liberals; on the other hand he was a man of great ability, whose prestige must be utilised so that he appeared to be a supporter of Government policy rather than a victim of it. Asquith knew that there would be considerable public disquiet if Kitchener was not found a post suitable for his proved ability. As a stop-gap, he invited Kitchener to rejoin the Defence Committee, from which he had withdrawn earlier. Kitchener accepted.

His old friend Birdwood hoped Kitchener might get the Turkish Embassy. He wrote: 'I have often wondered what might have happened if Kitchener had been our ambassador in Constantinople in 1914. He had, as I knew well, a remarkable influence—almost a dominating influence—on the peoples of the East and Near East.... I feel sure that he would have wielded enormous influence in Constantinople, even though the Turkey of 1914 was hardly the Turkey he had known in years gone by. Now it was strongly dominated by German influence, and Enver Pasha had undoubtedly made up his mind that Germany was invincible.'

Birdwood also described how, in that summer of disappointment of 1910, Kitchener came to buy his longed-for country house, Broome Park:

During that summer of 1910 Kitchener insisted on taking me off on a motor tour, the object of which was to find a suitable house for himself. We saw many places in Sussex, Hampshire, Dorset, and as far west as Devon, but none attracted him till he came across Broome Park, in Kent. He fell for it at once. I tried to put him off, saying it was really too big for him with its 476 acres of park, and pointing out it would need a lot of money spent on it after purchase. But he turned on me, asking why shouldn't he have a house of his own as everyone else had. This was the first suitable house he had found, and unless I could suggest a better he proposed to buy it. As soon as he entered the long, low hall, his builder's eye perceived that it was too low for its size, and he said he would have to raise it a foot, or eighteen inches, or even two feet.

I asked, how about the rooms above. He said they must look after themselves—and indeed the process involved lifting their floors to the level of the windows.... So Kitchener bought Broome and loved it.'

The house cost Kitchener £14,000. He lost no time in setting about alterations to it. But, as Birdwood said rather sadly, he was never able to live in it. On his death he left it to his nephew Toby, who became Viscount Broome, but Toby did not have sufficient money to complete the alterations or even to live in Broome in its unaltered state. He sold it. It became a hotel and is now a time-sharing house.

Having found Broome and established where he would put down roots, Kitchener decided he would be wise to take a long holiday before another job made that impossible. With Fitzgerald and a former ADC, Major A. McMurdo, he set off for Africa via Italy, Austria, Vienna and Turkey. He found that the Germans were powerful and influential in Constantinople, and that the British Ambassador counted for little. He was sure that he could change that, given sufficient funds. However, with Grey now as Foreign Secretary, it seemed highly unlikely that he would get the post or have the money to carry out his plans if he did. Grey was a supporter of Foreign Office career diplomats; furthermore he deplored the idea of the British Ambassador dabbling in bribery and corruption, which everyone else was practising successfully. Kitchener reluctantly decided that the Turkish Embassy was extremely unlikely to come his way, and moved on to Cairo. There he met the Khedive with whom he had had that brush in 1894 which had led to his threatening resignation.

From Egypt he went on to the Sudan where his reception pleased him. He was accorded the welcome of a deliverer, despite the strong rumours of plots to assassinate him. On his way to Uganda and Kenya he went on several hunting trips, where he was considerably more successful with elephants, lions and buffalos than he was at home with pheasant and partridges. In Kenya he found his old railway-building friend, now Sir Percy Girouard, who had become Governor. Kitchener, Fitzgerald, McMurdo, and another Sapper officer named Legget who had joined them, examined the possibilities of obtaining a grant of land to be developed by them jointly. The Kenyan government was trying to encourage settlers who would cultivate rich land which was merely being used for tribal grazing. They were allotted 2,000 acres each. The law governing these grants decreed that the owners should live in Kenya and either run the estate themselves, or employ a European to do so. Subsequently Girouárd granted another 3,000 acres to Kitchener on the basis that he was likely to be particularly active in its development. It was not an unreasonable assumption. Kitchener was no ordinary settler and his having a stake in Kenya would probably be of assistance to that country. But he could not be expected to settle there permanently yet awhile. In consequence, the three estates were put together to form the Songhor estate, and Legget, who had already taken up a separate allocation, was left to manage them.

In the event the outlay required to develop the estate proved more than any of the investors could manage. Kitchener obtained loans from the British East Africa Board, where he had influence, but even these were barely sufficient. After the death of Kitchener and Fitzgerald there was an outstanding debt of nearly six thousand pounds. Eventually Songhor became a private company, but still fell far short of the hopes of the original investors.

Kitchener returned to England in April 1911 to command the troops at the coronation of King George V, whose special request it was that he should do so. For the coronation ceremony Kitchener wore the GCSI Order. The Order has an extremely valuable jewel which hangs from a knot on the left side. When the coronation was over he noticed that the jewel had disappeared. Police and troops (still lining the streets) were alerted. Kitchener went off to change, but suddenly shouted, 'I've found it!' It had fallen off but had been caught in the flap of his field-marshal's boot. It was subsequently remarked: 'No one but Kitchener would have such luck,' recalling a remark of Salisbury's when asked to justify his choice of Kitchener to command the Sudan expedition, although there were several other officers senior to him: 'Kitchener has luck.'

Of all the attributes of successful generals, the phenomenon of luck is probably the most important. And perhaps Kitchener was even lucky to die at the height of his power and reputation.

Kitchener never bore resentment against his former opponents, with the possible exception of Curzon. As we have seen, he remained friendly with Hardinge when the latter had defeated him over the appointment of the new Viceroy, and now he found himself on friendly enough terms with Morley to ask the Minister to introduce him when he formally took his seat in the House of Lords. This could be interpreted as showing that Kitchener's eye for political or career advantage made him conceal his true feelings; but that view is hardly borne out by Morley himself, who was able to write of Kitchener: 'I had expected a silent, stiff, moody hero. Behold he was the most cheerful of men, and he hammered away loud and strong, with free gestures and high tones. He used the warmest language.' Although the two men had had a very different experience and held widely differing political views, this did not prevent them from liking and respecting each other. Kitchener also got on well with Asquith, who mentions him frequently in his correspondence with Venetia Stanley, and became nearly as close a friend of Mrs Asquith as he was of Lady Salisbury. By King George V he was, of course, liked and trusted. The Liberals were now at the height of their power; they had just established full control over the House of Lords by threatening to flood it with Liberal peers if it did not consent to having its powers drastically reduced. Kitchener steered clear of these political storms and, as his chances of further high-level employment appeared to be slight, began to devote more and more time to becoming an English country gentleman.

He encouraged the Boy Scouts, the creation of his old friend Baden-Powell, to camp at Broome Park, and himself became president of the North London Association. To his great pleasure he was invited to join the board of the London, Chatham and Dover Railway. This he felt was a first step to a post-service, business career. It also had the advantage that he could draw attention to the deficiencies of that part of the line which served Broome and have them remedied. Many holders of high rank in the services have a hankering to take up business careers and show they are as good at it as civilians, but few succeed in being more than mere impressive figureheads. Kitchener, with his engineering experience and shrewd appreciation of possibilities good or bad, might have been one of the rare successes. But the question of whether he would have displayed a talent for business was never resolved, for soon after this he was offered the post in Egypt with the resounding title of British Agent, Consul-General and Minister Plenipotentiary.

He returned to Egypt in civilian, formal dress, grey frock-coat and black silk hat, accompanied by his dogs. This was an attempt to make his presence seem not too obviously military, for Egypt, in the not too distant future, would be given self-government if the Liberals stayed in power in Britain. However, he was received with an impressive military turnout, which included a personal escort by the 21st Lancers. The regiment regarded him as one of its chief patrons: they might have thought very differently if he had court-martialled their commanding officer after the famous charge at Omdurman, as he had once seriously contemplated.

His ability to keep calm and impartial was tested from the moment of his arrival. War had just broken out between Italy and Turkey. Kitchener insisted that Egypt must be neutral, although for various reasons, not least that the country was predominantly

Moslem, they would have happily supported the Turks who, in any case, soon seemed to be winning.

Governing Egypt at this time was no sinecure. Kitchener's predecessor, Sir Eldon Gorst, in accordance with Liberal policy, had encouraged the Egyptians to look forward to responsible government. The idea that, after a period of educational development, instruction in democratic theory, and moderate industrial stimulus, any country would be able to run its own affairs harmoniously and successfully was an article of faith in nineteenth-century Liberal thought. Subsequent experience has shown that the path to successful responsible government is a stony one. Egypt, and Asquith's Cabinet, were already aware that Gorst's attempt to introduce democratic reform had encouraged the growth of small, fiercely nationalist groups which wanted self-government immediately with themselves in the key posts. Kitchener did not wish to concern himself too closely with constitutional affairs but preferred to concentrate on practical matters, such as improving agriculture, introducing sensible industry, and removing unjust laws which were a legacy from the past. Cromer supported Kitchener's view: he considered that responsible government should not be introduced too quickly. In consequence, the new constitution which Kitchener brought in on 21 July 1913 represented a cautious approach to representative government.

His economic measures were more progressive, more thorough, and longer lasting. The two most important reforms were the 'Five Feddan' law, and the Cantonal Courts law. The former protected the peasant holder of five feddans of land (just over five acres) from losing that land if he fell into debt; the second established small local courts where justice was related to local and traditional customs which the peasants understood. Previously the law had been applied in urban courts which the peasants could rarely attend, and could not understand if they did. Needless to say these provisions antagonised lawyers and financiers, but Kitchener paid no heed, believing both groups to be usurers and predators, who were responsible for most of the peasants' misery. Moneylenders were not permitted to charge more than 3%: Kitchener knew very well how easily whole peasant communities could fall into the power of extortionist money lenders who charged huge rates of interest and were backed in their practices by a corrupt judiciary. Then, having freed the peasants from their traditional shackles, he went on to help them develop their interests by large-scale drainage and irrigation schemes. He also established a mobile body of midwives to provide services in remote villages. He became 'Lord Kitchener—Friend of the Peasant'. He was regarded somewhat differently by foreign investors, who found some of their lucrative investments affected by his brakes on extortion. He spent government money on badly-needed public work such as hospitals (particularly eye hospitals), railways, roads; he also raised the height of the Aswan Dam. Not surprisingly, he spent money on preserving archaeological relics. Those who saw him at this time, moulding and developing a potentially great country, and assisting the population to live securely and happily, said that he had never looked more contented, not even after his great military victories.

Although an autocrat, he was completely approachable. Men from every level were allowed audience with him. However, he refused to see women on the basis that he was unable to distinguish between genuine and merely emotional pleas.

There were, of course, less harmonious occasions. The Gezira Club, which was open to both British and Egyptians (if they were able to afford it), had begun to foster groups of Egyptians who constantly talked politics and openly criticised Britain and the British. Kitchener listened to complaints about this, and finding they were justified, had himself made president of the club. From that position he called on all Egyptians to resign or be expelled, saying that there would be another club with joint membership shortly but by their conduct and remarks they had forfeited their membership of this one. A number of British members protested; some threatened to resign and others did so. When those who had resigned thought better of it and wished to withdraw their letters of resignation, Kitchener informed them that their resignations were irrevocable. He ignored criticism, knowing that he himself was neither nationalistic or racist. He considered that the privilege of membership of an established club had been abused and that there was no more to it than that.

By now he was quite different from the Kitchener who had been so socially inept when adjutant-general some twenty years before. He was noted for his affability, wit and charm. He became less serious, and read novels and books on the arts for amusement. He went shopping in the bazaars regularly, though he was a less formidable customer than he had been in India. His staff worked efficiently, not because they were afraid of his displeasure, but because they wished to show their appreciation of his consideration. His friends from England came out to see him and he was an excellent host to them. In the summer he took three months' leave in England and spent a good portion of it at Broome. Guests who came to stay there were not entirely pleased to find they were expected to work alongside him in the gardens, almost as apprentices. He also stayed in other people's houses. He was made welcome at Balmoral where he was able to stalk deer, though with less agility than in earlier years.

As Egypt began to prosper under his tutelage he became increasingly irritated with his old adversary the Khedive, whom he considered a major obstacle to complete reform. He considered that corruption in the Khedive's palace had gone beyond the limits of tolerance. Kitchener's predecessors, Cromer and Gorst, had both felt that interference with established corrupt practices could go too far. Kitchener disagreed. His particular target was the very considerable revenue from gifts which rich Moslems had made in past years for the purposes of education and other forms of social amelioration; this was constantly plundered and misappropriated by the Khedive and his friends. Kitchener acted decisively by appointing a Minister for Religious Charities, thus at a stroke removing these from the Khedive's control. He hoped that this might cause the Khedive to abdicate, but it did not. Kitchener therefore made an order that the Khedive's former absolute power to award titles and decorations was now null: instead he could endorse the recommendations of his ministers which would then, if approved, be countersigned by Kitchener himself.

Even this humiliation did not make the Khedive abdicate; there were some, like Cromer, who thought that Kitchener was pressing too hard on this issue. The Khedive was not especially corrupt by prevailing standards among oriental monarchs, and there was a danger that, if his abdication was forced, there would immediately be a wave of support for him from one of the nationalistic groups: the result for Egypt would be less satisfactory than if he had continued in his no longer influential office.

Unfortunately, to Kitchener the Khedive represented the last link of a thoroughly corrupt system, that of Turkish suzerainty over the Egyptian state. The sooner this was ended, Kitchener thought, the better for Egypt. Instead, Egypt and the Sudan should become a joint state and be ruled, like India, through a Viceroy. Eventually it should be allowed full responsible government under the British Crown. He felt that the first step towards this should be annexation by Britain. The Khedive, knowing that his position was threatened by Kitchener, decided that he would seek an audience with George V, explain his point of view, and hope to see some restraint exercised on Kitchener. Kitchener promptly took steps to prevent his obtaining such an audience, which could only be embarrassing for the King. The Khedive was informed unofficially that if he came to Britain the British monarch would not be able to see him. Instead, therefore, he went to Constantinople, where he found a more sympathetic reception.

This awkward situation was resolved, like many other apparently intractable problems, by the outbreak of the First World War. When that happened, Kitchener was in London and the Khedive was still in Turkey. Although Britain did not formally declare war on Turkey till 5 November 1914, war between the two countries had been almost inevitable since the outbreak, and after that date Britain declared a protectorate over Egypt. The Khedive issued an anti-British proclamation and was deposed. His uncle, Hussein, was installed in his place, but the long suzerainty of Turkey over Egypt was ended.

Kitchener never returned to Egypt from his summer leave, for he too was overtaken by events. On 5 August 1914, on the invitation of Asquith, he joined the Cabinet as Secretary of State for War. He was sixty-four and might well have preferred a lighter post.

There were many stories about Kitchener's conduct and bearing in Egypt but the best perhaps concerns an attempt to assassinate him which nearly succeeded. It occurred in July 1912. A nationalist, Taher Arabi, broke through the crowd in Cairo and levelled a gun, but before he pulled the trigger Kitchener walked steadily towards him and asked what he wanted. The man dropped the gun and fell on his knees. The guards then slashed him to pieces. It was in many parts of the world a time of assassinations. There was an attempt on Hardinge's life in which he was so badly wounded it seemed for a while that he might have to give up his post as Viceroy. It was suggested that, if he did so, Kitchener, who had proved himself in a similar capacity in Egypt, should replace him. Kitchener would no doubt have been delighted to accept, mainly because he would have enjoyed the opportunities for reform which the post offered but also, naturally, because he could then prove how wrong his former rejection had been. But another, almost unremarked, assassination put all prospects of India out of question. On 28 June 1914 an Austrian archduke was shot while on a visit to Sarajevo. It was not the cause of the war which would eventually kill millions, including Kitchener himself, but it was the event which made its outbreak inevitable.

The war came as no surprise to Kitchener. On the world tour he had taken after his service in India he had visited Australia and New Zealand with the brief of inspecting their forces and advising on military policy. He had made recommendations which would enable those countries to defend themselves if attacked, but at the same time he had indicated that the day might soon come when the whole Empire would be involved in a vast conflict.

Before leaving Egypt Kitchener had a further brush with the press.

169

Sydney Moseley, a British journalist, wrote a book, *With Kitchener in Cairo*,[1] which was ready for publication in early 1914 but did not appear until three years later. Moseley thought that Kitchener's original objection to the book may have been because he was under the impression that Moseley was a different man (who spelt his name without the second 'e' and was a severe critic of British policy). However, although Moseley made a number of very complimentary remarks about Kitchener, he also had some strong criticisms of his policies. One incident which had annoyed Moseley intensely, and Kitchener even more when it was discussed openly, was the manner in which a Russian resident in Alexandria named Adamovitch, who had organised a strike of Russian sailors (for more pay) back in 1906, was arrested and deported by the Russian consul. Existing Egyptian law gave foreign consuls power to take such action. Kitchener felt that this was an abuse which could only be dealt with in a thorough overhaul of the legal system and was extremely annoyed that Moseley should bring up an isolated case.

After Kitchener's death, Moseley wrote: 'Much that has been written about Lord Kitchener reveals a complete lack of understanding of the inner man. The late War Minister has been represented as a man of stone, a sphinx—a man of blood and iron. The human side of him has altogether been overlooked. Lord Kitchener , like many members of the human race, possessed characteristics that were distant and autocratic. He may have been stern and unyielding but he also had a broad outlook, a deep and genuine sympathy for the masses, and weaknesses without which he could not have held claim to his sex.'

What these masculine weaknesses were Moseley does not elaborate upon. However, as a journalist he was doubtless familiar with every detail of Kitchener's private life, even if he dared not publish his information. He went on: 'Critics of Lord Kitchener were few; for he mesmerised his critics. Therefore most pictures of him were distorted. To many of those whose familiarity with the late War Minister helped to nullify this paralysing influence, he only revealed himself at the heart-to-heart conference which was held just prior to his tragic death.' These were the chosen few: others never realised that Kitchener had changed much since his early days as a soldier in the field, and when he was War Minister 'wrote his way to victory in frock coat and a pair of pince-nez'.

Moseley described Kitchener's life. He was at one moment instituting much-needed reforms which had previously been thought

[1] (London, 1917).

170

impossible, at another entertaining on a lavish scale. As he had no wife, the duties of hostess were carried out by the Hon. Mrs Byng, wife of the commander of the British Forces. (General, later Field-Marshal, Byng was the commander of the Canadian Corps which captured Vimy Ridge and subsequently conducted the first great tank battle fought by the British army at Cambrai.)

Lord Kitchener's garden parties and balls were thronged with many hundreds of visitors, each individually lost in the great mass, but everyone, nevertheless, regarding himself as a person of increased importance as a result of being the invited guest of the famous soldier.

These were hardly occasions on which we could get a glimpse of the softer side of the great man. Like every host of importance, he was quickly and diplomatically snatched up by intimates, and tactfully hidden by them for the rest of the afternoon. Nevertheless, he often managed to greet you with a handshake and a 'How d'you do' before disappearing. I always wonder where he sprang from to greet me on the first occasion I went to one of his popular garden parties. I had a particular reason for not wishing to see him then. I therefore waited till the coast was quite clear so that I could slip in unobserved. I had to cross a lawn in order to reach the throng and I am positive that nobody was in sight. He certainly took me completely by surprise by suddenly appearing as it were from the earth, towering over me and holding out a friendly but overpowering hand.

There were more formal audiences too:

You sent in your card to the attaché, to whom you possessed a valuable letter of introduction. You were shown into the hall by a gorgeously attired dragoman, or maybe into the private dining room where stood conspicuously on the mantelpiece the silver cup won by Lord Kitchener, then a captain, in the polo tournament at Cairo in the year 1884. . . . Your reverie was interrupted by the unceremonious entrance of a tall, strongly built man wearing spectacles and smoking a cigar. 'Are you waiting to see me,' he asked, looking over the top of his spectacles and speaking in a tone which invited an answer to the affirmative.

It was not the attaché; it was Lord Kitchener.

Moseley mentioned an occasion when an impoverished village was not getting enough water. Somebody suggested writing to Kitchener and 'a missive of some sort was indeed sent'. To their amazement, the village elders were invited to come and discuss their grievances with him. This was unexpected and welcome news but it presented a problem because no one had clothes which they felt were sufficiently presentable and they could not easily afford new ones. By some means Kitchener heard of their dilemma and sent a note saying they must not incur any unnecessary expense, and that he would see them as they were.

According to Moseley, Kitchener 'was fond of music and never played bridge'. Others say that he was not particularly fond of music.

However, everyone was agreed that he was on the side of the fellaheen (the peasants). He was even described as 'the Lloyd George of Egypt', an expression which can hardly have flattered him. The fellaheen certainly needed protection. Not least of their afflictions was the number of bogus doctors who claimed to be able to cure their many ills. Most of the doctors had no qualifications at all, but had bribed their way to official recognition; others had simply taken over the diplomas of a dead doctor and used them as their own in order to obtain a licence to practise.

As a journalist and keen upholder of the right and freedom of the press, Moseley was at first startled by Kitchener's repressive measures: 'Lord Kitchener's known lack of sympathy towards the press made it an interesting speculation as to whether the soldier's sense of slaughter would be applied to Egypt's only medium of public expression. We were not long left in doubt. Through the Ministry of the Interior five vernacular journals soon received their quietus. No fuss was made: none of the inconvenient law-suits which waste so much time and money in countries where they are too sensitive about rights.'

But he went on to say that, reluctantly, he had concluded that Kitchener was right. Nowhere else in the world was there a press 'so enmeshed in the coils of officialism, exploiters and political adventurers. You can buy the opinion of any of these newspapers as you can buy drugs in Egypt.'

Freedom in Egypt, he believed, would simply lead to chaos. 'In Egypt the immediate emancipation of the press would be playing into the hands of the adventurous type of man, to whom Egypt is, or has been, a haven.

'Grievances on the face of it, are serious. But only on the face of it. After looking below the surface one comes to the conclusion that the time is not yet fully ripe.'

Egypt has certainly come a long way from those days when, as another writer sadly put it, 'the only unadulterated thing you could buy was poison.'

Chapter 11

The Cabinet Minister

Kitchener entered the War Office on 6 August 1914. He was asked to give a specimen signature. He took up the pen which had been brought to him. It refused to write. He flung it away. 'What a War Office,' he said. 'Not a scrap of Army and not a pen that will write.'

The regular Army, which the War Office hoped would be able, with its French allies, to check the German onslaught consisted of six infantry and one cavalry divisions, all well-trained according to pre-war standards. This made a total of approximately 125,000 men. There were another 60,000 regular troops overseas but these could not be brought back until replacements had been produced for them from local sources. There was also a territorial army of some fourteen divisions, but this was incompletely trained and ill-equipped. Its members had been enlisted on the basis that they were giving their services for home defence only and would not be required to serve overseas. This gave a total of 250,000 territorial forces which would be usable after more vigorous training. There were also a number of trained men in reserve but most of them were in other employment, and in any case would need some re-training. One of the most extraordinary features of the First World War was that while it was in progress some men who had enlisted in the regular Army came to the end of the period for which they had signed on, and were discharged. Often they were bachelors. Meanwhile married men with wives and children to support, or people working in vital industries such as agriculture were being called up, put through a period of training and then sent to the trenches.

Kitchener regarded the existing regular and territorial army with scorn. Knowing that the Germans were able to put a million and a half trained men into the field, he had only contempt for the politicians who thought that, even with the resources of the French, their numbers would be remotely adequate. He made little attempt to conceal his opinion of the Chief of the General Staff and his advisers in the War Office; he felt they had neglected their duty by letting the politicians of all parties remain unaware of the total inadequacy of our existing resources. He told his Cabinet colleagues that if the British had had a million trained men at their disposal, the Germans would never have dared to risk a war, but that now it had begun it would require far more than one million and, in fact, would only be won with the *last million* which would be thrown into the conflict. For many years he had believed that Britain should have conscription. He realised that conscription in peace-time was anathema to British ideas on personal liberty and had not therefore pressed his view when there seemed to be no immediate danger. But there was worse to come. Even if Britain had the right number of men, there would still be a desperate shortage of munitions. When the forces were expanded, and expansion would be a major problem in itself, it seemed highly unlikely that they would have sufficient ammunition and guns to make them effective against the enemy.

Unfortunately his disgust with the overall inadequacy of existing arrangements made him unable to see the areas where efficiency was commendable. Sir Henry Wilson had been Director of Military Operations at the War Office since 1911, and, though he was widely known to be conceited, disloyal and unscrupulously ambitious, he was also extremely capable. In consequence, the mobilisation and despatch of the six divisions went off without a hitch. Winston Churchill, who had now become First Lord of the Admiralty, deserved credit too, for he arranged the embarkation. But the success of these operations never received a word of praise from Kitchener. It was no excuse to say that both men had a sufficiently high opinion of themselves not to need anyone to add to it.

Kitchener was soon in conflict with the General Staff on the strategy of the war. He believed that the British Army should be concentrated around Amiens; they believed it should be seventy miles further forward at Maubeuge. The War Office view was that, with the Russians advancing on the eastern front and the French planning to produce a counter-thrust, the British should be well forward. In the event the French counter-thrust turned out to be a total disaster, which cost them enormous casualties, and the British Army had to make a hasty retreat from its exposed position. Kitchener had withdrawn his objections to the Maubeuge deployment because he understood that the French wanted Britain to agree to it and to conform to their strategic plans. When he

174

looked at the consequent disaster he was more firmly resolved than ever that if the country was to be saved from its folly he should not act against his own instinctive judgement again.

In the first year of the war Kitchener lived at 2, Carlton Gardens, a furnished house which had been lent to him by Lady Wantage. In March 1915 he moved to York House, St James's Palace, which had been offered to him by King George V; there is a plaque on the wall to commemorate his period of residence there. FitzGerald, his former ADC, had now become his Military Secretary and a colonel. They shared the same house, they were good friends, and worked in complete harmony. It has been suggested that they were more than friends, but there there seems no evidence at all to suggest homosexual tendencies in either man.

Having taken his seat in the Cabinet on the right of Asquith, Kitchener virtually assumed the rôle of wartime Prime Minister. Asquith still, of course, held the title but was well aware that in the matters that were then proceeding he was a novice. Kitchener insisted that this was not a war which could be won by sea power (though it could perhaps be lost at sea), as previous wars had been; it needed huge armies on the Continent and probably in other parts of the world too. He estimated that it would last at least three years, and as a first step to winning it he proposed to raise an army of a million men. His view was accepted by all except Sir Edward Grey; even Lloyd George, then Chancellor of the Exchequer, felt that this opinion was totally unrealistic. Churchill felt that Kitchener had so completely convinced the Cabinet of the soundness of his views that if he had promptly demanded conscription he would have met no opposition, either in Parliament or outside. But instead he proceeded cautiously with an appeal for a mere 100,000 volunteers.

'The First Hundred Thousand' were brought in by the posters featuring Kitchener pointing somewhat threateningly at them over the compelling statement: 'Your Country Needs YOU.' They came in such numbers that it was almost impossible to cope with the influx. Books of reminiscences of this period are full of amusing stories about bizarre improvisation, of learning by experience, of 'roughing it'. There were not enough uniforms or rifles and some men began drill in their civilian clothes carrying wooden rifles. Hindsight showed that it would have been better if the new recruits had come in via the territorials, and the latter had been asked at the outset whether they were willing to go abroad in spite of the terms of their enlistment. Kitchener's evident aim was to raise the army to seventy divisions, a total of some 1,400,000 men, of which the majority could be employed on front-line duties. But this vast number would place an incalculable strain on transport, munition supplies, and ancillary services: experience showed that for every fighting man at least eight were needed in support. There was a great shortage of instructors: most of those available were well out-of-date in their knowledge, for all the best men were taken away, even from the territorials, and sent to France. It was said that Kitchener realised the risks in creating an entirely 'New Army', but felt that a brand-new organisation would have a spirit of its own (which it did) and would be proud to be 'Kitchener's Army'. Unfortunately the policy was unfair to the achievement of the territorials who, though undertrained, had at least volunteered, and who went abroad willingly in large numbers. There were forty-seven battalions of them overseas by the end of 1914.

The worst aspect of the volunteer army, which had attracted two and a half million in eighteen months, was that it took the best and destroyed them in expensive trench battles. Recruits who would have made first-class officers and NCOs were slaughtered wholesale; in consequence the shortage of good leadership material became acute in the second half of the war. Men volunteered knowing that their expectation of life was probably three weeks from the day they landed in France; it seemed as if the youth of the nation had been chosen for sacrifice, and went to death with resignation. On many memorials erected after the war, the words 'The supreme sacrifice' appeared. They were apt.

Undoubtedly Kitchener's reputation as a successful general influenced many to join up. Sir Philip Magnus-Allcroft recorded that Mrs Asquith indiscreetly remarked that if Kitchener was not a great man he was, at least, a great poster, and that Kitchener retorted by telling his personal staff that all his colleagues repeated military secrets to their wives except Asquith, who repeated them to other people's wives. If Asquith had heard the remark he could have replied that he did not need to tell them to his own wife, as Kitchener was her close confidant. However, it would not have been quite true; Kitchener had no inhibitions about disclosing political secrets, but he would never betray military ones.

In spite of the flow of volunteers for the new armies, there was still a rush to join the territorials, probably because they had local identities and established names. This aspect of the territorials had no appeal for Kitchener, who felt that these regiments were all cluttered up with dead wood, with totally unsuitable people in senior posts. He believed that he had been let down by the amateurish, undisciplined attitude of many territorials in the Boer War; they contrasted sharply with their Boer opponents who were also peace-time volunteers. Any attempts to persuade Kitchener that he should adopt a more friendly attitude towards enlistment in territorial units met a very chilly response. If people wished to volunteer they should enlist in his new armies and act and be trained like regulars on short-term engagements.

Kitchener's disillusionment with British forces soon spread to include the French Army and its Commander-in-Chief J. J. C. Joffre, as well as the British Commander-in-Chief Sir John French, his old colleague of the Boer War. French wished to retire to the Seine, thus diverging from agreed Anglo-French strategy; he said that his army was in no condition to do otherwise. Kitchener felt this would be a disaster for Anglo-French solidarity and decided to go to France to insist that French kept the British Army in the line. With the blessing of the Cabinet he set off to see his former colleague, putting on his field-marshal's uniform. (The rank of field-marshal is unusual in that the holders do not retire; however, if in normal circumstances an ageing field-marshal were to don his uniform and start issuing orders in the Ministry of Defence, doubtless some remedy would quickly be found.) Kitchener was still very much the serving officer, although a Cabinet minister, and furthermore was senior to French. Believing that the heavy casualties the British Army had sustained had caused French to lose his nerve, he gave him a direct order that he must stay and support Joffre. He brushed aside French's protests that lack of information from Joffre had made that task virtually impossible. On his return, he persuaded the Cabinet that they should authorise the sending of our last remaining original infantry division, which was being held in reserve. (Although the bulk of the fighting was in France, it was by no means certain that this exhausted the German options and a surprise invasion launched across the sea to the north-east coast remained a worrying possibility.)

Fortunately the crisis passed. German strategy had been based on the Schlieffen Plan, by which their armies pivoted on Metz, and the two on the right flank, after violating Belgian and Dutch neutrality, should have swept round and encircled Paris. However, once this ambitious plan began, the extreme right flank started to outrun its supplies and its commander to lose his nerve. The line straightened and was checked by Joffre in a flank attack, which became the battle of the Marne. The Germans fell back to the Aisne. French stayed in command through several battles in which the British Army received staggering casualties for little gain, but was removed at the battle of Loos which ran from 25 September to 13 October 1914, and replaced by Sir Douglas Haig. (It is interesting to remember that the best-known commanders-in-chief of the First World War—French,

177

Haig, and Allenby—were all horse cavalrymen.) Although Kitchener and French were cordial enough when they corresponded or met in public, Kitchener subsequently made no secret of his disappointment in, and distaste for, French.[1]

Kitchener's burdens grew weekly, if not daily, as the war progressed. Lack of equipment was a major headache. Kitchener did not believe that any problem was insoluble, but some must have seemed exceptionally difficult to solve. Henry Wilson, his DMO, who early in the war moved to become deputy to Sir John French, was a friend of Foch and believed that British military policy should be subordinate to French strategy. In spite of his good record over the way mobilisation had been organised, Wilson was a difficult colleague and liable to upset otherwise harmonious arrangements. (He was a keen supporter of the idea of union between Britain and Ireland and thus incurred the enmity of the IRA, who assassinated him in London in 1922.)

During 1915 Kitchener showed that he was by no means inflexible. Before the war there had been no need to cater for the minority religious denominations in the Army, and they were therefore all classified under the broad heading of Church of England. But now, when there were protests about this, he gave way. He also gave way over the formation of Welsh and Northern Irish divisions, although he consistently turned down the proposal of John Redmond, a prominent Irish nationalist leader, that he should raise a Southern Irish division. When Redmond went ahead in disregard of Kitchener's veto and raised a division of Irish Roman Catholic volunteers, Kitchener refused to allow it to wear the Irish harp on its colours. This restriction was badly received, for he had approved of the Northern Irish Division using the red hand of Ulster.

Another instance of Kitchener's flexibility was in his dealings with French, of whose strategies he undoubtedly disapproved. But he attempted to get on with French and was not responsible for sacking him, as many have claimed. French had a high opinion of himself socially and tended to look down on Kitchener, although Kitchener's antecedents were at least as good as his own. Henry Wilson as French's deputy had done little to encourage mutual respect between the two men. Churchill, who had been impressed by Kitchener's realistic approach to the war from the beginning, tried to convince French that Kitchener's long-term policy was right and that his own efforts to finish off the war by suicidal attacks were more likely to eliminate his own army than achieve the results he intended.

[1] French delivered a sweeping attack on Kitchener in 1919—three years after Kitchener's death.

Churchill and Kitchener had now become good friends and supported each other. There was, however, a temporary setback to their mutual approval when Churchill came up with an adventurous scheme for breaking the trench deadlock. By 1915 it looked as if the war had settled into an unimaginative struggle of attrition and that the victors, if the survivors could be given that title, would only emerge when millions of men had been slaughtered on each side. The main theatre, in France, had had since 1914 a line of defensive works which stretched from Flanders in the north to the Swiss border in the south. The opposing lines were protected by barbed wire, machine-guns and artillery. Periodically, at heavy cost, one side or the other would make a small dent in the trench line opposite, only to lose in most cases the hard-won, blood-soaked territory in the next counter-attack. In addition, certain areas were fought for bitterly, not because they had good strategic or tactical value, but because they had acquired a dubious, macabre prestige. Ypres was one of them. However, until 1916 when the battles at Verdun and the Somme proved otherwise, there was always the hope that a swift, bold, large-scale attack might make a breakthrough in a vitally important strategic area. The theory behind this was that after artillery had pounded the enemy position and cut holes through the wire, the infantry would be able to pour through the gaps. Ammunition was conserved in order to make these bloodbaths possible, even though this resulted in shells being rationed so strictly that some German bombardments of British positions received inadequate retaliation, much to the disgust of the infantry. Later on, there was renewed support for the advocates of the theory of breaking through by sheer weight of shells and men, when the Germans did so in the spring of 1918, but by then conditions were very different from those in 1915.

At the time when Churchill conceived his bold plan for outflanking the Germans, the trench system had only just been consolidated. There was a chance, therefore, that if Britain could make a successful amphibious attack and invade at Ostend and Zeebrugge, German attention would be so diverted that French would be able to launch a mass attack in another sector of the line and break through. Kitchener at first approved of this plan, but when French asked for huge reinforcements, including fifty battalions from the new armies, Kitchener decided that the Zeebrugge plan was foolish and premature.[1] After consideration he felt that any available guns and shells

[1] Much later, in April 1918, a successful raid was made on Zeebrugge in order to cripple the German shipping which used it as a base, but this had nothing to do with land strategy.

179

should be sent to Russia in order to prevent that country collapsing and thus leaving Germany secure on her eastern front. He also believed that French was likely to squander vital resources. Nor was he happy about the amount of equipment which Churchill was collecting and, in his opinion, probably diverting from a better use. Churchill handed it all back when the Zeebrugge plan was disallowed but, feeling some frustration over the rejection of what he thought was an excellent tactical plan, looked for another area where such an attack might be made. His attention focused on a point at the other end of Europe—the Dardanelles.

A successful campaign in the Dardanelles would bring many advantages. Firstly, it would enable the western allies to supply Russia and prevent that country collapsing through lack of munitions. Secondly, it would put Turkey out of the war and end the drain on British manpower which was occurring in lesser campaigns, such as that in Mesopotamia. Thirdly, it would put an end to German plans for expanding to the Middle East and beyond. Fourthly, German counter-measures in Turkey could not fail to weaken them on the Western Front. Fifthly, Allied success there would influence Italy, Bulgaria and Greece. And so on. These were very good reasons for an Allied attack on the Dardanelles.

There were inevitably objections to the plan. The service chiefs had doubts about the practicability of a seaborne assault three thousand miles from base. Perhaps the spectre of the Crimean War lurked in the back of men's minds. Kitchener was in favour but, as he had allocated all available troops for the forthcoming spring offensive in France, regretted that he had none to spare for secondary campaigns. Once troops had been earmarked for certain areas and projects in the main theatre, they could not be re-deployed except in the event of dire emergency. The Dardanelles could never be anything but a secondary theatre. Victory in that area would enable us to help our Russian allies and to be very annoying to the Germans, but not to win the war. Final victory could only be achieved by a thrust into Germany. This point was clearly demonstrated in the Second World War when it was seen that the campaigns in North Africa, along the Mediterranean littoral and in Italy could never affect the outcome by themselves.

However, the inability to send seasoned British troops to the Dardanelles was not seen as an insuperable obstacle to the campaign. Somewhat optimistically, the service chiefs decided that a naval bombardment could demolish the Turkish forts and leave the way open to the Black Sea. Obsolete ships were to be used, so that if they were lost no harm would be done to our operational strength.

180

On 19 February 1915 a fleet of British warships and a few attached French ships bombarded the Turkish defences and destroyed their outer ring of forts. Had this attack been followed up promptly with landings, the whole enterprise would probably have succeeded. Instead a month was allowed to elapse before a further attack was made. No clearer warning could have been given of Allied intentions in the area, and in consequence the highly capable German general Liman von Sanders took over command of the Turkish defences. When an attempt was made to destroy the inner ring of Turkish forts on 18 March, success was minimal and three British ships were sunk by an unsuspected new line of mines.

At this point, Kitchener decided that in spite of his previous assessment there were now troops which could be spared for Gallipoli—in fact the regular 29th Division, which would be joined by a French division. Marshal Joffre immediately protested, on the basis that the divisions could not be spared; he feared that if he did not take an immediate stand, other divisions would follow these and his own command would be weakened. Kitchener, who had spent so much time in France that at times he saw a French point of view more clearly than he saw an English one, then supported him. He informed the Admiralty, even before he informed Churchill, that the 29th would not be going. Instead, he suggested the allocation of two divisions of untried Australian and New Zealand troops. This led to further meetings and calculations, and after much discussion the 29th Division, numbering some 19,000 men, a French division from the interior of the same size, the Anzac Corps of 30,000 and a Royal Naval Division of 11,000 were made available.

It is hardly surprising that Kitchener now began to show signs of the pressure upon him. From what he knew of Turkey he was well aware that, if Constantinople fell, Turkey would be out of the war. Even if that did not happen quickly, a revolt against Enver Pasha would achieve the same objective. The Germans knew this too and so did the Italians and Greeks. The latter now offered to supply three divisions to assist in the landings. This last promising development was promptly torpedoed by the Russians, who told the Greek government: 'In no circumstances can we allow Greek forces to participate in the Allied attack on Constantinople.' However, the British Cabinet was in favour of the attack continuing, although Lloyd George expressed doubt about expecting the Army to do something which the Navy had failed to do. General Sir Ian Hamilton was given command of the expeditionary force.

Knowledge of the terrain was, unfortunately, scarcely adequate for the venture. All that was available was an inaccurate map of the area, an obsolete report on the condition of the forts, and a 1912 Turkish Army handbook. Before one smiles at such inadequacies, one might perhaps reflect that British knowledge of Norway before a campaign began there in 1940 was based on old railway timetables and picture postcards; and that a key source of information about the possibility of tanks being able to mount the beach at Dieppe was a holiday snapshot. Those who fought against the Japanese in Malaya and Burma were much better placed. They could supplement their maps with excellent ones printed in Tokyo.

Most of the mistakes in the Dardanelles had been made before, and they are mistakes which have been repeated since. Some of the stores which would be needed first were packed at the bottom of the holds; wagons were loaded apart from horses; and shells separated from the guns which would fire them.

Although the Dardanelles expedition proved to be a costly failure, its many impressive features should not be overlooked. The attack began on 25 April 1915 and the troops fought tenaciously to retain and extend their footholds. At times the attackers came very near to success, in spite of being outnumbered and outgunned. But eventually it was decided that this difficult and expensive campaign was achieving nothing except huge losses, and the remnants of the force were withdrawn in January 1916. By the time the adventure was over the Allies had sustained 100,000 casualties—more than the sum total of the original landing force.

Like several other bold ventures in the First World War, a successful Dardanelles campaign would have shortened its duration, and thus saved hundreds of thousands of lives. It would possibly have averted the Russian revolution, if only by ensuing that the Russians' supply lines held. Not least of its effects were on Churchill and Kitchener. Both thought they had failed and let down their supporters. Undoubtedly they had failed, but the criticism levelled against them was uninformed.

One aspect of the Dardanelles campaign was illuminated many years afterwards. At Gallipoli the bombardment of Turkish positions had been relatively ineffective, because the correcting mechanism on the guns was inadequate for the purpose. This meant that when a ship was affected by waves or the firing of one section of guns, the other guns would fire inaccurately because they had not been automatically stabilised. An inventor named Arthur Pollen had designed a range-finder called the Argo Clock, incorporating a gyro, as early as 1905, and this had proved remarkably effective when ships were 'yawing', as rolling and pitching was called. However, Pollen's instrument, which was adapted after the war and fitted to all naval guns, was rejected in favour of a cheaper, less efficient version. Pollen's invention had its enthusiastic backers, who included Vice-Admiral Prince Louis of Battenburg and Admiral Lord Charles Beresford (who had commanded a gunboat in the Sudan expedition), but there were too many very conservatively-minded officers at the Admiralty who preferred the rival instrument. Among these was Admiral 'Jackie' Fisher, who had done much to drag the Navy into the twentieth century but failed on this particular issue. Fisher, who was First Sea Lord, resigned after the Dardanelles, having criticised Churchill's handling of the enterprise. He was not, of course, an entirely impartial judge, for he much preferred the idea of a landing in Schleswig-Holstein, after which, he thought, an expeditionary force would be able to march quickly to Berlin. The result of the rejection of the Argo Clock was that much of the firing at Gallipoli was insufficiently accurate: on one occasion British troops even found themselves fired on just as they had gained a difficult and vital objective. A year later, in 1916, lack of an efficient range-finder also contributed to ineffective gunnery at Jutland in 1916, when Jellicoe was reported as saying, 'What's the matter with our damned ships today!'

The combined effect of so many divergent views in 1915 made Kitchener's task exacting. On one side there was the Army which, with the French Army, believed the only way to victory was to smash an iron fist through the German trenches. Then there was Fisher with his theories about the Baltic; Grey, who thought more attention should be paid to Egypt and the Suez Canal; Lloyd George, who believed that a successful attack could be made via Syria; and the Russians, who felt that their claims for a bigger share of the ammunition pool were not being adequately considered. Kitchener looked very tired in 1915, 'showing signs of his age', it was said. He was sixty-five.

His colleagues must have seemed to him like beings from another world. Asquith was enamoured with a girl of less than half his age and spent much of his time writing indiscreet letters to her. French, whose mind might have been fully occupied with the responsibilities of commanding a battered British Army, was conducting an equally indiscreet correspondence with Winifred Bennet, the wife of a diplomat with whom he was having a passionate affair. (This liaison seemed faintly ludicrous to those who saw them together, for she was nearly a foot taller than he was.) Lloyd-George was engaging in affairs with all the discrimination of an amorous rabbit. To a person who had been brought up surrounded by politicians, these antics might have seemed normal

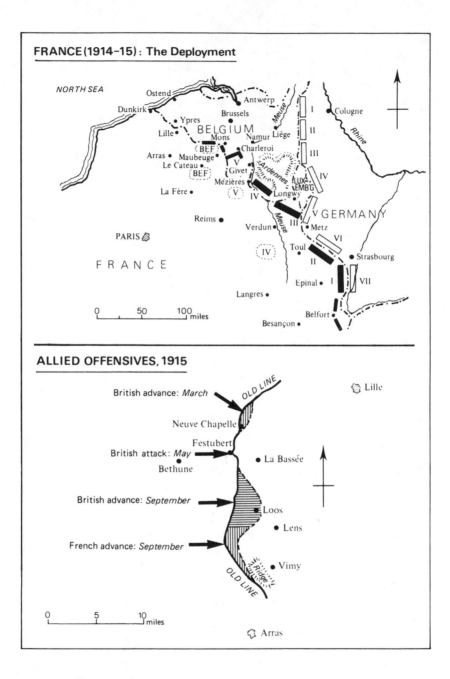

FRANCE(1914–15) : The Deployment

NORTH SEA

Ostend
Dunkirk
Antwerp
Brussels
Cologne
Ypres
BELGIUM
Lille
Mons
Namur Liège
Arras
Maubeuge
Charleroi
Le Cateau
BEF
Givet
Mézières
LUXEMB'G
Longwy
La Fère
Reims
Verdun
Metz
PARIS
Toul
FRANCE
Strasbourg
Epinal
Langres
Belfort
Besançon

Ardennes
GERMANY
Meuse
Rhine

BEF

I
II
III
IV
V
VI
VII

0   50   100 miles

ALLIED OFFENSIVES, 1915

British advance: *March*

OLD LINE

Lille

Neuve Chapelle

Festubert

British attack: *May*

Bethune

La Bassée

British advance: *September*

Loos

Lens

French advance: *September*

Ridge

Vimy

OLD LINE

0   5   10 miles

Arras

enough. To Kitchener, with a mildly puritan strain, they could not have been reassuring.

But the volunteers were coming in and the Allies still had a foothold, albeit a precarious one, in the Dardanelles. They still clung to the Ypres salient, even though the Germans had used gas in desperate attempts to push them off it. (It might have been better for the British if they had succeeded, for it was of little tactical value, and an enormous liability.) French, who had previously been so pessimistic, was now convinced that Ypres must be held, and it was—at a cost.

However, French cannot be blamed for the disaster at Loos (although he was, and it led to his being replaced by Haig). Joffre was now certain that the successful blow which most British and French commanders wanted could be launched against the Germans on a wide section of the front, including the Loos area, that autumn. Haig who, as the commander of the First Army, was responsible for executing the British part of the attack, had doubts, fearing that our guns and shells were still inadequate. Henry Wilson believed the attack was perfectly feasible, and supported Joffre. Robertson, who had now become chief of the general staff in the British Expeditionary Force, had similar doubts to Haig's. Certainly the German defences were still thin in the chosen sector, but they were being rapidly strengthened. Loos was a village set in a mining community; there was a canal in the area too. There did not seem to be grounds for too much optimism.

Yet Joffre's enthusiasm was still infectious. His prestige was high, as was his personal morale, after his remarkable success on the Marne which had stemmed the German attack. Now, he felt, was the time for a great offensive. The French First and Tenth Armies would attack in the Lens-Arras region, the Second and Fourth in the Champagne region, and with the British thrusting through the La Bassée-Loos area, the Allies were certain to make the necessary breakthrough. He was nothing if not highly optimistic: he allotted the cavalry, for example, an objective *fifty miles* east of Loos.

The ground over which the infantry must advance was described by General Rawlinson, the commander of two newly-raised Kitchener divisions—the 15th (Scottish) and the 47th (London), the first to be committed to a major battle—as being 'as flat as my hand'. But the palm of the hand is not noticably flat, and nor was the terrain, which consisted of long slopes with no cover and mineworkings laid at intervals.

The assault on all sectors was to be preceded by a ninety-six-hour bombardment of the German lines. The French had 117 guns to the mile: the British approximately sixty. Neither the British nor the French guns were sufficiently strong to cut the German wire or 'soften up' the defences, as the effects of devastating bombardments are nowadays called. (The Allies lagged behind in shell production too, which in England at that time was 22,000 a day, compared with 100,000 in France and 250,000 a day from Germany and Austria.)

Joffre's optimism proved unfounded. Loos lies directly north of Vimy Ridge and the important town of Arras. The battle which began on 25 September 1915 cost 60,000 casualties, most of which occurred in the first twenty-four hours. British troops captured eighth thousand yards of German trenches and in places penetrated up to two miles, but the main objective, a large-scale breakthough, was not achieved. It came very close to being so. General Richard Hilton, who during the battle was a Forward Observation Officer, wrote of it:

> A great deal of nonsense has been written about Loos. The real tragedy of that battle was its nearness to complete success. Most of us who reached the crest of Hill 70 and survived were firmly convinced that we had broken through on that Sunday, 25th September 1915. There seemed to be nothing ahead of us but an unoccupied and incomplete trench system. The only two things that prevented our advancing into the suburbs of Lens [the next town] were firstly the exhaustion of the 'Jocks' themselves (for they had undergone a bellyful of marching and fighting that day) and secondly the flanking fire of numerous German machine-guns, which swept that bare hill from some factory buildings at Cité St Auguste to the south of us.
>
> All we needed was more artillery ammunition to blast those clearly located machine-guns, and some fresh infantry to take over from the weary and depleted 'Jocks'. But, alas, neither ammunition nor reinforcements were immediately available, and the great opportunity passed.[1]

Having talked to his subordinate commanders Haig and Rawlinson, French had expressed doubts about the feasibility of the attack. Whereas Joffre thought of nothing except his success on the Marne, others recalled his costly failure in Artois. Why, it was subsequently asked, did Kitchener therefore overrule the British objections, on a visit to France in August, and tell French that 'we must act with all energy and do our utmost to help France in this offensive, even though by doing so we may suffer very heavy losses'?

[1] Letter to the author.

186

Various answers have been given to that question. One was that Kitchener knew that in the offing was a plan to have a supreme commander for the Allied Forces. Only one man was likely to be acceptable for that post, and it was himself, but he would be putting it out of his reach if he went against Joffre, who was supported by Foch, over this offensive. Liddell Hart, who does not necessarily endorse the view, pointed out that the *Official History* of the war commented: 'It is believed that Lord Kitchener himself had anticipated a call to this post.'

If he had, it would have been because he felt that only by having himself in that position could the war be won, with French clearly unfitted for the task and Joffre little better. But he himself was old and tired; his constitution was showing the effects of the rigorous life he had led and his eyes in particular were a source of trouble. Even if he did become supreme commander he would still have troublesome political superiors. If he was to have to continue to fight battles with politicians for more men and more guns, it would be better for him to fight them at close quarters in the Cabinet rather than in the battlefield with over half his attention taken by the need to watch the enemy.

Another explanation which has been proffered is that Kitchener believed that a successful battle in France would do much to dispel the public's sense of failure and disillusionment over the Dardanelles. This is probably partially true. But the most likely reason for his supporting Joffre is that he felt that this offensive offered a chance of winning a war which the British might otherwise lose. The soldiers were there, but the munitions were sadly deficient and, important though it was to have men for the trenches, men for the munitions factories were even more desperately required. During the early part of the war, munitions workers had been allowed to volunteer; later they were called up. The combination of these two factors so greatly affected production that when W. G. S. Adams of the Ministry of Munitions suggested that munitions workers should be exempted from the call-up, Kitchener immediately agreed.

Britain and the Empire could, Kitchener knew, produce sufficient manpower for British needs, when supplemented by the French. The latter were outnumbered in population by the Germans, but would fight doggedly for their homeland. The Russians had a vast reservoir of manpower—they were able to mobilise thirteen million men—but had sufficient arms for less than a tenth of that number. They had begun the war surprisingly well. Now they too were running short of munitions. There was a strong possibility that they would be defeated and there was no reason to suppose that the Germans would not recruit from the defeated armies and use the divisions thus formed against the Allies in France, Italy or the Middle East.

Nothing was now clearer to Kitchener than the fact that this war would be won by the nations with the greatest firepower. Even before the invention of gunpowder, this had been the decisive factor in battles. The ancients had had it in their bows; the Romans in their ballistas; the Civil War armies in their cannons which had knocked castles to pieces; and he himself had used it in the Sudan and South Africa. Whether it came from Maxim or Gatling, from *mitrailleuse* or *Minenwerfer*, it was the decisive factor. The subsequent history of warfare has produced nothing to vary that view. From the 88s and 5.5s of the Second World War, not forgetting the cargoes of bombs which are merely another form of it, to the rockets with nuclear warheads, there is very little argument about the effectiveness of sheer firepower. And Kitchener, in September 1915, knew that because of the superior firepower of the enemy the Allies could easily lose the war before our own resources were fully mobilised.

It was for this reason that he supported Joffre's highly speculative offensive and therefore bears some responsibility for the battle of Loos. He seems to have had greater faith in the French Army than was justified for their attacks made little headway. But two divisions of the new army Kitchener had created nearly won the battle: they fought better than veterans might be expected to do. Units in the 47th (London) Division with such unwarlike names as the 1/8th Post Office Rifles, and 1/15th Civil Service Rifles, the 1/17th Poplar and Stepney Rifles, surpassed all expectations. The 1/18th London Irish, who were also in the division, went into action by kicking a Rugby football ahead of them as they went forward from the trenches.

Extraordinary courage was shown that day. In the 15th (Scottish) Division, the 7th King's Own Scottish Borderers were virtually wiped out. Pipe-Major Robert MacKenzie, aged sixty, went on piping after he was wounded and until he was killed. As one Scottish unit advanced under fire, a soldier's kilt was caught by a loose strand of barbed wire. He freed it, being careful not to tear it, then ran forward to catch up his comrades and to die with them.

These were Kitchener's army. They had joined because he had asked them to do so, and they fought with magnificent spirit because they wanted to win a victory. Unfortunately many of these units contained men who should not have been there at all. There were medical students, scientists, engineers and chemists; one company in the 6th Cameron Highlanders was composed of the products of Glasgow High School and University. The skills which died with

188

them on that day were desperately missed later in the war, in technical arms.

French's misgivings persisted right up to and into the battle. On 24 April he wrote in his diary: 'I went to see Haig at his headquarters at 11.30 today. I intimated to him *the date*. I asked him to take every precaution to avoid waste of lives.

On 21 August he wrote: 'I had news from Kitchener late yesterday evening saying that they had it on the very best information that Germany was now very short of men. He asked me to urge Joffre to hasten his attack.'

It cannot, however, be said that French's handling of the battle, when it began, was inspired. On the night before it started, he was at Château Philomel, three miles south of Lillers and quite out of touch with the advancing troops. On the second day he spent some time in the field dressing station at Noeux-les-Mines, talking to the wounded and dying. This was an experience which might have turned the stomach of a weaker man, and was undoubtedly compassionate, but whether a dressing station was the correct place for a commander-in-chief in the middle of a battle which could still be won might be questioned.

Hindsight shows that this battle was badly handled at every stage. Troops moving up were misdirected, left unfed; when they made gains they were unsupported. Even so, they nearly won. Although Kitchener lacked the optimism of Joffre, he had an experience of winning wars and he felt that this was the critical time to win this one. If the Allies could break through now, Germany might collapse. Possibly he had absorbed the ideas of the cavalrymen all round him who believed that once there is a breakthrough it can be turned into a rout. This had been true of the eighteenth and nineteenth centuries; unfortunately it would not be true again till 1940, when the cavalry consisted of tanks and were led by gifted commanders such as Rommel.

After Loos Kitchener increased his efforts to produce more shells. There was little point in having guns if they had to be rationed to two shells a day, as had happened in some sectors earlier. He was appalled to find that, while men were dying in the trenches, those at home would go on strike for more pay, for better conditions. Sometimes the munitions workers workers worked so poorly that shells were defective. However, by appealing to workers personally in the factories—and he had never been a skilled orator—he achieved improvements. He persuaded the unions to accept previously unacceptable working practices and also to let women work in the factories.

But there were those who felt that this was not enough and that Kitchener should not be concerning himself with arms production at all. He had already been attacked by Northcliffe in both *The Times* and the *Daily Mail*. In the coalition government which had now been formed, Bonar Law, the Conservative leader who was now Colonial Secretary, joined forces with Lloyd George to try to oust Kitchener from power. But Asquith, very conscious of Kitchener's prestige in the eyes of the soldier and the general public, refused.

Conscription came in January 1916, but even after Loos Kitchener did not approve of it. Like many of his contemporaries, he believed that the voluntary system which had worked so well in the past was more suited to the national temperament and would still meet Britain's needs. Thus the voluntary system had continued under what was known as Lord Derby's Scheme. Derby had been made Director-General of Recruiting and had instituted a system of registration, where a man put his name down and was given a promise that he would not be called up until needed (and that unmarried men would go before married). But even this proved inadequate. There were still a million men who could volunteer but who showed no sign of wanting to do so, as indifferent to calls of patriotism as they were to the white feathers which were presented to them in the streets. There was some justification in this, since by now potential volunteers had learnt something of trench warfare, and of the losses in the Dardanelles. Even Kitchener's forceful personality was not enough to move men to volunteer.

Eventually, after considerable discussion, compulsory registration was brought in by the Military Service Act of 1916. Members of the Cabinet, who saw Kitchener as the symbol of autocracy, now saw a chance of getting rid of him. Churchill had resigned in the previous November, accepting the blame for the failure of the Dardanelles expedition. The Press, led by Colonel Repington of *The Times*, demanded that Kitchener should follow, blaming him for the lack of munitions, for his part in the Dardanelles plan, and for his support for the disastrous offensive at Loos. While recruitment had depended on Kitchener's name and personality, it would have been obvious folly to try to force him to resign. But now that everyone could be conscripted—a measure which many thought should have been brought in long before—there was no reason to retain him. Or so it seemed. Repington was undoubtedly the man who did most to rouse feelings against Kitchener. He was a friend of Sir John French's and explained French's failure as being entirely due to his having insufficient numbers of shells. He stated firmly: 'Kitchener did not comprehend the importance of artillery, took no effective measures to increase our supplies of it, and concealed the truth from his colleagues in the Cabinet.'

The irony behind the first part of this statement was that it was not Kitchener who had failed to grasp the importance of artillery: it was Henry Wilson and French who had both been in the War Office before 1914, and who were now denouncing him as being responsible for something they themselves should have remedied. And far from not taking measures to increase supplies, Kitchener had placed orders with so many firms that, by the time he met his death, shell production in Britain had increased by over fifty percent. He never received any credit for this increase in production. It was all attributed to a miracle performed by Lloyd George, who became Secretary of State for War a month after Kitchener's death. Undoubtedly Lloyd George did stimulate the production of munitions; but all the initial moves had been made by Kitchener.

The accusation that Kitchener 'had concealed the truth from his colleagues in the Cabinet' was not based on the production figures for munitions, but on the fact that he had despatched 20,000 shells to Gallipoli without broadcasting the fact. In view of the state of security at that time (a German spy was working in the censorship department of the British Post Office), it is hardly surprising that Kitchener was reluctant to disclose military moves to such a leaky audience as the Cabinet. At the time the Dardanelles shells were sent, French had no special need for them as his supplies were adequate.

By 1916 Kitchener was also being blamed by his colleagues for the apparent failure of the Salonika expedition, although this unhappy project had initially been the brainchild of Lloyd George. In January 1915 Lloyd George was Chancellor of the Exchequer, but the responsibilities of that post did not inhibit him from offering his views on strategy. They were original, if not entirely practicable. He suggested withdrawing the entire British Expeditionary Force from France and using it to invade Germany via the Balkans. This expensive ploy was too much for his colleagues to swallow, but through 1915 there was a growing conviction that Britain should take steps to frustrate German moves to crush Serbia. Serbia was the country which the Germans regarded as being responsible for the murder of the Austrian Archduke, for although the man who fired the shot was a Bosnian, he was a member of a Serbian secret society dedicated to revolution. Thus thoughts of vengeance had long been prominent in the thinking of the German high command. In October 1915 the moment seemed right and Serbia was crushed by the combined efforts of a Germany army invading from the north and a Bulgarian one from the east.

The Allies had foreseen the possibility of this German move for some time; they realised that it would probably involve Bulgaria, and that if that country joined Germany a possible supply route to Russia would be closed. And unless the Allies took appropriate action, Greece and Rumania would probably range themselves with Germany and her supporters. Surprisingly Joffre, who might have been expected to oppose any scheme which took troops away from France, now came out in strong support of an invasion of the Balkans and proposed that an attack force of a quarter of a million men should be landed at Salonika (Thessaloniki), a port and the chief city of Greek Macedonia.

It was too late. When the first French divisions landed and marched a hundred miles up to Krivolak they found that the Serbs had already been defeated and that the whole of the Bulgarian Army barred further progress. The French retired to a point some thirty miles north of Salonika, where British divisions were now installed. The invasion force was then built up to strength, incidentally requiring huge quantities of shipping to supply it. It stayed in that area for the next three years, making a few ineffective attacks but never any real progress. Subsequently, when excuses were sought for this wasteful enterprise, one was found in a statement which Hindenburg made when explaining the German defeat. He claimed that the German armies in France had been unable to sustain the Allied onslaught because too much of the Fatherland's energies were being diverted to supporting Turkey and warding off Allied assaults in the Balkans.

Kitchener had at first believed that another diversionary attack, when the Dardanelles expedition was in such deep trouble, would be the utmost folly. This was also the view of the British general staff. But, comforted by Joffre's enthusiasm, Kitchener at first wavered, then came out solidly in support. Joffre, it seems, felt that it was necessary for the Allies to appear to be taking positive action to win the war at that time, for peace parties in France were suggesting that the existing trench stalemate offered an ideal opportunity to begin negotiations with the Germans.

1915 had been a year of spectacular failures. There had been costly losses in France at Festubert, at Ypres, at Neuve-Chapelle and Loos; the Gallipoli expedition had been a chronicle of disaster, and the efforts to produce more munitions had so far fallen short of their target. None of these could be fairly blamed on Kitchener, but he *was* Secretary of State for War as well as the most visibly influential military figure so, inevitably, critical eyes fell on him. There exists a natural but not necessarily logical belief that if a country experiences

192

a series of disasters there must be a fault in its leadership. Thus in 1942, when British fortunes seemed at a very low ebb, the British armies had been defeated in Burma, Singapore, Crete and North Africa, Churchill was heavily criticised in Parliament. There were some who thought he should resign. One shudders to think of what might have happened if he had been forced to do so. But even in coalition governments, such as Britain had in both world wars, politicians never seem able to forget party politics. In 1915 Kitchener, a known Conservative, with the (false) reputation of opposing liberal ideas everywhere from Delhi to Whitehall, had few friends even among members of the party he supported. King George V, who was well aware of the pressures on the Secretary of State for War, appointed him a Knight of the Garter that summer, and wherever he went the general public and the troops cheered him, but these were not the places where real power lay. The press, which had a long-standing grudge against him, was not so much seeking revenge as seeing in him a target for a campaign. The press was now fully aware of its powers, though perhaps less of its responsibility. Journalists have to make a living by inducing people to buy their newspapers and few campaigns sell papers as well as does an attack on a previously respected public figure.

There was also the entirely natural view that once a man's reputation is linked with failure he should be replaced, even if the newcomer has a less distinguished record. The newcomer may have new ideas and new enthusiasms, with the energy to make his plans work. He might also be a more congenial colleague than his predecessor and that is good for everyone's morale.

'No man is indispensable', so the truism goes. Nevertheless, some men are considerably more dispensable than others, while some leave places which are very hard to fill. The fact that the war continued and was won after Kitchener's death shows clearly enough that he was not indispensable. It has, however, been suggested that if he had not died he would have continued to have an important influence on events. He *might* have prevented the disasters in Russia which led to the revolution and the humiliating Treaty of Brest-Litovsk; he *might* have influenced strategy in early 1918 and prevented the German breakthough; and it is thought that if he had been present at Versailles he would have influenced the treaty-makers to be less forthright and thus avoided the bitterness which prepared men's minds for the next conflict.

But in 1916 Kitchener's Cabinet colleagues had to make their plans on the basis that he would be with them for the remainder of the war unless efforts were made to remove him. They were tired of him—as he was of them. His only real friend was Asquith, yet not even Asquith would be able to resist a concerted move to send Kitchener to a different post, perhaps to India to become Viceroy at long last. Certainly he needed a rest. He was no longer the young man who was able to work all day and half the night, missing meals and never relaxing. When he went off to the Dardanelles in late 1915 he was as glad to go as his colleagues were to be rid of him for a while. He had never suffered fools (or what he thought to be fools) gladly, and he was too shy and reserved to make many friends. If an eminent man is incapable of making people feel at ease on first acquaintance, they are unlikely to put this down to his shyness: they are more likely to think he despises them and to hate him for it. Surrounded by politicians who were experts at making chance acquaintances seem like old and trusted friends, Kitchener seemed especially maladroit.

Seventy years later it is easy to forget the atmosphere of 1915. A Liberal government had been forced into declaring war by the violation of the neutral territory of its Belgian ally. Britain had been hopelessly unprepared and had only by the narrowest margin averted disaster when an apparently invincible German war machine swept forward to capture the French capital. Since those early, confusing days, the country had settled down on seeing the best of its youth sent to the trenches and steadily massacred. Attempts to vary the pattern at Gallipoli and Salonika had produced further sacrifice, added to humiliation. There had been disasters at sea, where previously Britain had been thought to be supreme. Rationing and the dislocation of war were making everyone's life less comfortable. The war which should have been over by Christmas 1914 now looked as if it would drag on till every able-bodied man in Britian and Germany had been killed. A general attitude of despondency had settled over the home front. Britain had been lucky to have a veteran commander in Kitchener, but even Kitchener seemed to have lost his ability to win victories and avoid heavy casualties in doing so. Perhaps he was, indeed, too old by now.

When the Germans launched their massive assault on Verdun in February 1916 the British Army was unable to do more than take over French sectors around Arras and thus release French troops for Verdun. A British offensive on the German lines in another sector, which would have helped relieve the pressure on Verdun and perhaps also make a significant breakthough, was simply not possible. Subsequently, when an attack *was* possible, at the beginning of July 1, in what became known as the battle of the Somme, Kitchener was already dead. So, not long after, were several thousand British troops who had been launched by Haig onto well-defended German positions. During the next few months a few miles were won at a cost of some 450,000 British casualties. It was still not enough. After their heroic defence of Verdun, and the loss of hundreds of thousands of men, the French Army began to disintegrate. The British were once more forced to take the offensive, this time in what became known as the battle of Passchendaele, a nightmare of mud, blood and confusion. It is easy to criticise what now seem to have been inept, rigid, callous policies, but the fact that both sides seemed to make the same mistakes suggests that the problems were greater than were men's ability to solve them. One excuse given for the relentless battering of the German lines in France is that the Allies were trying to reduce German pressure on Russia and prevent that country from making a separate peace. It is believed by some that if Kitchener had reached Russia he would have been able to talk to the opposition leaders and to persuade them to postpone the revolution till after the end of the war. There is, of course, no reason to suppose that he would have been successful, but it is worthwhile to remember that the first steps to revolution were taken by moderates.

By 1916 Kitchener was well aware that he had lost the confidence of his colleagues, but it did not cause him to think of resignation. Thoughts of resigning had occurred to many of his colleagues. Asquith himself would do so by the end of that year, but only after Lloyd George and several other ministers had also done so. But whereas they all thought that they would eventually return to positions of power and influence, Kitchener held no such conviction. He knew that if he left the Cabinet he would not take part in future war councils and, doubting the ability of others to shoulder burdens as effectively as he himself could even when old and tired, he intended hanging on to power as long as possible. Richard Kellet quotes him as saying to the Earl of Derby at this time: 'There is one thing I hope to live for, and that is to be on the British delegation when peace is made.'

When asked by Derby if he had any special views to put forward, he replied, 'Yes, not to take one country's territory and give it to another.'

'Would you take Alsace and Lorraine from Germany and give them to France?'

'No, there would be a war of revenge. And leave Germany with her colonies. They afford a safety valve; the Germans could go there peacefully and so not make war for the sake of new territory.'[1]

Wars usually seem to continue too long for there to be generous

[1] Quoted in *The King's Shilling*, a book distributed to Kitchener scholars (see Chapter 12).

peace treaties; the Boer War was an exception because Kitchener made it so. Any thoughts of generosity which might have existed in the minds of the Allies in 1916 had long disappeared by 1918. Clemenceau was talking of squeezing the German orange till the pips squeaked and this attitude, combined with woolly-minded ideas of re-drawing the map of Europe, prevailed. However, there was no more prospect of the First World War ending in 1916 than there was of the Second World War ending in 1942, when it too had reached the halfway point.

Chapter 12

The Final Stage

On 27 May 1916 the Czar sent Kitchener an invitation to visit Russia. Even though Kitchener's reputation was somewhat dimmed in Britain in 1916, it remained as bright as ever elsewhere. Sir George Arthur wrote: 'When the crisis came and Russia was stretched upon the rack, the name of the British Soldier-Statesman was familiar to rank and file hanging on grimly to trenches on the Dvina and in the Ukraine who had never heard of Joffre, and it was sounded in the workshops of Putiloff and Jula by artificers ignorant of the existence of Elswick and Essen.'[1] If this seems a sweeping claim, one may recall that during the Second World War the rank-and-file German and Japanese soldiers were well aware of the name of Churchill, and that Allied soldiers not merely knew the name and reputation of Rommel, but regarded him in many cases with more respect than they had for our own generals.

The party selected to make the visit, which was arranged almost immediately, added up to thirteen, including one detective-inspector and three servants. It was to embark at Scapa Flow on 5 June and sail to Archangel on the cruiser *Hampshire*.

Arrangements were apparently not finalised until the afternoon of 2 June. Kitchener spent the night of Saturday 3rd and the morning of Sunday 4th at Broome, where he dealt with personal papers, including some relating to the estate in Kenya. He expected to be back from Russia within three weeks, but not likely to be at Broome until a week later. He spoke of looking forward to seeing the rose garden at its summer best on his return. He went back to London that afternoon, and the same evening boarded the night train at Kings Cross. He was reported to have been somewhat pensive just before the train left, which caused speculation afterwards as to whether he

---

[1] Sir George Arthur, *Life of Lord Kitchener* (London 1920).

had a premonition that he might be setting off on his last journey. On arrival at Thurso the next day, the 5th, he boarded the destroyer *Oak* and then transferred to the *Iron Duke* at midday. In the flagship he was received by Admiral Sir John Jellicoe and lunched with the other flag officers of the fleet. He was spontaneously cheered by the sailors, who seemed delighted to see him on board.

The water was rough, for there was a north-east gale blowing, but this did not seem to trouble Kitchener, who had always been a good sailor. At 4.15 he left the *Iron Duke* and boarded the *Hampshire*. Jellicoe knew that however good a sailor a man is, a heavy buffeting in gale force winds imposes a strain which is better avoided, and therefore arranged that the *Hampshire* should sail on the leeside of the Orkneys and Shetlands, and avoid the worst of it. Arthur wrote of this: 'By an unhappy error of judgement an unswept channel was chosen for the passage of the cruiser and Kitchener—the secret of whose journey had been betrayed—was to fall into the machinations of England's enemies and to die swiftly at their hands.' Arthur, who had been Kitchener's military secretary, does not produce any evidence in support of his statement that 'the secret of his journey had been betrayed'. It is, of course, possible that the Germans knew of it, for they had spies in Russia as well as in this country, but the sinking of the cruiser was fortuitous. The mine which sank her had been in position before Kitchener had agreed to make the journey. It had been laid by U-boat No. 475 commanded by Lt-Commander Kurt Beitzen, along with twenty-one other mines, on 28 May, with the purpose of blocking one of the exits from Scapa Flow. At that time, the German high seas fleet was preparing to come out of harbour and range the North Sea. As soon as it emerged, it was certain to be intercepted by the British fleet, and the fewer units of the latter it encountered the better would be its chance of success.

The positioning of the mines seems to have been less effective than the Germans had at first hoped. When the German fleet set out on the morning of the 31st, with a plan to destroy the British by luring them into a situation where they would be vulnerable to attack by U-boats, the British had already swept the channels they intended to use when Admiral Scheer's ships made their long-awaited move. However, the channel which the *Hampshire* was destined to use had not been swept, as the Germans had not previously mined a channel so far north. It had been used by merchant ships before without mishap.

The weather worsened after the *Hampshire* set forth, but that was regarded as a good sign, for it meant that submarines would not be operating. The sea soon proved too heavy for the escorting destroyers; they could not keep station and were therefore ordered back. Had they stayed with the *Hampshire* a little longer, they could not have averted the disaster and might well have met one of their own, but they *might* have picked up a few more survivors.

At 7.40 p.m. an explosion almost cut the *Hampshire* in half, and she sank within ten minutes. She was a mile and a half off Marwick Head, where the coast consists of dark cliffs which rise sheer. There were fourteen survivors, all of whom got away on rafts, but two of them died of exposure before they were rescued. First Class Petty Officer Wilfred Wesson was one of the survivors and gave the following account immediately afterwards:

At 5 o'clock on the afternoon of Monday, June 5th, we embarked Lord Kitchener and his Staff on a special mission, but we did not know where we were going with them. The weather was very rough, so rough that the two destroyers which escorted us were sent back. At 8 p.m., while the watch below were standing by their hammocks ready to turn in, an explosion occurred. I was on the mess deck at the time. When the explosion happened all lights immediately went out and a terrible draught came rushing along the mess deck, blowing all the men's caps off. We did not know what had happened, so we walked aft to the only hatch that had not been battened down owing to the bad weather. While I was waiting with the others on the half-deck an officer came with Lord Kitchener from the captain's cabin. He called out: 'Make room for Lord Kitchener!' and the men opened out to let Lord Kitchener pass. He went on deck and I did not see any more of him after that.

Leading Seaman Charles Walter Rogerson carried the story a little further:

I was the last of the survivors to see Lord Kitchener before leaving the ship. In the papers I notice that his Lordship is said to have been drowned by the overturning of a boat, but this is not correct. Lord Kitchener went down with the ship. He did not leave her. I saw Captain Savill helping his boat's crew to clear a way to the galley. The captain at this time was calling to Lord Kitchener to go to the boat, but owing to the noise of the wind and the sea Lord Kitchener apparently could not hear him. When the explosion occurred Lord Kitchener walked calmly from the captain's cabin, went up the ladder and on to the quarter-deck. There I saw him walking quite coolly and collectedly up and down, talking to two of his officers. All three were wearing khaki without overcoats. In fact, they were dressed just as they were when they boarded the ship.

Lord Kitchener did not seem in the least perturbed, but calmly awaited the preparations for abandoning the ship, which were going on in a quiet, steady, and orderly way. The crew went to their stations, obeying orders steadily, and did their best to get out the boats, but that proved impossible. Owing to the rough weather no boats could be lowered; those that we got out were smashed up at once. No boats left the ship. What the people on shore thought to be boats leaving were three rafts. Men did get into the boats as they lay in their cradles, thinking that as the ship went from under them the boats would float. But the ship sank by the head, and when she did she turned a complete somersault forward, carrying down with her all the boats and those in them. I do not think Lord Kitchener got into a boat at all. When I sprang on to a raft he was still on the starboard side of the quarter-deck talking to his officers. I won't say he did not feel the strain of the perilous situation like the rest of us, but he gave no outward sign of nervousness, and from the little time that elapsed between my leaving the ship and her sinking I feel certain that Lord Kitchener went down with her, standing on the deck at the time. Of the civilian members of his suite I saw nothing.

Although I do not really know what happened, my belief is that the *Hampshire* struck a mine, which exploded under her fore-part. It could not have been a submarine in such weather. An internal explosion in one of the magazines would have ripped the ship apart. It was hard luck to come to such an end after going through the Horn Reef battle unscathed. In that battle we led the *Iron Duke* into action, and our shells sank a German light cruiser and two submarines. We did not have a single casualty on our ship, although big shells fairly rained into the water all around us.[1]

The Secretary of the Admiralty also published its own account of the conclusions arrived at as a result of the inquiry held into the loss of the *Hampshire*:

The *Hampshire* was proceeding along the west coast of the Orkneys; a heavy gale was blowing, with the seas breaking over the ship, which necessitated her being partially battened down.

Between 7.30 and 7.45 p.m. the vessel struck a mine and began at once to settle by the bows, heeling over to starboard before she finally went down about fifteen minutes after.

Orders were given by the captain for all hands to go to their established stations for abandoning ship. Some of the hatches

[1] Reported in *The Times*.

were opened and the ship's company went quickly to their stations.

Efforts were made without success to lower some of the boats, one of them being broken in half during the process and her occupants thrown into the water.

As the men were moving up one of the hatchways to their stations, Lord Kitchener, accompanied by a Naval Officer, appeared; the latter called out, 'Make way for Lord Kitchener,' and they both went up on to the Quarter Deck, and subsequently four Military Officers were seen on the Quarter Deck walking aft on the port side.

The Captain called out for Lord Kitchener to come up to the fore bridge near where the Captain's boat was hoisted; he was also heard calling for Lord Kitchener to get into the boat, but no one is able to say whether Lord Kitchener got into the boat or not, nor what happened to this boat, nor did any one see any of the boats get clear of the ship.

Large numbers of the crew used their life-saving belts, waistcoats, etc., which appear to have proved effective in keeping them afloat.

Three rafts were safely launched, and, with about fity to seventy men on each of them, got clear of the ship.

A private soldier appears to have left the ship on one of the rafts, but it is not known what became of him.

It was light up to about 11 p.m.

Though the rafts with these large numbers of men got safely away, in one case out of over seventy men on board, six only survived; the survivors all report that men gradually dropped off and even died on board the rafts from exhaustion, exposure, and cold. Some of the crew must have perished trying to land on the rocky coast after such long exposure, and some died after landing.

The news of Kitchener's death came as a stunning shock to the nation. Before the announcement, at midday on 6 June, the public had been quite unaware that he was not still in London. It was, for many, too great a shock to be believed.

Strange legends quickly grew up. The fact that his body was not among those washed up gave rise to the curious belief that he was a prisoner of the Germans. Some believed, rather more romantically, that he had found refuge in a cave under those dark and threatening cliffs and in due course would emerge like some Nordic god. One version of the same story was that he was now in an enchanted sleep, like Rip Van Winkle or Drake, and would wake at his country's hour of greatest need. Kitchener's sister Frances, known as Millie and now Mrs Parker, refused to believe that her brother could be dead, and frequently said so. She appears to have been a woman of strong convictions. She was a firm believer in a phenomenon which became known as 'the Unseen Hand'. 'The Unseen Hand' was believed to be a sinister but immensely powerful organisation which was dedicated to the downfall of Britain. At that moment it was controlled from Berlin but was not exclusively German. Among the many meetings held by people anxious to persuade the government to take action against this evil though intangible menace was one of the Women's Imperial Defence League, chaired by Millie Parker. And why not? The Unseen Hand had already encompassed the death of her brother, and was also hard at work subverting senior officers, politicians, journalists and anyone assisting Britain to win the war. An immediate and necessary first step was to eradicate people with any German-sounding name or German characteristics from all important posts. 'Important posts' were not limited to those in the government but also included the world of commerce; Millie Parker's injunction, if carried out, would have opened up promotion prospects considerably in both fields. The words 'Make Way for Lord Kitchener', which at first were repeated in awed tones, soon acquired a jocund flavour. They were shouted cheerfuly by soldiers when carrying burdens of one sort or another, and continued to be used in that way into the Second World War.

Later there were more appropriate memorials. A white marble statue of Kitchener was placed in St Paul's Cathedral in the memorial chapel and dedicated to him on 10 December 1925; there is another statue of him in the Horse Guards. Innumerable pictures and mementos of him were made and sold. There was a feeling that if his memory was kept alive, his spirit and wisdom would continue to guide the country. A number of books were written about him, but as the country was still at war the general pattern was of uncritical eulogy. Some, however, contrived to be balanced and fair. Subsequently the standard work was the three-volume study by Sir George Arthur, which was published in 1920. It was criticised as being a little too flattering and, in spite of its length, not quite comprehensive. It contained prefaces by the Marquis of Salisbury (son of the former Prime Minister) and Earl Haig. Both men knew him well, but Salisbury had had the opportunity of observing Kitchener the man as well as Kitchener the soldier. He described Kitchener as 'a solitary figure, solitary in the sense that he stood mentally and morally aloof from other men'. He continued: 'It is indeed true that he considered weakness a crime and sentiment as involving a danger to vigorous action, but probably this was his conviction because he was acutely conscious of the softer side of his own character.... Interwoven with firmness of purpose there was in him almost the quality of a child—the simplicity of a child and a measure of a child's irresponsible audacity—which created towards him amongst his intimate subordinates an attitude of affectionate amusement alongside of their profound admiration and respect.'

Others were not so generous, though appearing to be so. Viscount Esher published a book in 1921 entitled *The Tragedy of Lord Kitchener*. Of this, one could use Pope's words:

> Damn with faint praise, assent with civil leer
> and, without sneering, teach the rest to sneer.

After the First World War Kitchener gradually receded from the memory of the public. The memorials had been dedicated, the tributes given. He was almost forgotten when 'Sir Philip Magnus-Allcroft, writing under the name of Philip Magnus, published in 1958 a candid and comprehensive book with the title: *Kitchener: Portrait of an Imperialist*. Apart from one or two passages, it seems a fair portrait. But in his final chapter he delivered some judgements which caused annoyance. One of them ran: 'Kitchener's thoroughness constrained him to swing his boot into any system of administration, and to rend in pieces any established chain of command. His system was, in reality, the negation of any system; and his drive prompted him inexorably to centralise every species of authority in himself.' Critics who contented themselves with reading the first and last chapters of this book found the summary objectionable and unfair. But, although one might question the wisdom of labelling Kitchener as 'an imperialist' at a time when desperate attempts were being made to free the colonies as soon as possible (or even before), one cannot rightly describe this scholarly study as unfair.

Subsequently George H. Cassar, a Canadian professor at an American university, produced an even more comprehensive life, entitled *Kitchener: Architect of Victory*. Professor Cassar, who spent many years preparing this book, had clearly seen everyone and read everything which could illuminate the subject. The fact that his preface began with the words, 'No man since Wellington exercised so strong a hold as Kitchener had on the faith and loyalty of the English people', caused some disquiet. Potential readers wondered whether Cassar had heard of Wolseley, Roberts or Churchill. But Cassar's industry and scholarship are impressive and, if readers did not always agree with his judgements, this was on the whole because it is always difficult, if not impossible, for anyone reared on the other side of the Atlantic to understand what goes on in the British mind. Europeans face similar problems when trying to comprehend American opinions.

Cassar was very severe with Magnus. He described his book as having 'ignored key issues or treated them superficially'. He wrote: 'An almost contemptuous deprecation of Kitchener and his work pervaded this text. Disparagement was always conveyed with indulgent regret and always with a note, puzzling as well as tiresome, of intellectual superiority. The Kitchener of Sir Philip Magnus appeared more like a figure out of mythology than a human being.' Cassar continued, at length, to describe why he considered that Magnus's opinions were incorrect.

Among the many people who, at one time or another, formed and expressed opinions of Kitchener, few were as well qualified to do so as Sir William Robertson, who became chief of the general staff in December 1915. Robertson had had ample opportunity to separate the true from the false since he had enlisted as a cavalry trooper at the age of seventeen thirty-eight years earlier. On being offered the appointment of CIGS, Robertson felt somewhat apprehensive of the difficulties of working with Kitchener and requested to be left in France. Kitchener knew what this reluctance implied, said that he was well aware of his own 'unenviable reputation', but asked Robertson not to believe in it. Robertson then made several requests affecting his own new responsibilities and was surprised to find Kitchener making no objections. In Robertson's book *From Private to Field Marshal*, he wrote: 'He was easily the most outstanding personality at the Allied conference, and was listened to with more deference than was vouchsafed to any one else during the two and a half years that I attended these meetings. . . . Without quite knowing why sometimes, he had a wonderful knack of being right in the things which really mattered.

'For some months before his death it was common talk that his relations with certain members of the Government were far from happy and that intrigues were on foot to get him removed from the Cabinet . . . . I had not been a week in the War Office before I was warned by a friend that "they" hoped I would "down K". He did not say who "they" were and my reply was I was not concerned with "downing" anyone, and certainly not Lord Kitchener.

'Like some great men Lord Kitchener was exacting, and had no use whatever for those who raised petty difficulties at a time when prompt action was required; while as to his alleged habit of over-centralisation all I can say is that it was never displayed during the six months I had with him, and that he was as ready to listen to the advice of his departmental heads as were any of the other seven Secretaries of State under whom I have worked. Nor did he disclose any sign of that ruthless and domineering disposition attributed to him by those who wished to injure his good name. On the contrary he was a kind and delightful chief to serve, once his ways were understood, and I know that he many times stood up against opposition in high quarters so as to protect officers who were threatened with unfair treatment.'

Robertson considered that for Kitchener to have come to the Cabinet and succeed without any previous experience of politics was an astonishing achievement. He pointed out that not even the 'systematically prepared' Germans had foreseen the vast demand for munitions which the war would bring. But Kitchener, he said, was so alive to the necessity for increasing the output of munitions that 'when proposals of this kind were submitted to him he usually doubled the amount recommended, thus earning for himself the nickname of a "doubler" '. He added: 'On the whole I would say that the achievements and foresight of Lord Kitchener place him in a class entirely by himself, and they justify the conclusion that no man in any of the Entente countries accomplished more, if as much, to bring about the final defeat of the enemy.'

Robertson was a keen supporter of the idea of using tanks. The trials of the first tank, known as 'Mother', took place in February 1916 at Hatfield. Those present were doubtful about the use of this unwieldy monster in battle but Kitchener saw possibilities and agreed to Robertson's proposal that a hundred should be ordered. The following September fifty tanks went into action on the Somme. By then Kitchener had been dead for three months.

The most valuable memorial to Kitchener was undoubtedly the National Memorial Fund which was launched to provide for disabled officers and men of the Navy and Army. Its aim was to enable a disabled man to live at home, rather than be immured for life in an institution. It also provided for a number of scholarships which would enable young men to travel abroad. Later this was extended to cater for general educational needs. Scholarships were reserved for the sons of deceased and disabled officers and men. The Fund published a book of tributes to Kitchener. They came from Joffre, from Count Cadorna, chief of the general staff of the Italian Army, from Field-Marshal Lord Birdwood, from Arthur Henderson, the Labour MP who described Kitchener as being 'entirely free from the spirit of intrigue' and, in conversation, a man of 'good humour, homely sense, and frank comradeship.... A true soldier, he recognised that no sector of the nation contributed more in human wealth than did the working class. I found him free from prejudice and frankly and sincerely sympathetic in his attitude towards Labour.'

The book also contained extracts from Kitchener's own speeches in the House of Lords. It concluded with speeches made in Parliament by the Marquess of Lansdowne, Viscount French, H. H. Asquith, Bonar Law and G. J. Wardle, Chairman of the Labour Party. Wardle said, 'The working men of the country have a sure instinct for feeling worth and recognising worth when it is evident, and I believe in the case of Lord Kitchener there was no man, although to them he was largely a legend, in whom they had greater confidence and in whom they believed more firmly. They could rely upon his word, and it is that which in their hearts, I think, will be a much more imperishable monument than any monument of stone which this House may erect to his memory.' Kitchener would have been agreeably surprised to hear this opinion from such a quarter. But it is an appropriate epitaph.

Kitchener was an enigmatic figure. Perhaps his enormous popularity with the general public was the most extraordinary fact about him. Certainly his achievements in winning the Sudan campaign and the South African War were considerable, but they were in far distant countries and there was no reason why British public should have warmed to him as it did. His appearance was forbidding and his manner unsympathetic. His enormous moustache was greatly admired by many, but it seemed a barrier between the man and the outside world. Victorian fashion encouraged men to grow long beards, moustaches, and side whiskers, but these made their owner look unapproachable and severe. Kitchener, one feels, hid behind that huge moustache. Perhaps the secret of Kitchener's appeal to the public, to both men and women, was that he was the quintessential military figure, the strong, silent man. He was tall, had piercing blue eyes set widely apart, was accustomed to command and radiated confidence. He neither sought nor refused popularity. He had both foresight and forebearance. He was a soldier who knew how to make war, but he also knew how to make peace.

Appendix 1

Woolwich in the Kitchener Period

(The Story of a Batch, 1863 to 1865, told by one of them)

It seems a very short time since I went up for Woolwich in July, 1863. At that time the examination was always held at the Royal Hospital, Chelsea, where the dining-hall was fitted up for the reception of the candidates. Of these, 138 attended to compete for thirty-four cadet-ships. One was rejected as medically unfit, and one was dismissed for writing rude remarks on the papers! The medical inspection was held first; this was a good arrangement, as anyone found unfit was saved the trouble of going through the examination. The latter lasted from the 3rd to the 18th July, either one or two papers being given each day, and it was rather a relief when it came to an end.

We joined at Woolwich on the 12th August, thirty-six strong, a few days later than the older cadets.

At this time the course of study lasted two and a half years, or five terms. The year was divided up as follows: The winter vacation terminated about the last days of January. The first (or spring) term then commenced, and, with the exception of a break of a few days at Easter, continued until the beginning of June, when the term examinations were held. The 'Shop' broke up at the end of June, and then there was a vacation of six weeks until the beginning of August, when the second (or autumn) term commenced. This lasted until early in December, when study stopped for the examinations, the winter vacation being about the 22nd. The two terms and two vacations were therefore of equal length, and the division of each could be made very easily.

The Cadet Company was divided into the 'A', 'B', and 'C' Divisions, the first consisting exclusively of the first class, who were to be commissioned at the next examination. The 'A' Division worked completely apart from the rest of us, and had a separate dining-room—generally called the 'eating-house' to distinguish it from the dining-hall.

When we joined, the work of the day was divided as follows: Defaulters' parade at 6.15 a.m., which all cadets in arrest or undergoing punishment-drill had to attend. Breakfast at 7. For this meal, and for dinner and tea, each subdivision paraded separately; and, after being inspected by the subdivisional under officer, were marched up and paraded as a division. One of the subaltern officers then marched it to the dining-hall.

When breakfast was over, Mr. F–, the chaplain, came into the hall and read prayers. He was not a good reader, and always pronounced 'Amen' as if written 'Ow-wow!' Hence he was usually known as 'Ow-wow', and prayers as 'Ow-wow-stuff'. It was rather a relief when he was absent and the lieutenant on duty read prayers.

The first parade for study was at 8 a.m., when the cadets fell in by classes, not by divisions, and were marched to the class-rooms by the corporals on duty. The inspection of clothing was less minute than on drill and meal parades; but a serious matter—such as a button being off a tunic—was, of course, punished with an extra drill. Academy lasted until 11, when a quarter of an hour was given to get ready for drill parade. Drill usually went on from 11.15 to 12.45, its nature varying with the different classes.

At 1 p.m. the cadets paraded for dinner with the same formalities as for breakfast. The second parade for study was at 2 p.m., and we remained in Academy until 4. We were then free until 6; and hungry cadets could have lunch of bread and cheese and beer in the dining-hall from 4.30 to 5.30 p.m.

Third-study parade was at 6, and work went on for two hours. Then came tea parade at 8. After that we could do as we liked until 10.30 p.m., when all lights were put out.

The food was plain, but good and plentiful, and as we had to work pretty hard, the meals were very acceptable.

When I joined I was placed in a room in the front barracks with three other cadets. All the front barracks were similarly occupied, and it was rare that a cadet had a room to himself until his fourth term. Pocket-money was issued weekly to each cadet at the rate of 5s. for a responsible under officer, 3s.6d. for an under officer, 2s.6d. for a corporal, and 2s. for a cadet. This was supposed to come out of our pay; but, as the pay-sheets were usually in debt, it was really paid by the parents and guardians.

The course of study in the fifth class included mathematics, practical geometry, topography, drawing, French and German, gymnastics and infantry drill. Mathematics was always spoken of as

208

'swot', practical geometry as 'peter-stuff', because it was taught by Professor Thomas Bradley, generally known as 'Peter'. He was an excellent teacher who managed to get a good deal into the heads of the cadets. Topography was naturally called 'gore-stuff', as the professor was Major Gore.

Battalion drill was known as 'of-stuff', a word of which the following was the derivation: The sergeant-major of artillery who instructed us, and who did so very efficiently, had a loud voice, and, when a cadet made a mistake, always shouted, 'What are you a-doing of?' Naturally he was known as 'Of', and his special subject as 'of-stuff'. I do not know whether the word is maintained as an Academy tradition. If so, probably the origin is lost.

When winter came on the hours were slightly altered. Breakfast was at 8.0 and the first Academy parade at 9 o'clock; otherwise the course of the day's work was the same. Fires were allowed in the bedrooms, but there was no hot water in the baths. Sometimes, if the first-comer, one had to break the ice. Shirking bath, however, cold the weather, was regarded by the cadets as a serious offence. I remember on one occasion a cadet, who was suspected of doing so, being taken after parade and immersed in his tunic and busby!

Our first examination was held on December 9th, 1863, and 'Duke's Day' on the 20th, after which we went home until February 2nd, 1864.

In the fourth class the course of study was the same as in the fifth, except that we had fortification in addition to the subjects already mentioned. We looked down with dignity on the 'last-joined'—the wretched 'snooker'—and felt we were really very old cadets! The term passed quietly, and I can remember no particular incident. Our class remained of the same number as before, as, though two had dropped out of it, two others had dropped into it from the class above. The examinations began on June 8th and the vacation on the 22nd.

When we rejoined on August 3rd, I had the satisfaction of being given a room to myself on the east wing. Our class had increased by four cadets joining it from the one above. We began surveying and higher mathematics, the latter under Professor Sylvester, a splendid mathematician, but totally incapable of teaching cadets. As a natural result, order was usually badly kept in his Academy, and sundry measures of annoying him were indulged in with success by the cadets. One plan, which was occasionally tried, was for a large number of them to drop down behind their desks. Sylvester would suddenly awake from the solution of some abstruse problem and see the class-room half empty. This made him rush up and down, a movement which was prepared for by sprinkling the floor round his table with wax matches, which went off in succession as he stamped round, driving him quite wild. Another trick was to fill his ink-bottle with chalk, which clogged his pens and made him mad! But with all his little ways, he could teach well if he was allowed his own method, and personally I owe a good deal to him

October, 1864, was rather an eventful month. It opened by a tremendous explosion on the 1st at the Erith Powder Magazine, when about eighty tons of gunpowder (at least, we believed that was the amount) blew up.[1] We were just getting ready for parade when we heard the explosion, which shook the Academy like an earthquake, and then saw a great column of black smoke rising slowly and spreading out into a cloud in the sky.

The following day, curiously enough, an uneasy feeling began to be manifest in the R.M.A. The first symptom was a disturbance in the class-room where Professor Sylvester presided. The corporal on duty failed to quell it, and the assistant inspector of studies had to be called in. Then followed a row of which I have forgotten the particulars, which ended in the rustication of two cadets.

A little later in the month came Charlton Fair, against attending which there were very strict orders. Two cadets were seen by an officer to be at the fair, and placed in arrest on their return to barracks. After due investigation of the case, they were added to the rusticated, and when the order was read out on parade, it was received with a loud murmur. This, of course, was a very serious military offence, and, in consequence, one class was placed in arrest, and all the other cadets were confined to barracks. This was regarded as an unfair proceeding, as it punished the innocent as well as the guilty.

That night the disturbance culminated. One of the field-guns on the parade was fired towards the Governor's house, and all the swords which the cadets carried during punishment drill were thrown into the reservoir. One of the two cadets who had been rusticated, but had not yet been sent away, left his barrack-room and, jumping over the ditch, made his escape. He was pursued by two of the drill sergeants, who jumped into the ditch after him, and then grappled together, each thinking the other was the delinquent cadet. The latter, in the meantime, got away!

Matters were then regarded as very serious by the authorities, and on the following day a Board of Inquiry was sent down from London to investigate. The first step taken by them was a very sensible one,

[1] There were two magazines. The exact quantity of powder was never ascertained, but it was roughly calculated to be over 200 tons.

to remove the ban of confinement to barracks. The Board sat for some days and examined a number of cadets to try and find out the reasons for the row. I really do not think there were any valid ones, and can only suppose that it was due to a bacillus of unrest which developed itself about once in two years, generally in October.[1] The final result was that one cadet was sent away for good, others were rusticated, and some corporals reduced to the ranks.

The row ended rather unsatisfactorily for me, for, although not due for promotion until the following term, I was made a corporal in place of one of those who had been broken, and was sent to the front barracks to take charge of a four room. I thus lost my single room in the wing for the rest of the term, and having to take my tour of duty, had less spare time than before. One or two small ebullitions of feeling succeeded, but the unquiet spirit had worked itself out by the middle of November, when all settled down to work for the December examinations. In these, the examinations in mathematics, practical geometry and drawing were final, and the marks for them were carried on to the end of the whole course. As a natural result the third-class examinations went a long way in deciding which cadets were to get sappers and which were to become gunners. The competition, therefore, was very keen in the upper half of the class.

On the 22nd of December the Duke of Cambridge came down as usual, but the proceedings were of rather a different character from the customary course. The cadets were all paraded in undress uniform and marched into the gymnasium, where the Duke addressed them as to the iniquities of the past term. This well over, the usual full-dress parade, inspection, and prize-giving were held, and the Academy broke up for the winter vacation.

We rejoined on the 31st January, 1865, and as my batch had now attained the dignity of the second class, we had to take charge of the discipline of the R.M.A. I was made responsible under officer of 'B' Division, a position that might have been troublesome in the previous term, but a peacable spirit had come over the establishment now.

Of course, our studies became more practical, and we took up artillery, surveying, chemistry, and—what a good many liked best of all—riding. It was a great improvement having so much work in the open air, and the half-year passed quickly. The June examinations were succeeded by the usual vacations, and we met again for the last

[1] Possibly in commemoration of the mutiny of 1861. The tradition that a great victory over the authorities had then been gained had been handed down—probably strengthened by the subsequent change of governors and company officers.

term on the 2nd August. My class became the senior, or 'A' Division, and our interests separated from the rest of the Academy, as we always paraded and had our meals by ourselves.

This term a change, which was regarded as a great innovation, was introduced into the 'B' and 'C' Divisions, who were allowed to have tea in their rooms instead of being marched into the dining-hall. But in the 'A' Division we decided by a large majority against the alteration, as we could not see the advantage of messing about with food in our bedrooms, and preferred being saved the trouble of preparing the meal. There was another change, however, which I, as senior responsible under officer, pressed upon the authorities, but without success. That was, to allow smoking in moderation and not to treat it as a military offence. It was well known that many cadets indulged in smoking, but *it was a crime to be found out.* When the restriction was removed some years later, I have heard that the practice considerably diminished.

In September we went to Shoeburyness for a week to go through a course of artillery practice, and had a pleasant time there. We lived in the soldiers' barracks, and the only matter of complaint was that there was only one bath for about forty cadets, so that the juniors had to begin at a pretty early hour!

October and November were devoted to hard work for the final examination, and fortunately passed very quietly, though there was a sort of uneasy feeling that the troubles of the previous year might be repeated.

At the final examination I was first, and received the Pollock Medal, but the Sword was given to the second man although I was 'senior responsible'. This was commented upon in rather a strong manner by some of the newspaper reporters, upon which the Governor wrote to my father explaining that I was entitled to it, but that it had been decided that the same cadet would not get both if the second had done well also.

At the final examination our class was thirty-eight in number, of which ten received commissions in the Royal Engineers and twenty-eight in the Royal Artillery. Of the twenty-eight, twenty belonged to the batch which had passed into the Academy in July, 1863, and eight had dropped in from senior classes. It may be interesting to note the future history of the batch.

Of the ten sappers, eight reached the rank of colonel, and six are still serving on full-pay (1900).

Of the twenty gunners, five reached the rank of colonel and two are still serving, one in the Royal Artillery and one in the Indian Staff Corps.

If our batch, therefore, can be taken as a fair example, it would appear that the chance of long service is much greater in the Royal Engineers than in the Royal Artillery, and that cadets who mean to make the Army a profession for life should do their best to get into the former. But perhaps I am a little prejudiced, as, after thirty-four years' service, I am quite convinced that the corps of Royal Engineers is the best of all professions!

Appendix 2

Report on the Sudan and its Future by Major Kitchener
DĚBBEH, April 30, 1885

SIR—I have the honour to acknowledge the receipt of your telegram of to-day directing me to send you a Report, 1st, on my present idea of the political situation here; and, 2nd, on the possibility of establishing in the country some Government subsidised by Egypt.

1. PRESENT SITUATION

It appears to me that Mohammed Ahmed [the Mahdi] will not in the future be able to call upon Kordofan for recruits. He led the Bagara Arabs down to Khartum by playing successfully on their religious fanaticism and their greed. Religion supplied one motive, and further support was gained through the new relationships which he formed by marrying the daughters of the principal chiefs. But perhaps the greatest of the influences which he exercised over the majority of the Arabs was the prospect he held out of great loot in Khartum. It needed all his efforts to keep them there during the long siege, when they suffered much both from smallpox[1] and from want of food and other necessaries; and the final promise—great treasure and loot—had to be kept constantly dangled before their eyes. When at last the place fell, the Arabs found their mistake and were greatly disappointed. The result was a reaction of feeling disastrous to the Madhi's power in Kordofan, many sheikhs attempting to leave him. This he resented, and by harshness drove them into open revolt. During the Mahdi's absence from Kordofan the numerous merchants and natives who have been ruined by the stoppage of all trade fostered the feeling against Mohammed Ahmed and his cousin and Vakil the Sherif Mahmud in El Obeid. The result is a very general revulsion of feeling throughout Kordofan.

---

[1] Perhaps more accurately typhus.

214

Mohammed Ahmed, seeing the great danger to his future projects and prestige is now exerting all his power to recover Kordofan. All Gordon's black troops have been sent under Nur Angara, with many guns; and, if reports are true, they have suffered a similar fate to that which befell General Hicks and his army. Anyway they have not succeeded, and reinforcements under Nur Angara are to be sent up immediately from Khartum. Pending the settlement of this trouble, the Mahdi has given up all efforts to take Sennar, though, if vigorously attacked, the place would without doubt fall easily into his hands.

Whatever may be the result to the Mahdi's arms in Kordofan, I am of opinion that the Bagara Arabs will never in the future form the nucleus of Mohammed Ahmed's power. As it has been in Darfur, so will it be in Kordofan—Mohammed Ahmed delivers the people from Turkish oppression, and they deliver themselves from him.

Deprived of Kordofan the Mahdi will have to depend on the riverain population and such Arab tribes as the Hadendoa, Bisharin, Shukuriyeh, and Beni Amer. Of the riverain population the most devoted of his allies are the Jaalin, the bravest and most warlike of the tribes. Wad-el-Nejumi has now 3000 of these as a corps of observation at Metammeh, and doubtless many more have joined the Mahdi's standard.

Should, however, El Sidi Osman, by the power of the Shukuriyeh, move from Kassala on to the river at Shendy, his great influence over the Jaalin, coupled with his undoubted holiness and his true descent from the Prophet, will, I expect, cause many now in the ranks of the Mahdi to waver in their attachment to the man whom Sidi Osman had dubbed a false teacher. Sidi Osman wields a very great religious influence over the Sudan, but he does not arouse the fear by which Mohammed Ahmed compels those who disbelieve in him or dislike him to declare for him. Should Sidi Osman, however, arrive at Shendy with the Shukuriyeh Arabs, it will cause a great change in the feeling of the neighbourhood tribes.

Next to the Jaalin come the Shaikiyeh, who last year were on the Mahdi's side and fought for his envoy in the battles with the Mudir of Dongola. Since then they have received peace and have become loyal to the Government. The Mahdi has revenged himself on the Shaikiyeh found in Khartum, and on the many families of the tribe living on the river between Khartum and Metammeh. This ill-treatment of their relations and friends has caused a very bitter feeling against the Mahdi amongst the Shaikiyeh of the district, and I am of opinion that now, of all the riverain population, they are the most opposed to the Mahdi and his cause; although doubtless, if left unprotected, they would, under pressure from the enemy, make the best terms with him that they could.

The Dongolawi, although they have always remained loyal, are much more Mahdist at heart than the Shaikiyeh. Mohammed Ahmed is one of them, and has always treated them leniently and well, and they do not fear him; and some of them, too, are proud that a Dongolawi should have taken such a position in the world.

The old and very bitter blood-feud existing between the Shaikiyeh and the Dongolawi was the true cause of the Mudirate not being lost last year. It was not dislike of Mohammed Ahmed, but intense hatred of the Shaikiyeh, that made the Dongolawi to a man oppose the Shaikiyeh envoy who claimed to be their Emir.

The remainder of the riverain tribes have fought for Mohammed Ahmed and are still with him, but none of these are so important. Of the three large riverain tribes we at present hold two. Of the Arab tribes the Hadendoa and Bisharin have had almost enough of war; and they could not leave their hills and the road to Berber, which they guard. The Shukuriyeh, as already stated, are much under the influence of Sidi Osman, and it is very unlikely that they, or any large section of them, would follow Mohammed Ahmed out of their own country.

The Beni Amer I know little about.

Altogether, I think that, when the Kordofan Arab tribes leave Mohammed Ahmed, he will have very few real desert Arabs with him. I do not think the riverain tribes are anything like as warlike as the desert Arabs; not from want of pluck—they are just as fearless, I consider—but men with property, who have been used to living in houses, do not care to lose all without seeing where it will end. Religious enthusiasm carries them a long way, perhaps further than the desert Arabs; but belief in the Mahdi becomes after a time insufficient to compensate for the loss of all quiet and peace.

Food is getting very scarce throughout the country, and, if war goes on for another year in the producing districts, I have little doubt that there will be a famine. The numerous ruined water-wheels will not be repaired, and the cattle of those who have not been ruined are eaten by the fighting men. Without irrigation the country is a fruitless desert. It is said that the poor are already dying of hunger, and that grain is at famine prices. The greatest damper to religious enthusiasm is the having to pay pretty heavily for it.

Under these circumstances the addition of the rich province of Dongola, with its great supply of dates, and the money that the present Expedition has poured into it, would bring a great increase to the Mahdi's power and prestige; and in the future the Shaikiyeh and Dongolawi regiments would make no mean contingent amongst his forces.

Had it been possible to hold Berber, the Mahdi would, in my opinion, have disappeared very shortly, for advance is a necessity for him; he can neither stand still nor go back. It may perhaps be argued that the same effect would follow from the same cause if Wady Halfa and Assuan were held as frontier posts; but in this case the Mahdi's existence is much prolonged, for he has the whole of Sudan; no other influence is at work in the country; to those who may be driven to desperation by the simulated religious fervour they are forced to maintain no hope is held out that a brighter future may be attained by their own efforts.

The Mahdi's personal influence is paramount in the country, and until he leaves it I hardly think the people could free themselves. Of course this view may be wrong, and the people might emancipate themselves before the Mahdi was ready to take the next step forward; for, having prepared the way by his emissaries, he would doubtless expect at the right moment that the Frontier Force would find a more strategic frontier, with less length of lines of communication, where a determined stand should be made against the Mahdi's power, until next time. The Mahdi now has sent all his available forces to secure his rear. Should they fail to do so, his position would be, in my opinion, so critical that nothing but the cession of the Dongola province could save him.

II. Future government

Your telegram does not inform me whether the Government it is proposed to establish should be in any way protected by an armed force; but I take it that the intended problem is—how to establish a Government here that should be stable, with no other than money support. I consider it impossible to do this. I do not believe that any native Government that could be formed at a moment's notice would be sufficiently strong to resist the rebel advance following a retirement of our troops. Money, in this case, would, I believe, be powerless. The position of affairs was much stronger before the Expedition came up, and even then it could not have lasted long. Had there been no English force here, the Mudirate would have fallen after Khartum did, if not before.

If the English troops are needed elsewhere, and the English taxpayer does not like paying for putting down a false prophet and protecting Egypt, then I should take off the muzzle, and let Egypt act energetically for herself and her own preservation. Send up six Egyptian battalions to take the place of the English troops withdrawn, leaving three English battalions here. Reform the Egyptian cavalry and artillery. Let every post along the frontier be made as strong as possible by fortifications and guns. Send up Abdul-Kader Pasha as Governor, and make Cairo back him up. Let Abdul-Kader raise some native levies, and help him with money to be spent on subsidising the province. I think the present frontier, Merawi-Debbeh-Dongola, might be made strong and has many advantages.

But this is going beyond the subject you have directed me to report upon. I merely mention it as the only means, in my opinion, of saving the province from Mohammed Ahmed, and forming a stable Government in it.

In order to see what Government could have any chance of suiting this riverain population I think it is well to consider what their former Government was before the Turkish occupation. Doubtless in their hearts the people look back with feelings of pride to the time when they were free from the Turkish yoke.

The Dongola province was divided by two great tribes, the Dongolawi or Danagla and the Shaikiyeh, speaking different languages. Between these two endless war raged. The blood feud was most bitter and no year passed without raids, fights, and bloodshed. The blood feud is even still so strong that no Shaikiyeh notable will willingly pass through the Dongola country, the Shaikiyeh men pass themselves off as Danagla when they are in their enemy's territory. Some six years before the Turkish occupation the Shaikiyeh extended their influence over a portion of the Dongola country, and the only absolutely independent king was the Melek of Argo. This invasion was accomplished under the grandfather of Saleh Bey Wad-el-Mek, who was principal king of the Shaikiyeh, and the grandfather of Mohammed Bey Abud was his Prime Minister and Commander-in-Chief. Abud took the fortress at Hetani, and another at Raba, near Abu Gusi.

The Danagla then fell under the influence of the Shaikiyeh. About a year later the Sultan of Fertit in Jebel Nuba, grandfather of Said Agha, left his country for some unknown cause, and came down to Dongola with about 5000 slaves. He made an arrangement with the Danagla that, if he should deliver them from the Shaikiyeh, they would recognise him as their supreme king. He then went to work, and after six months' fighting retook Hetani and drove the Shaikiyeh back into their own country. Then he ruled the country as supreme king from Mahass to near Korti.

Then came the time of the Turkish occupation. The Melek of Berber made all the arrangements for the Turkish advance, so that Mohammed Ali Pasha was unopposed in the Danagla and Shaikiyeh countries. It is surprising to me that in the rebel ranks under the Mahdi, where one would have expected to see men ranging themselves under the banners of their former kings, they have not done so. I presume that it is religious fervour that marks as leaders men unknown before. I think, however, that the only chance of a Government being established is by taking the descendants, where fit, of the former ruling houses of the country.

With this view, I would divide the province into three Vakilates—(1) the *Shaikiyeh*, (2) *South Dongola*, (3) *North Dongola*. The Vakils to be, respectively, (1) Mohammed Bey Abud, son of Ibrahim Abud, and grandson of the former Prime Minister of the Shaikiyeh, who conquered the Dongolawi. Mohammed Bey is now at Dongola, having come with Khash'm-el-Mus Pasha's party across the desert. He bears a good character for intelligence and capability. The rightful king would be Saleh Bay Wad-el-Mek, who is at present a prisoner in the Mahdi's hands, and is therefore not available. (2) Said Agha, the present Hakim el Khot at Debbeh, who is grandson and heir of the late Sultan of Fertit, who ruled the Danagla. He is brave and intelligent; better educated than most of the notables, being able to read and write. I think he would be inclined to be cruel and warlike. (3) The Melek of Argo, descendant of the ancient kings, respectable and quiet, but without any prominent characteristics.

These three would have to be placed under one head, and, in order to keep the authority, the title of Mudir should be retained. Without a head there would be no confidence, no one to settle disputes between the Vakils. Each Vakil would suspect that either of the others was making terms with Mohammed Ahmed, and would try to be first in the field to gain his favour.

I can only think of Khash'm-el-Mus Pasha for the position, if he would accept it. I consider that this is a very weak point in the project. Placing a Shaikiyeh at the head might create difficulties, and would certainly not be popular among the Dongolawi; they rose and fought against the Mahdi's Shaikiyeh envoy, and might do so again.

I think if a stranger to both could be appointed, it would be much better; but I do not know where to find the man; a Sudani that can be trusted, and is energetic and capable and of good family, is what is required.

The native and black regular troops of the Mudirate would be needed to aid the new Government on the withdrawal of the Turkish garrisons, and sufficient money would have to be supplied to the Mudir, to raise as many soldiers as possible from his district.

The division of the Vakilates might be subsequently decided, but the following gives a rough idea of it: (1) *Shaikiyeh*.—Northern boundary, Ambukol; residence, Merawi. (2) *South Dongola.*—Ambukol to Ordeh; residence, Handak. (3) *North Dongola.*—Ordeh to the boundary of the Wady Halfa district, which would probably be changed slightly from its present position; residence, Argo. The Mudir to reside at Ordeh; to have under his direct orders all steamers and troops, except levies raised by his permission by the Vakils for service in their districts. He should not have power to dismiss or replace the Vakils, who should be appointed from Cairo.

The Mudir and Vakils must be well paid: I should say, Mudir, £150 per month or more; Vakils, £60 per month, would meet the case.

The subsidy required would probably amount to about £15,000 a year. I would suggest the Mudir to dispose of £9000 and the Vakils to have each £2000 for the protection of their districts.

I am, Sir,

Your Obedient Servant,

(Signed)   H. H. KITCHENER,

Major.

The Chief of the Staff, Dongola.

Appendix 3

The Kitchener Advertising Campaign

Sir Hedley Le Bas, who organised the advertising campaign for Kitchener's armies, pointed out that advertising for recruits had begun at least a hundred years earlier. Century-old advertisements claimed that recruits would be envied by their fellow men, and courted and adored by women. 'Would you make your fortune with the sex?' the potential recruit was asked. Abroad, best port wine was threepence a quart, rum, gin, brandy were tenpence. . . .

However, Le Bas realised that this type of advertisement would not do for Kitchener, 'whose stern conception of soldiery did not permit the son of Mars being attracted by the low price of spirits in the country in which he was likely to operate, or his prospects with the fair sex as a soldier of fortune'. Even the more modest approach 'To the Young Women of London' to make their boy friends enlist startled Kitchener, but he was quick to appreciate the efficacy of advertising's brash style.

'The last thing in Lord Kitchener's mind was the glorification of his own name', but he knew it would produce results. 'For,' said Le Bas, 'Kitchener was beloved by the public, and very justly so. The people trusted him. They turned instinctively to him for reassurance when the terrible crash came. . . . The right to use the name made the enormous task of finding a new army all the easier.'

G. R.

Your King and Country need You

A CALL TO ARMS

An addition of 100,000 men to His Majesty's Regular Army is immediately necessary in the present grave National Emergency.

Lord Kitchener is confident that this appeal will be at once responded to by all those who have the safety of our Empire at heart

TERMS OF SERVICE.

General Service for the period of the war only. Any men so enlisting will be discharged with all convenient speed as soon as the war is over.

Age of enlistment between 19 and 30

HOW TO JOIN.

Full information can be obtained at any Post Office or Labour Exchange in the Kingdom or at any Military Barrack

GOD SAVE THE KING.

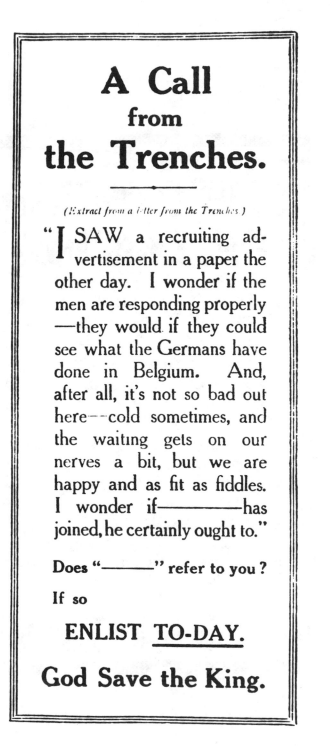

A Call
from
the Trenches.

(Extract from a letter from the Trenches.)

"I SAW a recruiting advertisement in a paper the other day. I wonder if the men are responding properly —they would if they could see what the Germans have done in Belgium. And, after all, it's not so bad out here——cold sometimes, and the waiting gets on our nerves a bit, but we are happy and as fit as fiddles. I wonder if————has joined, he certainly ought to."

Does "————" refer to you?

If so

ENLIST TO-DAY.

God Save the King.

TO THE
YOUNG WOMEN
OF LONDON

Is your "Best Boy" wearing Khaki? If not don't **YOU THINK** he should be?

If he does not think that you and your country are worth fighting for—do you think he is **WORTHY** of you?

Don't pity the girl who is alone—her young man is probably a soldier—fighting for her and her country—and for **YOU.**

If your young man neglects his duty to his King and Country, the time may come when he will **NEGLECT YOU.**

Think it over—then ask him to

JOIN THE ARMY TO-DAY

5 Questions to men who have **not** enlisted

1. IF you are physically fit and between 19 and 38 years of age, are you really satisfied with what you are doing to-day?

2. Do you feel happy as you walk along the streets and see other men wearing the King's uniform?

3. What will you say in years to come when people ask you—"Where did you serve" in the great War?

4. What will you answer when your children grow up, and say, "Father, why weren't you a soldier, too?"

5. What would happen to the Empire if every man stayed at home like you?

Your King and Country Need You.

ENLIST TO-DAY.

At any Post Office you can obtain the address of the nearest Recruiting Office

God Save the King.

5 Questions to those who employ male servants

1.   HAVE you a Butler, Groom, Chauffeur, Gardener, or Gamekeeper serving you who, at this moment should be serving your King and Country?

2.   Have you a man serving at your table who should be serving a gun?

3.   Have you a man digging your garden who should be digging trenches?

4.   Have you a man driving your car who should be driving a transport wagon?

5.   Have you a man preserving your game who should be helping to preserve your Country?

A great responsibility rests on you. Will you sacrifice your personal convenience for your Country's need?

Ask your men to enlist TO-DAY.

The address of the nearest Recruiting Office can be obtained at any Post Office.

God Save the King.

Appendix 4

Letter from Mrs Florence Marc (Kitchener's cousin, 'My dear Flo') to her sixteen-year-old son

Nov 7th 1916.

Dear Son,

Today is the day when England is collecting a big fund in memory of your 2nd cousin Herbert Horatio Kitchener and the thought comes over me, that one day I too shall be beyond your voices and that many tender memories of the heroic figure of these heroic times may be forgotten.

It is a proud thing, my dear Son, to be related to such a hero and to bear his name. You will read many histories of him and many biographies & they will all speak of his greatness but it will not be recorded, perhaps it is known to few, how great too was his kindness of heart. It was in the rare glimpses of family life that this kindness would show itself.

It is all so familiar to me and so bound up in my memory, that it is difficult to remember that it is not the same to you—So I am going back a long time ago—

When your dear Grandmother Emma Day (née Kitchener) was only a little girl of 12 years old (1839) she went to Aspall Hall, & there she formed a lifelong friendship with Fanny Chevallier. They did lessons together and were most devoted friends.

Now *I* always understood that when Uncle Henry [Colonel Henry Horatio Kitchener] went to see her—his favourite niece, he fell in love with her friend Fanny Chevallier, but I think the family of Chevallier claim an earlier knowledge of one-another.

Be that as it may Uncle Henry married Fanny Chevallier and so the tie between your Gd Mother and her friend became even closer. and the 4 sons were ever welcome in my old home (Cousin Herbert was the 2nd son). My first recollection of Cousin Herbert is distinct. He came to see us from Woolwich I believe about 1870, a very tall stripling—I think I must have been between 5 & 6 years of age but I remember that he distinctly bumped his head in our nursery doorway at 10 Manchester Square!

The next thing I clearly remember was seeing him 'stamping' with my elder brother 'Tom'. I can see the stamp book now which belonged to him, a dark sort of maroon brown. My brother was an invalid & I remember someone had given him a beautiful red leather stamp album. Before Cousin Herbert went away (I think to Palestone) he gave Tom his collection (about 1875). Three years ago I recalled the story of Cousin Herbert. He remembered it perfectly and he said 'I should like to see those stamps again, some were good, I remember perfectly making up my mind to give them to Tom.'

The next recollection was his return from Palestine. He gave me a gourd tied with red braid & Palestine written on it, and he gave me a card with little pressed flowers from the Holy Land. And he gave your Gd Mother his book of photographs with writing, and had both taken & written them himself.

Then he surveyed Cyprus.

Then the Egyptian campaign.

The next time I saw him I was still in my teens, I remember I was dressed in white in a white satin bonnet. He offered to sit for me and he said 'You might get it into the Academy.' Soon he was made Sirdar & he wrote and asked Granny to take Maggie and me to Cairo. (Auntie Maggie was too ill & we could not go).

Then came a big interval. I was married before I saw him next time at Christ's College Lodge when your Uncle Jim was Vice-Chancellor. He came to take an honorary degree & was tremendously fêted. He seemed at the zenith of his fame. Then came the S. African war & all its glories & then India.

Now it was upon his return from India that he came to stay a fortnight with your Father and me & then I learnt to know him better than ever before. His grand simplicity struck me & his total absence of guile. He had a most delightful laugh & he always liked my stories and listened to them & called me a 'raconteuse' & he was not at all particular about their accuracy & always upheld me in a good story.

For quite a long time he left us his big dog 'Bang' to take charge of & he gave Francie her dog 'Bangle'.

At this time he was looking out for a place & decided upon Broome Park (whilst he was staying at Champneys). I have the telegram he sent me when he had completed the transaction.

We had some fun about getting some reduction in the price! Having completed the sale he became very interested in finding furniture & we used to sally forth in the motor to all sorts of shops—sometimes starting at 10.30 and returning at 3 p.m. He told me I was like Granny. He used upon these excursions to be like a schoolboy—so happy—& he said to me several times that he had got 'the Antiquarian microbe' badly. This was a very happy fortnight & we used to get out our pencils & make plans for Broome—And he used to explain it to me.

About this time I asked Hal to come & stay & one day he said he would take some snap shots of Cousin Herbert & me. We went on the lawn together & we sat on the old teak seat & Hal took ever so many because Cousin Herbert said 'If you take several one of them may be good.' Alas, Hal, used an old roll & not one came out!

Then Cousin Herbert was appointed to control the traffic & make the military arrangements for the Coronation. He told me afterwards that he had hardly got mounted on his horse on the day of the coronation than he felt something hurting his foot most frightfully. When he was undressing after the ceremony he missed some star from his uniform & it was ultimately found in his boot!! He also told me that upon this occasion he was nervous about Lord Roberts & the long standing in the Abbey, he said 'I did not say anything to Roberts but I was ready if he fell.'

He told me too that something the King had to have removed when he was crowned would not come undone, but Lord Crewe produced a little pr. of scissors & the garment was cut.

Then came his civil appointment to Egypt 'British Agent'. Before he left he asked me if I knew of someone who could design & collect the necessary information for an heraldic window which he wished to have for Broome. I wondered and then said 'No'—'I do' he said 'You could do it well.' I answered I should be afraid but he said 'You do it, I leave it to you to take charge.'

As you know I took charge & I went to Aspall to see the hatchments & I collected information from Uncle Frank & I got measurements from Western (his agent), & I made little careful sketches & finally entrusted the completion of the designs to Mr Krüger. And very delighted he was when he found it done to his entire satisfaction.

I also 'took charge' of the big ceiling executed by Cowtan—with Mr Krüger's help we got that done too. I have many interesting letters from Herbert upon the subject. Cousin Herbert paid several visits to Champneys once when there were big manoeuvres in our district. We dined, he & your father & I at Lord Rothschilds & he told me he had been vastly entertained listening to me talking French to a french Marquis who was objecting to the Self made man & I was disagreeing!

When he was last home from Egypt, he wrote that he would come to luncheon with me July 1914. He wrote he would be in our

229

neighbourhood. The Sunday came! I was in bed at 10.30 in the morning when an urgent letter was brought in a motor car for me from Lady Brownlow. She wrote that they had fixed a luncheon in honour of their guest, Lord Kitchener that day, & that only at breakfast he had announced that he was coming to luncheon with me. Lady Brownlow begged me to come with your Father to them instead (obviously that they might hold their guest). At 11 o'ck Cousin Herbert arrived at Champneys & said he was going to stay with me! I drew him aside (Col Store was with him) & I said I feared we must go to Ashridge tho' I would greatly prefer not.

He reluctantly consented & we went. Lady Brownlow had a big luncheon & I was exalted above all the peeresses. After a little protest I was *made* by *him* to consent to have the honours of the day. Lady Brownlow gracefully advanced & said 'You will wish to take your cousin in' & he said 'Thank you I shall'!

I sat between Lord B & Herbert & I felt from Lord B's manner that I had caused a lot of perturbation, innocent as I was. After luncheon we strolled to the conservatory & Lady B said to Colonel Store 'Will you take Mrs Marc round the garden.' Cousin Herbert advanced & said 'No Store I'll take my cousin & you fetch my hat'!

We went away from what he called 'the crowd' & we sat by a purple vine & he was pleasanter & kinder than I had ever known him—looking at me affectionately. He talked of Broome, of Egypt. He made plans for my coming to Broome & for further old furniture hunts & he planned for a picnic at Broome on my birthday. I was to stay at Greenhill & we were to go to shops together. He wrote down these engagements & he said he would spend 10 days with us in Sept & then he said something very strange & mysterious 'Do you know Flo, sometimes I wonder why I am doing all this at Broome. I often think I shall never sleep under that roof.' (Little did we know a world war was upon us, & what it would mean.) I hastily said that I was thinking of how much he would enjoy it & that he was still young.

Then I came away, a cloud over me, & I told your Father what he had said. He said goodbye to us, saw me off, & I never saw him again.

A few days after he wrote predicting the war & saying he could not come to me, & then on August 4th he wrote again saying 'Goodbye' to me, & that evening when I got his letter I read in the evening papers that he had been recalled. (He was starting for Egypt) I was very thankful.

He wrote to me several times during the war & on April 27th 1916 he wrote & asked me to have luncheon at York House & if not he would try & come & see us. That was the last letter I ever had from him. And then you know, my dear Son, what happened & how that great heroic figure met with the Viking's death.

I have jotted down this that you may know in years to come, how much I admired him as a man as well as a nation's hero.

You will never forget too how he asked me to let you sit up late when you first wore your Osborne uniform & how you played 'The Army against the Navy' & how you nearly won! And in the morning he said to me 'We must get your boy onto a good ship' & he also said 'I like your boy'—

He lived a grand life & he died a grand death. He lived to raise a mighty army & we should be thankful for his wonderful life—but we mourned him for your Father & I cared deeply for him. You and I shall never forget when we stood together in St Paul's, & just as we were leaving poor Western told us that Cousin Herbert had never allowed the card with our names on to be taken away.

Perhaps he wanted to be reminded that you were soon to be appointed to a ship—or perhaps it was one of those little gleams of family affection which steal into the lives of even the greatest of men.

Your loving
Mother

Appendix 5

Extracts from some of Kitchener's writings and speeches

From a speech made on Army policy in India
Two years ago in this Council I explained that my policy of redistribution did not contemplate the massing of large numbers of troops on the North-West Frontier, and that I was entirely opposed to any such policy. Notwithstanding that declaration, I see that recently a distinguished General Officer, formerly Military Member of the Viceroy's Council, has stated, in a letter to the papers, that he knows far better than I do what my policy meant, and that the massing of troops on the frontier was the real intention of my redistribution scheme. I can only say that, if such was the case, I have signally failed in carrying it into effect; for I have only allotted £285,600 for accommodation on the frontier out of the total of £958,400 spent.

From a speech made at Johannesburg, 18 June 1902
And, gentlemen, what have we learnt about our enemies? We were told that the Boers would all run away. Well, they ran away very often, but they always came back again. We were told they would never hold together in any cohesive formation, and I fully believe that there is no one more self-confident of his own individual opinion than the Boers. And yet what have we seen? That they have subordinated themselves to their leaders and have worked with discipline through a long and protracted war. We have seen them courageous in attack and retreat. They have always shown such marked ability as to be a lesson to us all. There is another character-istic they have displayed which, if we are true descendants of our forefathers, we ought to be most capable of fully appreciating. I refer to that wonderful tenacity of purpose, that 'don't-know-when-you-

are-beaten' quality which they have so prominently displayed in this war. There may be individuals amongst them whose characteristics and methods we do not like and do not approve of but judged as a whole I maintain that they are a virile race and an asset of considerable importance to the British Empire, for whose honour and glory I hope before long they may be fighting side by side with us.

Kitchener's message carried by each soldier of the BEF in 1914
You are ordered abroad as a soldier of the King to help our French comrades against the invasion of a common enemy. You have to perform a task which will need your courage, your energy, your patience. Remember that the honour of the British Army depends on your individual conduct.

It will be your duty not only to set an example of discipline and perfect steadiness under fire, but also to maintain the most friendly relations with those whom you are helping in this struggle. The operations in which you are engaged will, for the most part, take place in a friendly country, and you can do your own country no better service than in showing yourself in France and Belgium in the true character of a British soldier.

Be invariably courteous, considerate, and kind. Never do anything likely to injure or destroy property, and always look upon looting as a disgraceful act. You are sure to meet with a welcome and to be trusted; your conduct must justify that welcome and that trust.

Your duty cannot be done unless your health is sound. So keep constantly on your guard against any excesses. In this new experience you may find temptations both in wine and women. You must entirely resist both temptations, and, while treating all women with perfect courtesy, you should avoid any intimacy.

Do your duty bravely,
Fear God,
Honour the King.

KITCHENER,
Field-Marshal.

From a speech to Parliament in 1915
Labour may very rightly ask that their patriotic work should not be used to inflate the profits of the directors and shareholders of the various great industrial and armament firms, and we are therefore arranging a system under which the important armament firms will come under Government control, and we hope that workmen who work regularly by keeping good time shall reap some of the benefits which the war automatically confers on these great companies. I feel

strongly, my Lords, that the men working long hours in the shops by day and by night, week in and week out, are doing their duty for their King and country in a like manner with those who have joined the Army for active service in the field. They are thus taking their part in the war and displaying the patriotism that has been so manifestly shown by the nation in all ranks, and I am glad to be able to state that His Majesty has approved that where service in this great work of supplying the munitions of war has been thoroughly, loyally, and continuously rendered, the award of a medal will be granted on the successful termination of the war.

Kitchener's speech on the part of the civilian army, 1 March 1916
If it be true, and it certainly is true, that this is a war of nations, then the whole nation is fighting, and we have two great armies, not only the Army in the field, but the other army consisting of the whole of the civilian population at home. As a representative of the Army in the field, I want to appeal on their behalf to the civilian army at home, for it is vital to the Army in the field that the civilian army at home should also strenuously play its part. The Army in the field could not last one single day without the efforts of the civilian population behind it. Our soldiers depend wholly on the civilian population for their food, their clothing, and the unlimited munitions and equipment that they must have if they are success-fully to meet their enemies. Whether they can get all these vital things in sufficient quantities, and continue to do so, depends absolutely and entirely upon whether every man and woman at home shows the utmost economy in production, and the utmost economy in consumption. If men or women are not producing all they can by their labour or skill, or are consuming either in food or clothes, or anything else more than they need, they are making it so much the more difficult to meet the needs of our soldiers and our Allies, and therefore they are doing something to help our enemies to win just as much as a soldier who refuses to do his utmost on the field of battle.

It is not only money that our Armies require. We want just as many men as we can get as soldiers. Therefore we are bound to take all the men that can possibly be spared, whether from industry, agriculture, or commerce. We want an unceasing supply of guns and shells, rifles and cartridges, and all other munitions of war. We want very large supplies of other military requirements, such as food, clothing, and transport. We want to provide as much munitions, supplies, and equipment as possible for the use of our Allies.

The question is, How can we do all these things at the same time?

How can we take millions of men from our workshops, farms, banks, and offices and yet provide not only all the things that the whole nation consumes under peace conditions, but also the vast mass of war material which now requires millions of men and women for its production? Now that our working population is so much smaller owing to the millions of soldiers in the field how can that smaller population produce vastly more? If those left behind are going to work only as hard as they worked before, and each man and woman is to produce only as much as before, and if all the civilian population are going to consume as much as they did before, then our problem will be insoluble. If everyone is to go on living as if times were normal, either we shall be unable to get all the men we require as soldiers, or we shall be unable to produce enough for our civilian population as well as what our Armies must imperatively have in order to carry through their tremendous task.

Hitherto, finding that we could not produce nearly enough for the wants of our Army and our Allies, and for our own needs, we have filled up the gap by vast importations from foreign countries. It is essential for the strength of our financial system, and for the main-tenance of our foreign exchanges, that we should rely much more upon ourselves. We cannot possibly produce enough to meet all our ordinary peace-time requirements as well as our military needs. Therefore, either the civilian population must go short of many things to which it is accustomed in time of peace, or our armies must go short of munitions and other things indispensable to them. Which is it to be? Are the civilians at home prepared to let their brothers and friends in the trenches sacrifice their lives and endure hardships of all kinds, and yet themselves not be ready to undergo the small sacrifi-ces in the way of harder work, increased effort, and increased economy which alone can with certainty provide our armies with all that they require until the end of the war?

First, if we employ less labour in meeting the wants of the civilian population then we can release more men for the fighting forces. Secondly, if we import less for consumption by the civil population then we lessen the difficulties of sea transport. Those difficulties as you know are very great at present. Thirdly, by importing less for the civilian population we also relieve the serious congestion at our docks in this country. Fourthly, by carrying less for the civilian population we also relieve the congestion on our railways. Fifthly, by a general reduction in the consumption of commodities by the civilian population we do much to limit the increase in the cost of living. Lastly, by consuming less ourselves we set free labour and capital to be employed in making what our own armies and those of our Allies need. Therefore the military needs of this country urgently demand the strictest economy on the part of all citizens of this country.

Let those who are making large profits and receiving large wages, and are therefore tempted to extravagance, remind themselves that such profits and such wages are only made possible by the sacrifices of our Navy and Army, and that money made at such a cost should be used or invested for the nation's benefit and not spent in personal indulgence. Economy in everything is desirable, and particularly of course in such articles as coal, food stuffs, intoxicating liquors, petrol and oils, tea and coffee, tobacco, and clothing of all kinds, especially woollen articles.

Economy is only one side of the picture. Both economy and productive energy are required of all workers, and both are of equal importance. If every man and woman work their hardest to produce everything the Army needs, then they are doing their bit. And if every man and woman receiving higher wages owing to the war or enjoying an independent income save all they possibly can and invest it in Government securities they are equally doing their bit. But if they do not work their hardest and do not save as much as they can, so far from contributing to the national cause, they are in fact directly injuring it, and also are hindering their friends and relations in the trenches.

Kitchener's speech on the Military Service Bill, 23 May 1916
My Lords, on this the final stage of the Bill it may be appropriate for me to say that its smooth and rapid passage through your Lordships' House will prove most beneficial to the Army. As soon as the measure has received the Royal Assent we shall be able to regulate the flow of recruits to the Colours, and get rid altogether of those sudden fluctuations in recruiting which were so prejudicial alike to military and industrial interests. Further—and I emphasise the point—the process of recruiting will now be carried out with a minimum possible inconvenience to the men themselves.

The idea has apparently been prevalent in certain quarters that for some wholly inexplicable motive the military authorities are prone to crowd and even to congest the ranks with men physically unfit to bear arms. No suggestion could be wider of the truth. Under the provisions of this Bill we can call up men for medical re-examination; but this power will be used not to absorb the physically unfit, but to secure the physically efficient. Some of these men are undoubtedly sheltering themselves behind certificates acquired in an unsatisfactory way or under a temporary condition of ill-health.

The terms of this Bill will enable us to make use of the men who were discarded on account of physical disability for active service but who are suitable for home service, clerical work, and the like. In a word, the Bill, in purport and in effect, makes directly and unmistakably for equality of sacrifice in the national cause. The Army Council will, for their part, use every endeavour to render it as easy as possible for the men to be called up. We shall keep the groups open for voluntary attestation until the appointed date.

There is no doubt that the Armies in the field will welcome this measure with intense satisfaction. Generals and Staffs will be able to count with moral certainty on their receiving the necessary drafts and reinforcements, and the rank and file will be encouraged by the thought that all their countrymen at home are prepared to support them to the utmost of their power. Our Allies also will, I believe, recognise in our acceptance of obligations which are undoubtedly such a marked departure from our national traditions that this country is prepared to throw into the scale without reserve the whole of our resources against the common foe. The conviction deeply and universally felt that we have engaged in a just war and the patriotism of our people gave us, under the voluntary system, a far larger Army than we could ever have contemplated. This Bill will enable us to maintain its numbers in a manner and to a degree not hitherto possible, and thus take our fair and full share in the great conflict on the issue of which our position as a nation and the future of our race depend.

Appendix 6

Ludendorff on the death of Kitchener

In 1925 V. W. Germains published a book entitled *The Truth About Kitchener* and added the following letter:

In similar fashion as in the history of the Emperor William I, apart from Bismarck and Moltke, the name of the Prussian Minister of War, and great army organizer, Von Roon, but for whom the three victorious wars of that epoch would have been inconceivable, has been too little mentioned, so it appears to me, that in the history of the world-war Lord Kitchener has not yet received the appreciation due to him if we are to perceive the great historical events in clear perspective.

Lord Kitchener became the organizer of the British Army after England had entered the world-war. He created armies out of next to nothing, trained and equipped them. Through his genius alone, England developed side by side with France, into an opponent capable of meeting Germany on even terms (vollmächtiger Gegner für Deutschland) whereby the position on the front in France in 1915 was so seriously changed to Germany's disadvantage.

His great organizing powers alone would have sufficed to render Lord Kitchener one of the most remarkable and important of the military personalities of the world-war, perhaps the most distinguished England had ever had.

His mysterious death was the work neither of a German mine nor of a German torpedo but of that power which would not permit the Russian army to recover with the help of Lord Kitchener because the destruction of Zarist Russia had been determined upon. Lord Kitchener's death was caused by his abilities.[1]

(Signed) LUDENDORFF.

[1] Author's italics.

Germains commented:

I have italicized the concluding passage of this remarkable letter because deep as will be the interest with which Englishmen will read the words soldierly acknowledgment of Lord Kitchener's great military capacities which come from the enemy-leader, the phrase, *Lord Kitchener's death was due to his abilities*, must acquire a tragic significance when we remember the dark stories which have so long been circulating, alleging that this greatest of Englishmen met his death by treachery. Courtesy towards a distinguished enemy general, who has gone as far probably as he *could* go, in unravelling the mystery of the *Hampshire*, must forbid us from dotting the i's and crossing the t's of his statement too narrowly. But Englishmen who remember the uncommonly close relationship which existed in those days between the Russian revolutionary committees and the German intelligence service, may be forgiven for drawing their own conclusions.

Bibliography

The books listed below are only a small selection of those with references to Kitchener. Most of the histories of the period 1850–1916 make some comment, long or short, on his achievements. there have been numerous biographies, of varying merit. Many of them are now out of print, and have also disappeared from library shelves. I have therefore listed the ones most likely to be obtainable.

Amery, L. S. (ed.), *The Times History of the War in South Africa, 1899–1902* (London 1905–9)

Arthur, Sir George, *Life of Lord Kitchener* Vols I–III (London 1920)

Arthur, Sir George, *General Sir John Maxwell* (London 1932)

Ashmead-Bartlett, E., *The Uncensored Dardanelles* (London 1928)

Asquith, H. H., *Memories and Reflections 1852–1927* (London 1929)

Asquith, Margot, *More Memories* (London 1933)

Ballard, C. R., *Kitchener* (London 1930)

Beaverbrook, Lord, *Politicians and War* (London 1960)

Begbie, H., *Kitchener: Organizer of Victory* (New York 1915)

Beloff, Max, *Imperial Sunset: Britain's Liberal Empire 1871–1921* (London 1969)

Birdwood, Field-Marshal Lord, *Khaki and Gown* (London 1942)

Blake, Robert, *The Unknown Prime Minister* (London 1955)

Buckle, G. E. (ed.), *The Letters of Queen Victoria 1866–1901* (London 1932)

Burleigh, Bennet, *Khartoum Campaign 1898* (London 1899)

Calwell, Maj-Gen Sir C. E., *Sir Henry Wilson: His Life and Diaries* (London 1927)

Cassar, George H., *Kitchener: Architect of Victory* (London 1977)

Churchill, Winston S., *The River War* (London 1899)

Cook, Sir Edward, *The Press in War Time* (London 1920)

Cromer, Earl of, *Modern Egypt* (London 1908)

Daiches, Dr Samuel, *Lord Kitchener and his Work in Palestine* (London 1915)

Dewar, G. A. B., *The Great Munitions Feat* (London 1921)

De Watteville, Lt-Col H., *Lord Kitchener* (London 1939)

Dilks, David, *Curzon in India* (London and New York 1969)

Dugdale, B. E. C., *Arthur James Balfour* (London 1936)

Edwardes, M., *High Noon of Empire: India under Curzon* (London 1965)

Elgood, Lt-Col P. G., *Egypt and the Army* (London 1924)

Elton, Lord, *General Gordon* (London 1954)

Esher, Reginald Viscount, *The Tragedy of Lord Kitchener* (London 1921)

Falls, Cyril, *The First World War* (London 1960)

Field, Eric, *Advertising: The Forgotten Years* (London 1959)

Fraser, Peter, *Lord Esher* (London 1973)

Germains, V. W., *The Truth about Kitchener* (London 1925)

Germains, V. W., *The Kitchener Armies* (London 1930)

Gilbert, Martin, *Winston S. Churchill* (London 1971 et seq.)

Godwin-Austen, A. R., *The Staff and the Staff College* (London 1927)

Gordon, Hampden, *The War Office* (London 1935)

Green, Lt-Col Howard, *The British Army in the First World War* (London 1968)

Grew, E. S., *Field Marshal Lord Kitchener* (London 1916)

Hamilton, General Sir Ian, *Gallipoli Diary* (London & New York 1920)

Hay, Ian, *The First Hundred Thousand* (London 1915)

Higgins, T., *Winston Churchill and the Dardanelles* (London 1963)

Holmes, R., *Little Field-Marshal: Sir John French* (London 1981)

Jackson, H. C., *Behind the Modern Sudan* (London 1955)

Jenkins, Roy, *Asquith* (London 1964)

Jerrold, W., *Earl Kitchener of Khartoum* (London 1916)

Joffre, T. *Personal Memoirs* (tr. T. B. Mott) (London 1932)

Kedourie, E., *England and the Middle East* (London 1956)

Kruger, R., *Goodbye Dolly Gray* (London 1959)

Liddell-Hart, B. H., *History of the First World War* (London 1970)

Lloyd-George, David, *War Memoirs* (London 1933)

MacMichael, Sir Harold, *The Anglo-Egyptian Sudan* (London 1934)

Magnus, Philip, *Kitchener: Portrait of an Imperialist* (London 1958)

Marshall-Cornwall, Sir James, *Haig as a Military Commander* (London 1973)

Maurice, Maj-Gen Sir F., *British Strategy* (London 1929)

Meintjes, J., *De la Rey: Lion of the West* (Johannesburg 1966)

Meintjes, J., *General Louis Botha* (London 1970)

Meintjes, J., *President Steyn* (Capetown 1969)

Middleton, Earl of, *Records and Reactions 1859–1939* (London 1939)

Minto, Mary, Countess of, *India, Minto and Morley 1905–1910* (London 1934)

Morley, John, Viscount, *Recollections* (London and New York 1917)

Nicolson, Harold, *King George V* (London 1952)

Nutting, Anthony, *Scramble for Africa: The Great Trek to the Boer war* (London 1970)

Phillips, W. C., *The Loss of HMS Hampshire and the Death of Lord Kitchener* (London 1930)

Repington, Lt-Col C. á Court, *The First World War 1914–1918* (New York 1921)

Rickards, M., *Posters of the First World War* (London 1968)

Robertson, Field-Marshal Sir W., *From Private to Field Marshal* (London 1921)

Rose, K., *King George V* (London 1983)

Selby, John, *The Boer War* (London 1969)

Spender, J.A. and Asquith, Cyril, *Life of H. H. Asquith* (London 1932)

Steevens, G. W., *With Kitchener to Khartoum* (London 1898)

Taylor, A.J. P., *English History 1914–1915* (London 1965)

Turner, E. S., *Dear Old Blighty* (London 1980)

Von Falkenhayn, Gen E., *General Headquarters 1914–1918 and its Critical Decisions* (New York 1920)

Von Hindenburg, Marshal P., *Out of My Life* (tr. F. A. Holt) (New York 1921)

Von Sanders, Liman, *Five Years in Turkey* (Annapolis 1927)

Warner, Philip, *Dervish: the Rise and Fall of an African Empire* (London 1973)

Warner, Philip, *The Battle of Loos* (London 1976)

Watkins, O., *With Kitchener's Army* (London 1899)

Wingate, Reginald, *Mahdiism and the Egyptian Sudan* (London 1968)

Wingate, Ronald, *Wingate of the Sudan* (London 1955)

The most comprehensive collection of papers relating to Kitchener are the Kitchener papers which were deposited in the Public Record Office by the Field-Marshal's great-nephew, the present Earl Kitchener.

Also at the Public Record Office is additional information in the Cabinet Papers, the Cromer Papers, the Dardanelles Commission Report and the Foreign Office Archives.

Further material may be found in the archives of the National Army Museum, the Imperial War Museum, the India Office Library, the Bodleian Library, the Cambridge University Library, King's College London Library, the Beaverbrook Library, and the Durham University Library.

Index

PHILIP WARNER joined the British Army in 1939 after graduating from Cambridge and served throughout the Second World War, mainly in the Far East. Subsequently he was a Lecturer for the British Council in Spain and a Senior Lecturer at the Royal Military Academy, Sandhurst. He is an experienced military historian, among whose works are *The Crimean War, The D-Day Landings, Alamein,* and a widely praised biography of Field Marshal Sir Claude Auchinleck, published in Great Britain in 1981. He lives and writes in Surrey.